Maui Travel Guic

All You Need to Know Before You Go with Top Recommendations on Must-Visit Beaches, Things to Do, Hidden Gems, Where to Stay, Places to Eat, and Ways to Save

Sebastian Felix

Disclaimer Notice

The information provided in this book is intended for general informational purposes only and reflects the author's research and personal experiences. While every effort has been made to ensure the accuracy and reliability of the content, the author and publisher make no guarantees or warranties regarding the completeness, timeliness, or applicability of the information contained herein. Readers are encouraged to seek professional advice and conduct their research before making decisions based on the contents of this book. The author and publisher shall not be held liable for errors, omissions, or actions based on the information presented.

Contents

Chapter 1: Introduction

Welcome to Maui

Welcome to Maui, the Valley Isle, known for its stunning natural beauty, diverse landscapes, and rich Hawaiian culture. Whether you are looking for adventure, relaxation, or a taste of the island's history and traditions, Maui offers something for everyone. From the scenic Road to Hana and the majestic Haleakalā National Park to the beautiful beaches and charming towns, Maui promises an unforgettable experience.

Natural Wonders: Discover Maui's diverse landscapes, including volcanic craters, lush rainforests, cascading waterfalls, and pristine beaches.

Cultural Heritage: Explore Maui's rich Hawaiian heritage, from ancient Polynesian traditions to modern-day celebrations of island culture.

Outdoor Activities: Enjoy a wide range of outdoor activities, such as snorkeling, surfing, hiking, and whale watching, amidst Maui's breathtaking scenery.

Island Hospitality: Experience the warm aloha spirit, with friendly locals eager to share their traditions, stories, and hospitality.

Overview of Maui

Geography: Maui is the second-largest island in Hawaii, located in the central Pacific Ocean. It is known for its varied landscapes, from the volcanic terrain of Haleakalā to the lush Hana rainforest and the sandy shores of Wailea and Kaanapali.

Regions: Maui is divided into several distinct regions, each offering unique attractions:

West Maui: Home to the historic town of Lahaina, the luxurious resorts of Kaanapali and Kapalua, and beautiful beaches.

South Maui: Known for its upscale resorts, sandy beaches, and snorkeling spots in Wailea and Kihei.

East Maui: Featuring the scenic Road to Hana, lush rainforests, and waterfalls.

Central Maui: Includes the island's main airport in Kahului, the commercial hub of Wailuku, and the isthmus connecting West and East Maui.

Upcountry Maui: Located on the slopes of Haleakalā, known for its farms, ranches, and the Haleakalā National Park.

Population: Maui has a population of approximately 167,000 people. The largest towns are Kahului and Wailuku, with smaller communities scattered across the island.

Economy: Maui's economy is primarily driven by tourism, agriculture, and retail. The island is famous for its sugarcane and pineapple plantations, as well as a growing focus on diversified agriculture, including organic farming and renewable energy.

Transportation: Maui is served by Kahului Airport (OGG), with smaller regional airports in Hana and Kapalua. The island has a well-maintained road network, with rental cars being the most popular mode of transportation for visitors. Public buses and shuttle services are also available.

History of Maui

Ancient Hawaiians: The Polynesians were the first to settle on Maui, bringing their culture, traditions, and agricultural practices. The island's history is rich with legends and historical sites related to ancient Hawaiian chiefs and deities.

European Contact: The first European to visit Maui was Captain James Cook in 1778. The arrival of Europeans led to significant changes in the island's society, economy, and culture.

Kingdom of Hawaii: Maui played a crucial role in the unification of the Hawaiian Islands under King Kamehameha I. The town of Lahaina served as the royal capital of the Kingdom of Hawaii in the early 19th century.

Missionary Influence: Christian missionaries arrived in the early 19th century, influencing local culture and education. The Baldwin House in Lahaina is a notable historical site from this period.

Plantation Era: The sugarcane and pineapple industries boomed in the late 19th and early 20th centuries, bringing immigrants from Asia and Europe, which contributed to Maui's diverse cultural heritage.

Modern Maui: Today, Maui is a popular tourist destination known for its natural beauty, luxury resorts, and outdoor activities, while also preserving its cultural heritage and natural resources.

How to Use This Guide

This guide is your essential companion for exploring Maui, offering practical advice, insider tips, and recommendations to help you make the most of your visit.

Planning Your Trip: Essential information on when to visit Maui, entry requirements, travel insurance, health tips, currency exchange, and packing essentials for different seasons.

Getting to and Around Maui: Detailed guides on arriving in Maui by air, sea, or land, as well as navigating the island efficiently using rental cars, public transportation, and tour services.

Where to Stay: Recommendations for accommodations across Maui, from luxury resorts and beachfront hotels to charming bed and breakfasts and budget-friendly hostels.

Top Attractions: A comprehensive list of must-see sights and activities, including natural parks, historic towns, beaches, museums, and scenic drives, with tips for exploring each destination.

Cultural Experiences: Insights into Maui's rich cultural scene, including traditional Hawaiian festivals, music performances, hula shows, and local crafts.

Dining and Nightlife: Recommendations for dining out in Maui, from gourmet restaurants and food trucks to traditional Hawaiian luaus and beachfront bars, as well as nightlife spots and entertainment options.

Outdoor Activities: Suggestions for outdoor enthusiasts, including hiking trails, snorkeling and diving spots, surf breaks, whale-watching tours, and golfing.

Family-Friendly Activities: Fun-filled attractions and activities for families, including interactive museums, animal sanctuaries, kid-friendly beaches, and educational tours.

Practical Information: Useful tips on tourist information centers, emergency contacts, local customs and etiquette, internet connectivity, and postal services in Maui.

Maps and Navigation: Detailed maps of Maui's regions, public transportation networks, and tourist routes, facilitate easy exploration and navigation during your stay.

Final Tips and Recommendations: Insider advice on hidden gems, lesser-known attractions, seasonal events, and local insights to enhance your visit to Maui and create lasting memories.

Appendices: Additional resources, including a glossary of Hawaiian phrases, conversion charts, emergency phrases, recommended reading, and an index for quick reference.

With this guide, you'll embark on a journey through Maui's natural wonders, vibrant culture, outdoor adventures, and warm hospitality, ensuring an enriching and unforgettable experience on this beautiful Hawaiian island.

Why Visit? Top Reasons to Visit Maui, Hawaii

1. Spectacular Beaches

Maui is home to some of the world's most beautiful beaches, each offering unique experiences. Ka'anapali Beach is perfect for snorkeling and sunbathing, while Wailea Beach boasts luxury resorts and calm waters ideal for swimming. For those seeking adventure, the black sand beach at Waianapanapa State Park provides a stunning and unique coastal experience. Whether you're looking to surf, snorkel, or simply relax, Maui's beaches cater to all preferences.

2. The Scenic Road to Hana

The Road to Hana is one of the most scenic drives in the world, offering breathtaking views of lush rainforests, cascading waterfalls, and dramatic coastal cliffs. This winding route takes you through 620 curves and over 59 bridges, with numerous opportunities to stop and explore. Highlights include the Seven Sacred Pools at Oheo Gulch the Hana Lava Tube, and the vibrant flora of the Garden of Eden Arboretum.

3. Haleakalā National Park

Haleakalā National Park is home to the world's largest dormant volcano. Visitors can hike through the surreal landscapes of the crater, which resembles a lunar surface, or drive to the summit to witness a sunrise that paints the sky with vivid colors. The park also offers a variety of trails, ranging from easy walks to challenging hikes, allowing visitors to explore diverse ecosystems and encounter unique flora and fauna.

4. Diverse Marine Life

Maui's surrounding waters are a haven for marine life, making it one of the best places in the world for snorkeling and diving. Molokini Crater, a partially submerged volcanic caldera, is one of the top snorkeling destinations, where you can swim with tropical fish and observe coral reefs. During the winter months, the waters around Maui are teeming with humpback whales, and whale-watching tours offer the chance to see these magnificent creatures up close. Additionally, the island's many bays and coves, such as Honolua Bay and Turtle Town, provide excellent opportunities to spot sea turtles, dolphins, and other marine life.

5. Rich Hawaiian Culture and History

Maui is steeped in rich Hawaiian culture and history, and there are many ways to experience this on the island. Visit Lahaina, a historic town that was once the capital of the Hawaiian Kingdom and a bustling whaling village. Today, it's a cultural hub where you can explore historic sites, art galleries, and museums. The island is also home to several heiau (ancient Hawaiian temples), such as Pi'ilanihale Heiau in Hana, which is the largest in Hawaii. Attending a traditional Hawaiian luau is another way to immerse yourself in the local culture, where you can enjoy hula performances, Hawaiian music, and a feast of traditional foods.

6. Adventure Activities

For those seeking adventure, Maui has no shortage of thrilling activities. Zip-lining through the island's lush forests offers a bird's-eye view of the stunning landscapes, while helicopter tours provide a unique perspective of Maui's hidden valleys, waterfalls, and rugged coastline. Surfing is another popular activity, with beaches like Ho'okipa Beach Park being renowned for their excellent waves. If you prefer to stay on land, hiking trails in places like Iao Valley State Park and the Pipiwai Trail in Haleakalā National Park offer breathtaking views and challenging terrain. Maui's diverse geography means that every day can be a new adventure.

7. Luxurious Resorts and Spas

Maui is known for its world-class resorts and spas that offer the ultimate in luxury and relaxation. Areas like Wailea and Kapalua are home to some of the most prestigious resorts in the world, including the Four Seasons Resort Maui and the Ritz-Carlton Kapalua. These resorts offer top-notch amenities such as beachfront locations, infinity pools, gourmet dining, and full-service spas.

Many resorts also offer unique experiences like golf courses with ocean views, guided cultural activities, and access to exclusive beaches. Whether you're looking for a romantic getaway or a family-friendly resort, Maui has accommodations that cater to every need.

8. Maui's Farm-to-Table Dining

Maui is a foodie's paradise, particularly for those who appreciate fresh, locally sourced ingredients. The island's farm-to-table dining scene is vibrant, with many restaurants partnering with local farms to offer dishes that highlight Maui's unique flavors. Visit O'o Farm in Upcountry Maui, where you can tour the farm and enjoy a meal made from the produce grown on-site. The Maui Brewing Company offers locally crafted beers that pair perfectly with their farm-fresh menu. For a truly unique experience, try the Maui Chef's Table at The Mill House, where you can enjoy a multi-course meal prepared by top chefs using ingredients sourced from the island.

9. Vibrant Art Scene

Maui has a thriving art community that is reflected in its numerous galleries, art festivals, and cultural events. The Maui Arts & Cultural Center in Kahului is the island's premier venue for the visual and performing arts, offering everything from concerts and theater productions to art exhibitions. In Lahaina, the Friday Night Art Walk is a popular event where galleries open their doors to showcase local artists. The island is also home to several artisan markets, such as the Maui Swap Meet and the Upcountry Farmer's Market, where you can find handmade crafts, jewelry, and artwork. The natural beauty of Maui provides endless inspiration for artists, and visitors can take home a piece of the island's creative spirit.

10. Welcoming Aloha Spirit

Perhaps the most compelling reason to visit Maui is the warmth and hospitality of its people. The Aloha Spirit is a way of life in Hawaii, characterized by kindness, generosity, and respect for others. From the moment you arrive, you'll be greeted with a warm Aloha and a friendly smile. The locals are eager to share their culture, traditions, and knowledge of the island, making your stay in Maui truly special. Whether you're attending a community event, participating in a cultural activity, or simply chatting with a local, the Aloha Spirit will leave a lasting impression on your heart.

Chapter 2: Know Before You Go

Best Time to Visit

Maui is a destination that offers year-round appeal, thanks to its tropical climate and diverse attractions. However, the best time to visit can depend on various factors such as weather, crowd levels, and specific activities you want to experience. Here's a detailed guide to help you decide the best time to plan your trip to Maui.

Weather Considerations

Winter (December to February)

Weather: Winter in Maui is mild with temperatures ranging from the mid-60s to low 80s Fahrenheit (18-27°C). Rain showers are more frequent, especially in the northern and eastern parts of the island.

Pros: This is the peak season for whale watching as humpback whales migrate to Maui's warm waters. Winter also offers a respite from the cold weather on the mainland.

Cons: Higher prices and larger crowds due to holiday travel and winter vacations.

Spring (March to May)

Weather: Spring brings pleasant temperatures ranging from the mid-60s to mid-80s Fahrenheit (18-29°C). Rainfall decreases compared to winter.

Pros: Lower hotel rates and fewer tourists make it an excellent time to visit. The island's flora is in full bloom, offering beautiful scenery.

Cons: Some activities, like whale watching, may be less available as the season progresses.

Summer (June to August)

Weather: Summer temperatures range from the low 70s to the high 80s Fahrenheit (21-31°C). The weather is dry, and the ocean is calm.

Pros: Ideal conditions for water activities like snorkeling, diving, and surfing. Families find it convenient due to school vacations.

Cons: Peak tourist season leads to crowded attractions and higher accommodation prices.

Fall (September to November)

Weather: Fall temperatures are similar to those in spring, ranging from the mid-60s to mid-80s Fahrenheit (18-29°C). The weather is generally dry.

Pros: Another great shoulder season with fewer crowds and lower prices. Excellent time for outdoor activities and enjoying the beaches.

Cons: The risk of hurricanes is slightly higher in early fall, although direct hits are rare.

Crowd Levels and Accommodation Prices

Peak Season: The busiest times are during winter holidays (December through February) and summer (June through August). Expect higher prices for flights and accommodations.

Shoulder Season: Spring (March to May) and fall (September to November) are considered shoulder seasons with moderate crowds and more reasonable prices. These periods offer a balance of good weather, fewer tourists, and better deals.

Off-Peak Season: While Maui doesn't have a true off-peak season, the months of April and May, as well as September and October, tend to be less crowded and more affordable.

Events and Festivals

Winter: The Maui Whale Festival in February celebrates the annual return of humpback whales.

Spring: The East Maui Taro Festival in April highlights the island's cultural heritage with traditional foods and music.

Summer: The Kapalua Wine & Food Festival in June and the Maui Film Festival in June-July are notable events.

Fall: The Aloha Festivals, which span multiple islands, often have events in Maui during September and October, celebrating Hawaiian culture with parades, music, and dance.

Activity-Specific Timing

Whale Watching: Best from December to April, peaking in February and March.

Surfing: Winter months are best for experienced surfers on the north shore, while summer offers gentler waves suitable for beginners on the south shore.

Snorkeling and Diving: Summer provides the calmest waters and the best visibility.

Hiking: Trails are accessible year-round, but the dry season (April to October) offers more predictable weather.

Best Time to Visit the Maui Based on Interests and Preferences

Choosing the best time to visit Maui depends on your interests and what you hope to experience during your trip. Here's a detailed breakdown based on various interests:

Beach and Water Activities

- **Best Time:** April to October

These months offer the warmest ocean temperatures and calmest waters, making it ideal for swimming, snorkeling, scuba diving, and other water sports. South and west shores, such as Kaanapali and Wailea, are particularly favorable during this period.

Whale Watching

- **Best Time:** December to April

Humpback whales migrate to Maui's warm waters during winter. The peak months are January to March. Whale-watching tours operate from Lahaina and Maalaea Harbor, providing opportunities to see these magnificent creatures up close.

Surfing and Windsurfing

- **Best Time:** November to March (north shore), June to August (south shore)

Winter months bring larger swells to the north shore, particularly around Paia and Ho'okipa Beach. Summer offers smaller but consistent waves on the south shore, around Kihei and Lahaina.

Hiking and Exploring Nature

- **Best Time:** March to May, September to November

During these shoulder seasons, temperatures are moderate, and there's less rainfall compared to winter. Trails in Haleakala National Park and the Iao Valley are less crowded, offering a more serene experience.

Avoiding Crowds

- **Best Time:** April to early June, September to mid-November

These periods are outside the peak tourist seasons (summer and winter holidays), resulting in fewer crowds. Accommodation and activity prices are also generally lower.

Cultural Festivals and Events

- **Best Time:** Year-round (specific events have fixed dates)

Maui Film Festival: Usually held in June in Wailea.

Hawaiian Slack Key Guitar Festival: Typically, in June.

Maui County Fair: Usually in October in Wailuku.

Aloha Festivals: Held in September, celebrating Hawaiian culture.

Check local event calendars for exact dates and additional events.

Budget-Friendly Travel

- **Best Time:** April to mid-June, September to mid-December

These shoulder seasons offer lower airfare and accommodation rates compared to peak tourist seasons. You can enjoy the island's beauty without breaking the bank.

Photography and Scenic Beauty

- **Best Time:** Year-round

Maui's diverse landscapes are stunning any time of year. However, the golden hours (sunrise and sunset) provide the best lighting for photography.

Sunrise at Haleakala Crater and sunsets in Lahaina or Kaanapali are particularly breathtaking.

Golfing

- **Best Time:** Year-round

Maui's climate is suitable for golfing any time of the year. However, spring and fall offer the most pleasant weather with moderate temperatures and less humidity, making it comfortable for extended hours on the golf course. Courses in Wailea and Kapalua are renowned for their stunning views and challenging play.

Family Travel

- **Best Time:** June to August, December to January (school holidays)

These periods coincide with school vacations, making it convenient for families with children. Summer offers excellent weather for beach activities, while winter provides opportunities for whale watching and holiday events. Family-friendly resorts often have special programs during these times.

Romantic Getaways

- **Best Time:** February (Valentine's Day), May (spring bloom), September to November

February is popular for romantic getaways due to Valentine's Day, while May offers beautiful spring flowers. The fall season, with fewer crowds and moderate weather, is also ideal for a romantic escape. Consider visiting secluded beaches like Makena Beach or taking a sunset cruise.

Adventure and Outdoor Activities

- **Best Time:** April to October

These months provide optimal weather for outdoor adventures like zip-lining, paragliding, and ATV tours. The Road to Hana is also best explored during this time, with less chance of rain making the drive safer and more enjoyable.

Festivals and Cultural Experiences

- **Best Time:** Year-round (specific dates for events)

Maui hosts numerous cultural events throughout the year. For example:

Maui Arts & Cultural Center Events: Year-round performances and exhibitions.

Maui Onion Festival: Usually in May, celebrating the famous Maui onions.

Makawao Rodeo: Typically held around the Fourth of July, showcasing Hawaiian paniolo (cowboy) culture.

Keeping an eye on local event calendars will help you plan your visit around these enriching cultural experiences.

Health and Wellness Retreats

- **Best Time:** Year-round

Maui offers numerous wellness retreats focusing on yoga, meditation, and holistic health. Many resorts and wellness centers offer retreats throughout the year. The tranquil environment of Maui's beaches and tropical forests provides a perfect setting for relaxation and rejuvenation.

Eco-Tourism

- **Best Time:** Year-round

Eco-friendly tours and activities are available throughout the year. Visiting during the off-peak seasons (spring and fall) can enhance your experience with fewer tourists. Participate in conservation activities, such as beach clean-ups or volunteering at local wildlife sanctuaries.

Month-by-month Guide to Visiting Maui

January

January is a popular month to visit Maui, especially for those looking to escape colder climates. The weather is generally warm with daytime temperatures averaging in the low 80s°F (around 27°C). However, it's the rainy season, particularly in the northern and eastern parts of the island. This makes the lush areas like Hana exceptionally green and vibrant. Whale-watching season is in full swing, making it a prime time for those interested in seeing humpback whales. Beaches in the south and west tend to be sunnier and less rainy, providing great conditions for sunbathing and swimming.

February

February continues the whale watching season, offering some of the best opportunities to see these magnificent creatures. The weather remains warm, with occasional showers, especially in the afternoons. Surfing conditions are ideal on the north shore, particularly in places like Peahi (Jaws) where big wave surfers gather. It's still the high tourist season, so popular spots might be crowded, and accommodations can be pricier.

March

March sees a slight increase in temperatures, making it a pleasant time for beach activities and exploring the island. The rain begins to taper off towards the end of the month. The tail end of the whale watching season still offers sightings. The spring break period can bring an influx of visitors, particularly families, so planning and booking accommodations in advance is advisable.

April

April is a transition month with fewer tourists and a drop in accommodation prices. The weather is warm and relatively dry, making it an ideal time for hiking, snorkeling, and exploring Maui's natural beauty. The landscapes are still lush from the winter rains, and the ocean conditions are calm, perfect for underwater activities.

May

May offers a balance of good weather and fewer crowds. Temperatures are consistently warm, averaging in the mid-80s°F (around 29°C), and rainfall is minimal. This month is great for outdoor adventures like hiking in Haleakalā National Park or driving the scenic Road to Hana. The ocean is usually calm, providing excellent conditions for snorkeling, diving, and other water sports.

June

June marks the beginning of the summer season. The weather is hot and dry, with temperatures often reaching the high 80s°F (around 31°C). The ocean is warm, making it ideal for swimming, surfing, and other water activities. Summer brings more tourists, so popular attractions and beaches can become crowded. This is a good time for family vacations, with many family-friendly activities and events.

July

July is one of the hottest months on Maui, with temperatures frequently hitting the high 80s and sometimes the low 90s°F (32-34°C). The weather is dry, and the ocean is perfect for all types of water sports. This is the peak of the summer season, so expect larger crowds and higher accommodation prices. The Fourth of July celebrations in Lahaina are a highlight, featuring parades, fireworks, and local festivities.

August

August continues the summer trend with hot and dry weather. It's one of the busiest months due to school holidays, leading to crowded beaches and tourist spots. Ocean conditions remain excellent for water activities, but it's advisable to book tours and accommodations well in advance. Despite the heat, the trade winds provide some relief, especially in the evenings.

September

September sees a decrease in tourist numbers as the summer season winds down. The weather is still warm and pleasant, with less humidity than in peak summer. This is a great month for those looking to enjoy Maui's beauty without the crowds. Hotel rates begin to drop, making it a more budget-friendly time to visit. The ocean remains warm, ideal for swimming and snorkeling.

October

October is considered one of the best months to visit Maui. The weather is consistently warm, with daytime temperatures in the mid-80s°F (around 29°C) and minimal rainfall. The summer crowds have dwindled, making it a perfect time for a more relaxed and peaceful visit. The ocean conditions are excellent for diving and snorkeling, with clear waters and abundant marine life.

November

November marks the beginning of the winter season, with slightly cooler temperatures and an increase in rainfall, especially towards the end of the month. Early November can be a great time to visit due to fewer crowds and lower prices.

The island starts to prepare for the holiday season, and the landscapes remain lush and green from the rains. It's a good time for hiking and exploring Maui's natural attractions.

December

December is a festive month in Maui, with holiday decorations and events creating a vibrant atmosphere. The weather is warm, with temperatures in the low 80s°F (around 27°C), but there's an increase in rainfall, particularly in the northern and eastern parts of the island. The high tourist season returns, with many visitors seeking to spend their holidays in a tropical paradise. Whale-watching season begins again, adding another exciting activity to the itinerary. Prices for accommodations and flights can be high, so early booking is recommended.

Getting to Maui

Reaching Maui, one of Hawaii's most beloved islands, requires some planning, especially considering its remote location in the central Pacific Ocean. Here's a detailed guide on how to get to Maui:

Flights to Maui

Major Airports

Maui is served by two main airports:

Kahului Airport (OGG): The primary airport located on the north shore of Maui. It handles most of the island's long-distance flights and serves as the main gateway for tourists.

Kapalua Airport (JHM): A smaller airport on the west side of Maui, near the resort areas of Kaanapali and Lahaina. It mainly handles inter-island flights and private charters.

Direct Flights

Many major airlines offer direct flights to Kahului Airport from various U.S. mainland cities. Popular departure points include:

West Coast: Los Angeles (LAX), San Francisco (SFO), Seattle (SEA), Portland (PDX)

Other Major Hubs: Denver (DEN), Chicago (ORD), Dallas (DFW), Phoenix (PHX)

Connecting Flights

For travelers coming from other parts of the U.S. or international destinations, connecting flights are often necessary. Common layover cities include:

Honolulu (HNL): Many flights route through Honolulu International Airport on Oahu, which is the largest airport in Hawaii. From Honolulu, you can catch a short, 30–40-minute inter-island flight to Maui.

West Coast Cities: Major west coast hubs like Los Angeles, San Francisco, and Seattle often serve as layover points for flights to Maui.

Airlines Serving Maui

Several airlines provide regular service to Maui, including:

- Hawaiian Airlines
- Alaska Airlines
- American Airlines
- Delta Air Lines
- Southwest Airlines
- United Airlines
- Inter-Island Travel

If you are visiting other Hawaiian Islands as part of your trip, you can reach Maui via inter-island flights or ferries.

Inter-Island Flights

Hawaiian Airlines: Offers frequent flights between Maui and other Hawaiian Islands, including Oahu, Kauai, and the Big Island.

Southwest Airlines: Recently started offering inter-island flights, providing an additional option for travelers.

Ferry Services

Expeditions Lanai Ferry: Provides service between Lahaina on Maui and Manele Bay on Lanai. This is a great option for day trips or multi-island itineraries.

Molokai Ferry: Although currently not in operation, there have been ferry services between Maui and Molokai in the past. It's worth checking for any updates or new services before your trip.

Private Charters and Yachts

For a more luxurious or customized travel experience, private charters and yachts are available. These can be arranged through specialized travel agencies and provide a unique way to arrive in Maui.

Getting Around the Island

Once you arrive in Maui, you'll need transportation to explore the island.

Car Rentals

Renting a car is the most convenient way to get around Maui, offering flexibility to explore at your own pace. Major rental companies operate out of Kahului Airport and other locations around the island.

Public Transportation

Maui Bus: The public bus system provides service to various parts of the island, including major tourist areas. It's a cost-effective option but can be less convenient than renting a car due to limited routes and schedules.

Taxis and Rideshares

Taxis: Available at the airport and in major tourist areas, though they can be more expensive for longer distances.

Rideshare Services: Uber and Lyft operate on Maui, providing convenient and often cheaper alternatives to taxis.

Shuttle Services

Many hotels and resorts offer shuttle services to and from the airport and popular attractions. Check with your accommodation to see if this service is available.

Tips for Air Travel to Maui

Book Early: Flights to Maui can fill up quickly, especially during peak travel seasons. Booking early can help you secure the best fares and preferred flight times.

Check for Deals: Airlines often have sales or offer discounted fares during certain times of the year. Sign up for fare alerts and keep an eye out for promotions.

Travel Insurance: Consider purchasing travel insurance that covers flight cancellations, delays, and other unexpected issues, especially if traveling during hurricane season.

Visa and Entry Requirements

Maui, being a part of the state of Hawaii, follows the entry requirements of the United States for international travelers. Here are the comprehensive details regarding Maui visa and entry requirements:

Visa Requirements for Maui

Visa Waiver Program (VWP) Eligibility:

Most travelers visiting Maui, as part of Hawaii and the United States, can enter under the Visa Waiver Program (VWP), provided they meet the following criteria:

Citizenship: Travelers must be citizens of one of the countries participating in the Visa Waiver Program. This includes most European countries, Australia, Japan, South Korea, and others. A full list of eligible countries can be found on the official website of the U.S. Department of State.

Purpose of Visit: Travelers must intend to visit for tourism, business, or certain other specified purposes (e.g., medical treatment, short-term study).

ESTA Authorization: Before travel, travelers must obtain approval through the Electronic System for Travel Authorization (ESTA). ESTA is an automated system that determines the eligibility of visitors to travel to the United States under the VWP.

Visa Requirements for Non-VWP Countries:

Travelers from countries not eligible for the Visa Waiver Program must apply for a visa at a U.S. embassy or consulate. The type of visa required depends on the purpose of the visit (e.g., tourist visa, business visa, etc.). Detailed information on visa categories and application procedures can be obtained from the nearest U.S. embassy or consulate.

Important Notes:

Passport Validity: All travelers, regardless of nationality, must have a passport valid for at least six months beyond their intended stay in the United States.

Entry Conditions: Entry to Maui (Hawaii) is considered entry into the United States. Travelers must comply with U.S. immigration and customs regulations.

Transit Passengers: Travelers transiting through U.S. airports en route to another destination must also comply with U.S. entry requirements.

Customs and Immigration Procedures

Arrival Procedures:

Upon arrival in Maui (Hawaii), travelers are required to proceed through immigration and customs control. Procedures typically include:

Immigration Inspection: Presenting a valid passport and completed arrival/departure form (Form I-94 or electronic equivalent).

Customs Declaration: Completing a customs declaration form and declaring any goods or items being brought into the United States.

Customs Regulations:

Duty-Free Allowances: There are limits on the value and quantity of goods that travelers can bring into the United States duty-free. Items exceeding these limits may be subject to customs duties and taxes.

Prohibited Items: Certain items, such as agricultural products, firearms, and certain medications, may be restricted or prohibited. It's important to review and comply with U.S. customs regulations to avoid penalties or confiscation of items.

Departure Procedures:

When departing from Maui (Hawaii), travelers are required to go through security checks and may be subject to additional screening procedures before boarding their flight.

Health and Safety Considerations

Health Requirements:

Vaccinations: No specific vaccinations are required for entry into Maui unless travelers are arriving from or have recently visited a region with specific health risks. It's advisable to check with a healthcare provider for recommended vaccinations.

COVID-19 Requirements: During the COVID-19 pandemic, additional health protocols may be in place, such as testing requirements or quarantine measures. Travelers should check the latest requirements from both the U.S. government and relevant authorities in their home country.

Travel Insurance:

Travelers are advised to have adequate travel insurance covering medical expenses, including potential COVID-19-related costs, as healthcare in the United States can be expensive for non-residents.

Budgeting and Costs

Planning a budget for a vacation to Maui involves considering various factors such as transportation, accommodation, food, activities, and unexpected expenses. Here's a detailed guide to help you manage your travel costs effectively:

1. Flights to Maui

Booking Tips:

Timing: Prices for flights to Maui can vary significantly depending on the season. Aim to book tickets well in advance, ideally 2-3 months before your travel dates, to secure the best fares.

Comparison: Use flight comparison websites or apps to find the most competitive prices across different airlines.

Flexible Dates: Being flexible with your travel dates can help you find cheaper options.

Cost Range: Flights to Maui from mainland USA typically range from $300 to $800 round-trip per person, depending on departure city and time of booking.

2. Accommodation Costs

Types of Accommodation:

Resorts and Hotels: Luxury resorts in areas like Wailea and Kaanapali can range from $300 to $600+ per night.

Vacation Rentals: Condos and vacation homes can vary widely in price depending on location and amenities, averaging $150 to $300 per night.

Budget Options: Hostels and budget hotels are limited on Maui but can start from around $100 to $200 per night.

Booking Tips:

- **Off-Peak Travel:** Consider traveling during shoulder seasons (spring and fall) for lower accommodation rates.
- **Longer Stays:** Some rentals offer discounts for longer stays, so consider staying a week or more if possible.

3. Transportation Costs

Rental Cars: Recommended for exploring Maui as public transportation is limited. Prices for rental cars vary by type and company, averaging $50 to $150 per day.

Booking Tips: Book in advance and compare prices from different rental agencies. Prices can fluctuate, so check regularly for deals closer to your travel dates.

Gasoline Costs: Expect to pay around $4 to $5 per gallon for gas in Maui. Plan your driving routes efficiently to minimize fuel expenses.

4. Food and Dining

Average Costs:

Meals: Dining out in Maui ranges widely. Breakfast can cost $10 to $25 per person, lunch $15 to $30, and dinner $30 to $75+ at mid-range restaurants.

Groceries: If staying in a vacation rental, budget $50 to $100 per day for groceries depending on dietary needs and preferences.

Saving Tips:

- **Cooking:** Opt for accommodations with kitchen facilities to prepare some meals yourself.
- **Local Eateries:** Explore food trucks, local markets, and casual dining spots for more affordable options.

5. Activities and Excursions

Popular Costs:

Snorkeling Tours: $50 to $150 per person depending on duration and included amenities.

Hiking Permits: Some areas like Haleakala National Park require entrance fees of $30 per vehicle or $15 per individual.

Budgeting Tips:

- **Bundle Activities:** Look for package deals or bundles for activities like snorkeling, ziplining, or guided tours.
- **Free Activities:** Enjoy beaches, hiking trails, and scenic drives which are often free or have minimal costs.

6. Miscellaneous Expenses

Souvenirs: Budget varies widely, but plan for $50 to $200 depending on personal shopping habits.

Tips and Gratuities: Tipping is customary in Hawaii, typically 15% to 20% in restaurants and for tour guides.

Emergency Funds: Keep a buffer of $200 to $500 for unexpected expenses or medical needs.

7. Total Estimated Budget

Daily Budget Range: Depending on accommodation and dining choices, plan for $200 to $400 per day per person as a general guideline.

Total Trip Budget: For a week-long stay in Maui, excluding flights, budget around $2,500 to $5,000 per person for a comfortable experience, adjusting based on personal preferences and planned activities.

Travel Insurance

When traveling to Maui, it's generally recommended to have travel insurance to protect yourself against unexpected events that could disrupt or affect your trip. Here are some key points to consider regarding travel insurance for Maui:

Coverage Essentials

Trip Cancellation and Interruption: Covers non-refundable trip costs if you need to cancel or cut short your trip due to covered reasons, such as illness, injury, or severe weather.

Medical Coverage: Provides coverage for medical expenses if you become ill or injured during your trip. This includes doctor visits, hospitalization, and emergency medical evacuation if needed.

Baggage and Personal Belongings: Covers loss, theft, or damage to your luggage and personal items during your trip.

Travel Delays: Reimburses you for additional expenses due to travel delays, such as accommodation and meals, if your trip is delayed for a covered reason.

Emergency Assistance Services: Provides access to 24/7 emergency assistance services, including medical and travel assistance.

Specific Considerations for Maui

Outdoor Activities: If you plan to engage in outdoor activities like hiking, snorkeling, or surfing, ensure your insurance covers these activities. Some insurers may require additional sports or adventure coverage.

Natural Disasters: Given Maui's geographical location, it's wise to check if your insurance covers disruptions caused by natural disasters such as hurricanes or volcanic activity.

Rental Car Coverage: If you plan to rent a car in Maui, consider insurance coverage for rental vehicles, which can protect you against accidents and damage to the rental car.

How to Choose the Right Policy

When selecting travel insurance for Maui, consider the following factors:

Coverage Limits: Ensure the policy limits are sufficient to cover potential expenses, especially for medical emergencies and trip cancellation costs.

Exclusions and Limitations: Review the policy exclusions carefully to understand what is not covered, such as pre-existing medical conditions or risky activities.

Provider Reputation: Choose a reputable insurance provider with a strong track record of customer service and claims processing.

Policy Cost: Compare premiums and deductibles across different policies to find one that fits your budget while offering adequate coverage.

Policy Flexibility: Look for policies that offer flexibility in terms of coverage duration and optional add-ons for specific needs.

Where to Get Travel Insurance

Travel Insurance Providers: Many travel insurance providers offer comprehensive plans that cater specifically to travelers visiting Hawaii, including Maui. Compare plans to find one that suits your needs.

Credit Card Benefits: Some credit cards offer travel insurance as a benefit when you use the card to purchase travel expenses. Review your card's terms and conditions to see if it includes adequate coverage for your trip.

Travel Agencies and Online Platforms: Travel agencies and online booking platforms often offer travel insurance options during the booking process. Compare coverage and prices to find the best option for your trip to Maui

By securing appropriate travel insurance, you can enjoy peace of mind knowing that you are financially protected against unforeseen circumstances during your visit to Maui. Always read the policy details carefully to understand what is covered and any exclusions that may apply.

Chapter 3: Accommodation

Types of Accommodation in Maui

Maui offers a diverse range of accommodation options to suit various budgets and preferences. Here's a comprehensive guide to the different types of accommodations you can find on the island:

1. Luxury Resorts

Maui is renowned for its luxury resorts, which offer world-class amenities, including oceanfront views, fine dining, and private beach access. Located primarily in Wailea and Kaanapali, these resorts often feature sprawling pools, golf courses, and spa services, making them ideal for a high-end vacation experience. The resorts are designed with Hawaiian-inspired architecture, blending indoor and outdoor living. Room types range from elegant suites to private villas, some with direct beach access. Prices typically start at $500 per night and can go up to several thousand dollars for more exclusive options.

2. Condominiums and Vacation Rentals

Condominiums and vacation rentals are popular choices for those seeking a more home-like atmosphere. These accommodations are scattered throughout Maui, with concentrations in Kihei, Lahaina, and Kapalua. They offer the convenience of self-catering facilities, such as fully equipped kitchens and laundry rooms, making them perfect for families or longer stays. Many condos are part of resort complexes, giving guests access to shared amenities like pools and fitness centers. Depending on location and amenities, prices range from $150 to $400 per night.

3. Boutique Hotels and Inns

Maui's boutique hotels and inns provide a more intimate and personalized experience than larger resorts. Often family-owned, these accommodations are usually located in quieter areas like Paia, Hana, and Upcountry Maui. They feature unique decor and offer a more authentic Hawaiian experience, often with fewer rooms and a focus on local culture. These hotels may not have the extensive amenities of larger resorts, but they excel in charm and character. Prices generally range from $200 to $600 per night.

4. Bed and Breakfasts

For a cozy, home-like atmosphere, Maui's bed and breakfasts offer personalized service and a chance to experience local hospitality. Typically located in residential areas such as Makawao, Haiku, and Hana, these accommodations provide comfortable rooms with homemade breakfasts. Many B&Bs are in charming, historic homes or unique properties with beautiful gardens and scenic views. Guests can enjoy a more laid-back and authentic experience, often with the opportunity to interact with local hosts. Prices usually range from $150 to $350 per night.

5. Budget Hotels and Motels

For travelers on a budget, Maui offers a selection of budget hotels and motels, primarily located in central areas like Kahului and Wailuku. These accommodations provide basic amenities, such as free Wi-Fi, parking, and air conditioning. While they may lack the luxury of resorts, they offer clean and comfortable lodging at a fraction of the price. Some budget hotels also feature on-site dining or are conveniently located near restaurants and shopping centers. Prices typically range from $100 to $200 per night, making them a great option for budget-conscious travelers.

6. Camping and Eco-Lodges

For a more adventurous experience, Maui's campgrounds and eco-lodges offer a unique way to connect with nature. Campgrounds are available in state parks like Hosmer Grove and Kipahulu, offering basic facilities such as restrooms and picnic areas. Eco-lodges, often located in remote areas like Hana and Upcountry Maui, focus on sustainability and provide rustic accommodations surrounded by natural beauty. These options are ideal for those who enjoy outdoor activities and want to experience Maui's stunning landscapes firsthand. Prices for camping are very affordable, usually under $50 per night, while eco-lodges can range from $100 to $300 per night, depending on the level of comfort and amenities offered.

7. Villas and Private Homes

For those seeking privacy and a more exclusive stay, renting a villa or private home is an excellent option in Maui. These accommodations are often located in upscale areas like Wailea, Kapalua, and Kaanapali, offering spacious living areas, private pools, and fully equipped kitchens. Many homes also boast stunning ocean views and direct beach access.

Villas and private homes are ideal for families or groups, providing the space and amenities needed for a comfortable, extended stay. The experience is akin to having a luxurious home away from home, with added perks such as housekeeping services and concierge assistance available in some properties. Prices for villas and private homes typically start around $500 per night and can exceed $5,000 per night for the most luxurious estates.

8. Hostels and Shared Accommodations

Maui's hostels provide an affordable and social lodging option, particularly for solo travelers or backpackers. Found mainly in Paia, Wailuku, and Lahaina, these accommodations offer dormitory-style rooms with shared bathrooms, kitchens, and communal spaces. Some hostels also provide private rooms for a bit more privacy. Hostels often organize group activities like hiking tours, surf lessons, and social events, creating a community vibe among guests. This is a great way to meet other travelers and explore the island on a budget. Prices range from $30 to $100 per night, making them the most economical choice for accommodation in Maui.

9. Cottages and Bungalows

Maui's cottages and bungalows provide a charming and often secluded retreat, perfect for those looking to escape the crowds. These standalone accommodations are typically found in serene locations such as Hana, Kula, and Upcountry Maui. Cottages and bungalows offer a cozy, rustic atmosphere with features like private lanais (porches), garden views, and sometimes even outdoor showers. They are often surrounded by lush tropical gardens or set in peaceful countryside settings, offering a more tranquil experience. Many come with kitchenettes, allowing guests to prepare their meals. Prices generally range from $150 to $400 per night, depending on the location and level of comfort.

10. Agritourism Stays

For a unique and immersive experience, consider an agritourism stay in Maui, where guests can stay on working farms or ranches. These accommodations are typically located in Upcountry Maui and Hana, providing a rustic and educational experience. Guests can participate in farm activities, such as harvesting crops, tending to animals, or even making local products like honey or coffee. Agritourism stays offer a deeper connection to the island's agricultural heritage and are ideal for those who appreciate sustainable living and local food.

Accommodations range from simple farm stays to more luxurious farmhouses, with prices varying from $100 to $300 per night.

11. Timeshares

Maui is home to several timeshare properties, offering a blend of resort amenities with the comforts of a private condo. These accommodations are particularly popular in areas like Lahaina, Kaanapali, and Kihei. Timeshares often come with multiple bedrooms, full kitchens, and living areas, making them ideal for families or groups. Guests typically have access to resort-style amenities such as pools, fitness centers, and on-site dining. Timeshare stays provide a home-away-from-home experience with the flexibility of a resort. Prices for timeshare rentals can vary widely depending on the season and location, typically ranging from $200 to $500 per night.

12. Wellness Retreats

For those seeking rejuvenation and relaxation, Maui's wellness retreats offer a holistic experience focused on health and well-being. These retreats are often nestled in secluded areas like Hana and Upcountry Maui, providing a serene environment surrounded by nature. Accommodations at wellness retreats range from simple, minimalist rooms to luxurious suites, all designed to promote relaxation and healing. Guests can partake in yoga classes, meditation sessions, spa treatments, and organic meals sourced from local ingredients. These retreats often offer personalized wellness programs tailored to individual needs. Prices vary depending on the level of luxury and the services offered, generally ranging from $300 to $1,000 per night.

Tips for Booking Accommodation in Maui

1. Book Early, Especially for Peak Season

Maui is a popular destination year-round, but peak seasons, such as winter (December to March) and summer (June to August), see a significant influx of visitors. To secure your preferred accommodation, it's advisable to book at least 6-12 months in advance, especially for high-end resorts, villas, or unique stays like cottages and bungalows.

2. Consider the Location

Maui is diverse in its landscapes and activities. Decide on the type of vacation you want—beachfront relaxation, hiking and exploring nature, or cultural immersion. Wailea and Kaanapali are known for their luxury resorts and beautiful beaches, while Paia and Hana offer a more laid-back, local experience. Upcountry Maui provides a cooler climate and access to hiking trails and farms. Choose your accommodation based on proximity to the activities you plan to enjoy.

3. Look for Package Deals

Many resorts and hotels in Maui offer package deals that include amenities like breakfast, car rentals, or even activities such as snorkeling or luau tickets. These packages can save you money and simplify your planning. Be sure to compare what's included in the package with booking everything separately to ensure you're getting a good deal.

4. Check Cancellation Policies

Given the unpredictable nature of travel plans, it's crucial to review the cancellation policies before booking. Some accommodations offer free cancellations up to a certain date, while others may charge a fee or require full prepayment. Flexible booking options are especially important during uncertain times, such as inclement weather or unexpected events.

5. Use a Reputable Booking Platform

When booking accommodations, use trusted platforms like Booking.com, Airbnb, or directly through the hotel's official website. These platforms often provide customer reviews, detailed descriptions, and secure payment methods. They also offer customer support in case you encounter any issues.

6. Read Reviews Carefully

Customer reviews can provide valuable insights into what to expect from your accommodation. Look for recent reviews to get a sense of the current condition and service. Pay attention to comments about cleanliness, staff friendliness, and the accuracy of the listing descriptions. Reviews can also reveal hidden gems or potential deal-breakers that you might not find in the official description.

7. Consider All Fees

When comparing prices, be sure to account for all additional fees, such as resort fees, cleaning fees (for vacation rentals), parking charges, and taxes. These fees can add up quickly and significantly increase the total cost of your stay. Ensure you understand the full cost before finalizing your booking.

8. Stay Flexible with Dates

If your travel dates are flexible, consider staying outside of peak travel periods or mid-week instead of weekends. This flexibility can often lead to better rates and more availability, especially in popular areas. Use booking platforms' flexible date features to see if shifting your stay by a day or two can offer better deals.

9. Contact the Property Directly

Sometimes, contacting the property directly can yield better rates or additional perks not available through third-party booking sites. You may also be able to request specific rooms or accommodations that meet your needs better than what's available online. It's also an opportunity to clarify any questions about the property or the area.

10. Consider Renting a Car

Maui is a large island, and many attractions are spread out. Depending on where you stay, renting a car may be necessary to explore the island fully. Some accommodations, particularly those in remote areas, may not be easily accessible without a car. Be sure to factor in car rental availability and cost when choosing your accommodation. Some hotels and resorts offer packages that include car rentals, so explore those options as well.

11. Check for Special Requirements

If you have specific needs, such as accessibility features, pet-friendly policies, or amenities like a kitchenette, verify that the accommodation meets these requirements before booking. Not all properties are equipped to handle special requests, so it's essential to confirm these details in advance.

12. Consider Alternatives to Hotels

Explore alternatives like vacation rentals, condos, and bed and breakfasts if you're looking for a more personalized experience. These options often offer more space, kitchen facilities, and a local feel that can enhance your stay. Vacation rentals, in particular, are great for families or longer stays as they provide the comforts of home.

Chapter 4: Top Experiences and Sights

15 Must-Do Experiences in Maui

Maui offers a wealth of natural beauty, cultural sites, and activities that make it a dream destination for travelers. Here are 15 must-do experiences on the island:

1. Watch the Sunrise at Haleakalā National Park

Haleakala Watching the sunrise at Haleakalā National Park is a breathtaking and unforgettable experience. Haleakalā, which means "House of the Sun" in Hawaiian, is a massive shield volcano that rises 10,023 feet above sea level. The park is renowned for its stunning sunrises, offering a spectacular view of the sun emerging over the clouds and casting a golden glow over the rugged volcanic landscape. To experience this natural wonder, plan to arrive at the summit well before sunrise. The park is a popular destination for sunrise viewing, so getting there early ensures you have a good spot to witness the awe-inspiring sight. The temperatures can be quite cold, especially in the early morning, so dress warmly and bring layers. The panoramic views from the summit are enhanced by the dramatic landscape of the crater, with its reddish, gray, and black rock formations. The play of light and shadow as the sun rises is a photographer's dream. Many visitors also take the opportunity to explore the short trails around the summit to fully appreciate the park's diverse landscapes.

Tips for Watching the Sunrise:

- **Check Sunrise Times:** Verify the sunrise time for the day of your visit and plan to arrive at least 30 to 60 minutes early.
- **Make Reservations:** If you plan to enter the park before sunrise, you may need a reservation or permit, depending on the time of year.
- **Dress in Layers:** The temperature at the summit can be freezing early in the morning, so wear warm clothing and bring blankets if needed.
- **Bring a Flashlight:** It will be dark before sunrise, so a flashlight or headlamp is useful for navigating and finding your viewing spot.
- **Be Respectful:** Keep noise to a minimum to maintain the tranquility of the experience for all visitors.

2. Drive the Road to Hana

Driving the Road to Hana is a quintessential Maui adventure, renowned for its stunning scenery and adventurous twists and turns. This 64-mile scenic drive winds along the northeastern coast of Maui, offering breathtaking views of lush rainforests, cascading waterfalls, and rugged coastline. Key highlights include the Twin Falls, Waianapanapa State Park with its black sand beaches, and the lush Oheo Gulch with its Seven Sacred Pools.

The journey can take 2.5 to 4 hours one way, depending on stops and traffic, so it's best to start early to fully enjoy the sights. The road features over 600 curves and 50 one-lane bridges, so driving requires focus and patience.

Tips for Driving the Road to Hana:

- **Start Early:** Begin your drive in the morning to avoid the crowds and make the most of daylight.
- **Plan Your Stops:** Research and plan your stops to maximize your time and experience.
- **Pack Essentials:** Bring snacks, water, and sunscreen, as amenities are limited along the route.
- **Drive Carefully:** Navigate the narrow and winding road cautiously and respect local traffic rules.
- **Check Weather Conditions:** Rain can make roads slippery and impact visibility, so check weather forecasts before you go.

3. Explore Lahaina's Historic Town

Spot Exploring Lahaina's historic town offers a fascinating glimpse into Maui's past, combining rich history with vibrant culture. Once the capital of the Hawaiian Kingdom, Lahaina is now a charming town filled with preserved landmarks and cultural sites. Start your visit at Lahaina Banyan Court Park, home to the largest banyan tree in the U.S., planted in 1873. The tree provides a picturesque setting for local art fairs and events. Nearby, visit the Lahaina Historic Trail, which features several important sites, including the Old Lahaina Courthouse and the Waiola Church, one of Maui's oldest churches. Stroll along Front Street, lined with historic buildings now housing shops, galleries, and restaurants. You'll also find the Lahaina Jodo Mission, known for its impressive Buddha statue and peaceful gardens. Don't miss the Wo Hing Museum, which offers insights into the Chinese immigrant experience in Hawaii, or the Baldwin Home Museum, the oldest house on Maui, showcasing early missionary life.

Tips for Exploring Lahaina:

- **Wear Comfortable Shoes:** You'll be walking a lot on historic streets and pathways.

- **Check Opening Hours:** Museums and historic sites may have varying hours, so plan your visit accordingly.
- **Bring Cash:** Some smaller shops and eateries may only accept cash.
- **Explore Early or Late:** To avoid crowds and enjoy a more leisurely experience, visit popular sites early in the morning or later in the afternoon.

4. Relax on Kāʻanapali Beach

Relaxing on Kāʻanapali Beach offers a quintessential Maui experience with its stunning scenery and tranquil atmosphere. Located on the western coast of Maui, Kāʻanapali Beach stretches for three miles of golden sand and clear turquoise waters. It's renowned for its soft sand, gentle waves, and picturesque backdrop of the West Maui Mountains. The beach is ideal for sunbathing, swimming, and snorkeling, with calm waters and excellent visibility for exploring underwater life. For a more active experience, you can try stand-up paddleboarding or take a sailing excursion from the nearby resorts. The beach is also well-equipped with amenities, including beachside restaurants, shops, and restrooms.

Tips for Enjoying Kāʻanapali Beach:

- **Arrive Early:** To secure a prime spot and enjoy the best light for photos, consider arriving early in the day.

- **Bring Essentials:** Pack sunscreen, a hat, and plenty of water to stay hydrated and protected from the sun.
- **Rent Equipment:** If you're interested in water sports, rent gear from local shops or hotel services.
- **Respect the Environment:** Follow beach rules and clean up after yourself to help preserve the natural beauty of the area.

5. Visit ʻĪao Valley State Park

Visiting ʻĪao Valley State Park offers a captivating glimpse into Maui's natural beauty and cultural heritage. Located in central Maui, this lush park is famous for its striking landscapes, particularly the iconic ʻĪao Needle, a 1,200-foot tall rock formation that rises dramatically from the valley floor. The needle, a remnant of an ancient volcano, is set against a backdrop of verdant rainforests and flowing streams, creating a stunning visual contrast. The park features several scenic trails that provide opportunities for leisurely hikes and exploration. The Iao Needle Lookout Trail is a short, paved path leading to a viewpoint where you can take in panoramic vistas of the valley and the needle. For a more immersive experience, the Ethnobotanical Trail offers insights into the native plants and their historical uses by the Hawaiian people.

Tips for Visiting ʻĪao Valley State Park:

- **Check Weather Conditions:** The park is often misty and can experience sudden rain, so dress in layers and bring a light rain jacket.
- **Arrive Early:** To enjoy a quieter experience and avoid crowds, try to arrive early in the morning.
- **Wear Comfortable Shoes:** Sturdy, comfortable footwear is recommended for walking on uneven or slippery trails.
- **Respect Park Guidelines:** Follow park rules to protect the natural environment and preserve its beauty for future visitors.

6. Snorkel at Molokini Crater

Snorkeling at Molokini Crater is a highlight of any Maui adventure, offering an exceptional underwater experience. Located about 3 miles off the coast of Maui, Molokini is a crescent-shaped volcanic caldera that is renowned for its crystal-clear waters and vibrant marine life. The crater, partly submerged, forms a protected marine sanctuary ideal for snorkeling and diving.

Snorkeling Experience:

Marine Life: The waters around Molokini are teeming with colorful coral reefs, tropical fish, and sometimes even larger species like manta rays and sea turtles. The visibility is often exceptional, ranging from 80 to 150 feet, providing a clear view of the underwater landscape.

Conditions: The crater's shape and location offer relatively calm waters, making it a great spot for both beginner and experienced snorkelers. However, conditions can vary, so it's always best to check the weather and sea conditions before your trip.

Tips for Snorkeling at Molokini Crater:

- **Book a Tour:** Most visitors reach Molokini via boat tours departing from Maui's harbor. Ensure you book in advance, especially during peak seasons.
- **Wear Proper Gear:** Bring or rent high-quality snorkeling gear, including a mask, snorkel, and fins. Some tours provide equipment, but it's good to check beforehand.
- **Bring Sunscreen:** Use reef-safe sunscreen to protect your skin and the marine environment.
- **Follow Safety Guidelines:** Listen to your guide's instructions on safety and marine conservation to ensure a safe and respectful snorkeling experience.
- **Stay Hydrated and Eat Light:** Bring water and a light snack for the trip, as you'll need energy for snorkeling and boat travel.

7. Attend a Traditional Hawaiian Luau

Attending a traditional Hawaiian luau is a quintessential experience that offers a deep dive into Hawaii's rich culture. A luau typically begins with a welcoming lei greeting, followed by an elaborate feast featuring dishes like kalua pig (slow-cooked in an underground oven called an imu), poke, poi, and tropical fruits. The highlight of the evening is the live entertainment, which includes hula dancing, traditional Hawaiian music, and the dramatic Samoan fire knife dance. These performances are not only entertaining but also serve as a cultural storytelling medium, preserving and sharing Hawaiian legends and traditions.

Tips for Attending a Luau:

- **Book in Advance:** Luaus are popular and can sell out quickly, so it's wise to book your tickets in advance.
- **Arrive Early:** Arriving early allows you to enjoy the full experience, including pre-dinner activities like lei-making or traditional Hawaiian games.
- **Dress Comfortably:** Wear comfortable clothing, preferably with a Hawaiian touch, like an aloha shirt or a floral dress. Don't forget your camera to capture the vibrant performances.
- **Try Everything:** Be adventurous with the food and try all the traditional dishes to get a true taste of Hawaiian cuisine.
- **Respect the Culture:** Remember that a luau is not just entertainment but a cultural ceremony. Show respect for the traditions and the performers.

8. Explore the Maui Ocean Center

Exploring the Maui Ocean Center offers an immersive and educational experience of Hawaii's marine life.

Located in Ma'alaea Harbor, this state-of-the-art aquarium showcases the rich biodiversity of the Pacific Ocean through interactive exhibits and informative displays.

Highlights of the Maui Ocean Center:

Living Reef: This exhibit features vibrant coral reefs and their inhabitants, including a variety of tropical fish, sea anemones, and other reef dwellers. It provides insight into the delicate balance of these ecosystems and their importance to marine life.

Sharks and Rays: The center is home to a variety of shark species and rays, showcased in a 750,000-gallon Open Ocean Exhibit. The tank's large acrylic viewing tunnel allows visitors to walk through and observe these majestic creatures up close.

Tide Pool: The interactive tide pool exhibit offers hands-on experiences, where visitors can gently touch and learn about starfish, sea urchins, and other intertidal animals.

Hawaiian Marine Life: Dedicated exhibits highlight the unique marine life native to Hawaiian waters, such as Hawaiian green sea turtles and Hawaiian monk seals.

Tips for Visiting the Maui Ocean Center:

- **Plan Your Visit:** The center is typically open daily from 9:00 AM to 5:00 PM. Check the website for any seasonal changes or special events.
- **Purchase Tickets in Advance:** To avoid lines and ensure entry, consider buying tickets online before your visit.
- **Wear Comfortable Shoes:** The center involves walking and standing, so comfortable footwear is recommended.
- **Explore the Gift Shop:** The on-site gift shop offers unique souvenirs, including educational toys and marine-themed merchandise.
- **Respect the Marine Life:** Follow the center's guidelines for interacting with exhibits to ensure the well-being of the animals.

9. Zipline Through Maui's Forests

Ziplining through Maui's forests offers an exhilarating way to experience the island's lush landscapes from a unique vantage point.

Several companies provide zipline tours, allowing you to soar above verdant valleys, dense rainforests, and cascading waterfalls. On a typical zipline tour, you'll be fitted with a harness and safety gear before embarking on a guided adventure through the treetops. As you glide along the ziplines, you'll enjoy panoramic views of Maui's natural beauty, including breathtaking vistas of the island's rugged terrain and tropical vegetation. Some tours even include multiple lines, with varying lengths and speeds, to provide a thrilling experience.

Tips for Ziplining:

- **Check Weight and Health Restrictions**: Ensure you meet the weight and health requirements set by the tour operators for safety reasons.
- **Wear Appropriate Clothing:** Opt for comfortable, weather-appropriate clothing and closed-toe shoes. Avoid loose items that could get caught during the ride.
- **Listen to Your Guides:** Pay close attention to safety instructions and guidelines provided by your guides to ensure a safe and enjoyable experience.
- **Book in Advance:** Zipline tours are popular, so book your spot ahead of time to secure your preferred date and time.

10. Enjoy a Farm-to-Table Dining Experience

Enjoying a farm-to-table dining experience in Maui is a delightful way to savor the island's fresh, local produce and support sustainable agriculture.

These dining experiences focus on using ingredients sourced directly from local farms, ensuring that you enjoy the freshest flavors while also supporting the community. Restaurants like The Mill House and Mama's Fish House are renowned for their farm-to-table approach. At The Mill House, you'll dine on dishes crafted from ingredients grown on the on-site farm, with a menu that changes seasonally to highlight the best produce. Mama's Fish House offers an authentic taste of Maui with its seafood caught by local fishermen, ensuring freshness and flavor in every bite. The experience often includes a farm tour, where you can see firsthand where the ingredients are grown, followed by a meal featuring dishes made from those very ingredients. This connection between farm and plate enhances your appreciation of the food and the effort involved in its production.

Tips for Farm-to-Table Dining:

- **Make Reservations:** Farm-to-table restaurants can be popular, so booking ahead ensures you get a spot.
- **Ask About the Farm:** Inquire about the local farms and producers featured in your meal to learn more about the source of your food.
- **Be Adventurous:** Embrace the seasonal menu and try new dishes that highlight local ingredients.

11. Hike the Pipiwai Trail

The Pipiwai Trail, located within Haleakalā National Park on Maui, is a must-do hike for nature enthusiasts. Spanning about 4 miles round trip, this trail offers an immersive experience through Maui's lush rainforest. As you ascend, you'll pass by the enchanting Bamboo Forest, where the towering bamboo stalks create a serene, almost otherworldly atmosphere. The trail also takes you past the stunning Makahiku Falls and culminates at the awe-inspiring Waimoku Falls, a 400-foot waterfall cascading down a sheer cliff. The trail is moderately challenging, with some steep sections and rocky terrain, so sturdy footwear is recommended. The hike typically takes about 2 to 3 hours to complete, depending on your pace and how long you linger at the scenic spots. Be sure to bring plenty of water, and don't forget your camera to capture the incredible views along the way.

12. Tour a Coffee Farm in Upcountry Maui

Touring a coffee farm in Upcountry Maui offers a unique insight into the island's agricultural heritage. Nestled on the slopes of Haleakalā, these farms benefit from the rich volcanic soil and cool climate, ideal for growing high-quality coffee beans. A typical tour begins with an introduction to the coffee-growing process, from planting to harvesting. You'll walk through rows of coffee trees, learning how the beans are carefully cultivated and picked by hand. Next, you'll visit the processing facilities where the beans are sorted, pulped, and dried.

Many tours also include a demonstration of roasting, where you can smell the rich aroma of freshly roasted coffee. The experience often concludes with a tasting session, where you can sample different coffee varieties produced on the farm, each with its distinct flavor profile.

Tips for Touring a Coffee Farm:

- **Book Ahead:** Tours can fill up quickly, especially during peak tourist seasons, so it's advisable to book in advance.
- **Dress Comfortably:** Wear comfortable shoes for walking through the fields and bring a hat and sunscreen, as you'll be outdoors for much of the tour.
- **Ask Questions:** Don't hesitate to ask the farmers about their techniques and the coffee-making process—they're usually happy to share their knowledge.

13. Whale Watching (Seasonal)

Maui Whale watching in Maui is a spectacular seasonal activity, typically peaking from December to April. During these months, humpback whales migrate from Alaska to the warm waters of Hawaii to breed, calve, and nurse their young. This annual migration transforms Maui into one of the best places in the world for whale watching. Several tour operators offer whale-watching excursions, which provide an up-close view of these majestic creatures in their natural habitat. These tours range from smaller, more intimate boats to larger vessels equipped with viewing platforms and knowledgeable guides who share insights about whale behavior and conservation efforts.

During the tour, you may witness various whale behaviors, including breaches (where whales leap out of the water), fluke dives (where they raise their tails high), and spouting (the mist of water vapor released when they exhale).

Tips for Whale Watching:

- **Book Early:** Whale-watching tours are popular, especially during peak season, so it's wise to book your tour well in advance.
- **Dress Appropriately:** Wear layers and bring a jacket, as it can be cooler on the water than on land. Don't forget sunscreen and a hat.
- **Bring Binoculars:** While tours usually provide spotting scopes, binoculars can enhance your viewing experience.
- **Follow Safety Instructions:** Listen to the crew's safety briefings and guidelines to ensure a safe and enjoyable experience.

14. Kayak and Paddleboard in Maui's Waters

Kayaking and paddleboarding in Maui's waters offer a unique and immersive way to experience the island's stunning coastline and marine life. Whether you're gliding over crystal-clear waters or exploring secluded coves, these activities provide both adventure and tranquility.

Kayaking

Maui's coastline offers several excellent spots for kayaking. Popular areas include:

Makena Beach: Known for its beautiful waters and scenic views, this area is great for both beginners and experienced kayakers. The nearby Molokini Crater can be reached for a more adventurous excursion.

Kihei: The calm waters of Kihei are ideal for a leisurely paddle. You might spot sea turtles and various fish species as you explore the coastline.

Lahaina: Kayaking here offers views of historic Lahaina Town and opportunities to spot marine life. Early morning is a great time to go, as the waters are calmer and wildlife more active.

Paddleboarding

Stand-up paddleboarding (SUP) is another popular way to enjoy Maui's waters. Some top spots include:

Kaanapali Beach: With its calm, clear waters and picturesque setting, Kaanapali is perfect for paddleboarding. You can paddle along the coast and enjoy views of luxury resorts and lush landscapes.

Napili Bay: This bay offers calm conditions and clear water, making it ideal for beginners. Paddle out to the rocky outcrops for a chance to see marine life up close.

Wailea: Known for its beautiful scenery and calm waters, Wailea is a great spot for a serene paddleboarding experience.

Tips for Kayaking and Paddleboarding:

- **Check Weather Conditions:** Wind and waves can affect your experience, so check the forecast before heading out.
- **Wear Appropriate Gear:** Use sunscreen, wear a hat, and bring a water bottle. It's also helpful to wear a swimsuit or quick-dry clothing.
- **Stay Hydrated and Energized:** Bring a small snack and plenty of water, especially if you plan to spend a few hours on the water.
- **Respect Wildlife:** Maintain a safe distance from marine animals and avoid disturbing their natural behavior.

- **Follow Safety Guidelines:** Wear a life jacket and follow local safety regulations, particularly if you're new to kayaking or paddleboarding.

15. Take a Helicopter Tour of Maui

Taking a helicopter tour of Maui provides a breathtaking bird's-eye view of the island's diverse landscapes, from lush rainforests and volcanic craters to stunning coastlines and waterfalls. These tours offer an unparalleled perspective of Maui's natural beauty and are an unforgettable way to explore the island.

Tour Highlights:

Scenic Views: Experience panoramic vistas of famous landmarks like the Haleakalā Crater, the Road to Hana, and the West Maui Mountains. The aerial view showcases the island's varied terrain, including hidden waterfalls and pristine beaches.

Expert Commentary: Many tours include informative commentary from knowledgeable guides, providing insights into Maui's history, geology, and ecology.

Duration: Tours typically range from 45 minutes to 1.5 hours, offering various options depending on your time and budget.

Tips for Taking a Helicopter Tour:

- **Book in Advance:** Helicopter tours are popular and can fill up quickly, so it's best to book your flight well in advance.
- **Dress Comfortably:** Wear comfortable, layered clothing and closed-toe shoes. The temperature in the helicopter can vary, and it's often cooler at higher altitudes.
- **Bring a Camera:** Ensure your camera or smartphone is fully charged to capture the stunning views. Most helicopters have large windows for unobstructed photography.
- **Arrive Early:** Arrive at the departure location early to complete any required paperwork and receive a safety briefing.
- **Follow Safety Instructions:** Listen carefully to the safety briefing provided by the tour operator and adhere to all instructions during the flight

Chapter 5: Getting Around Maui

Renting a Car

Renting a car in Maui is an experience that can significantly enhance your vacation, giving you the freedom to explore the island's diverse landscapes, from stunning beaches to lush rainforests and towering volcanoes, at your own pace.

Why Renting a Car is Essential in Maui

Maui is an island full of natural wonders, from the lush rainforests along the Road to Hana to the volcanic landscapes of Haleakalā National Park and the beautiful beaches of West and South Maui. These attractions are spread out, and public transportation on the island, while available, is limited in terms of routes and schedules. Renting a car allows you to explore the island at your own pace, visit off-the-beaten-path locations, and make spontaneous stops to soak in the breathtaking views.

Without a car, you may find it challenging to access some of Maui's most iconic sites. For example, the famous Hana Highway is best experienced with the flexibility to stop at waterfalls, beaches, and small towns along the way—something that's difficult to do with a bus or tour. Similarly, reaching the summit of Haleakalā for sunrise or sunset requires driving up the mountain in the early hours or late afternoon, times when public transport isn't available.

Choosing the Right Vehicle for Your Maui Adventure

When renting a car in Maui, you'll have a variety of vehicle options to choose from, depending on your travel plans, group size, and budget. Here's a breakdown of the most common types of vehicles available and the benefits of each:

Economy and Compact Cars:

These smaller, more fuel-efficient vehicles are ideal for solo travelers or couples looking to explore Maui on a budget. They are perfect for driving around town, visiting beaches, and navigating the island's main roads. While they may lack the power and space of larger vehicles, they are easy to park and get better gas mileage.

Midsize and Full-Size Sedans:

If you're traveling with a small family or a group of friends, a midsize or full-size sedan might be a better fit. These vehicles offer more legroom and trunk space, making them comfortable for longer drives, such as the Road to Hana or trips to Upcountry Maui. They still offer good fuel efficiency while providing a smoother ride.

SUVs:

An SUV is a popular choice for families, groups, or anyone planning to explore more rugged areas of the island. With higher ground clearance and more powerful engines, SUVs are better suited for driving on unpaved roads or through areas that may require a bit more traction, such as certain parts of the Road to Hana after heavy rain. They also provide ample space for luggage, beach gear, and other essentials.

Convertibles:

For those who want to fully embrace the tropical vibes of Maui, renting a convertible can be an exciting option. Imagine cruising along the coastline with the top down, enjoying the warm breeze and panoramic views. While convertibles typically have less storage space and can be pricier, they offer a unique and memorable way to experience the island's beauty.

Jeep Wranglers:

Jeeps are especially popular in Maui, particularly for those planning to tackle the Road to Hana or explore more remote areas like the backside of Haleakalā. The rugged build and off-road capabilities of a Jeep Wrangler make it an excellent choice for adventurous travelers. Keep in mind that while Jeeps offer great off-road performance, they are not the most fuel-efficient option.

Minivans:

If you're traveling with a large family or group, a minivan might be the best choice. Minivans offer seating for up to seven or eight passengers, along with plenty of room for luggage and other belongings. They are a practical choice for families with children, providing easy access to car seats and extra space for strollers, beach gear, and snacks.

Luxury Vehicles:

For those looking to travel in style, Maui offers a selection of luxury vehicles, including high-end sedans, SUVs, and sports cars. These vehicles provide a premium driving experience with advanced features, superior comfort, and a touch of sophistication. Renting a luxury car can add an extra layer of enjoyment to your Maui vacation, especially for special occasions.

Rental Car Companies and Locations

Maui has a wide range of rental car companies to choose from, including major international brands like Hertz, Avis, Enterprise, Budget, and Alamo, as well as local agencies. Most rental car companies have offices at Kahului Airport (OGG), which is the main entry point for visitors to the island. There are also rental locations in popular tourist areas like Lahaina, Kaanapali, Kihei, and Wailea.

Kahului Airport (OGG):

Renting a car directly from the airport is the most convenient option for most travelers. After landing, you can easily pick up your car and start your journey without the need for additional transportation to your accommodation. The airport rental car facility is located just a short shuttle ride from the terminal.

Lahaina/Kaanapali:

If you're staying in West Maui, you may find it convenient to rent a car from one of the local agencies in Lahaina or Kaanapali. This option is ideal for those who want to spend a few days relaxing in the area before venturing out to explore the rest of the island.

Kihei/Wailea:

For visitors staying in South Maui, there are rental car offices in Kihei and Wailea. This is a good option if you plan to explore the beaches and attractions of South Maui before heading to other parts of the island.

Costs and Pricing

The cost of renting a car in Maui can vary significantly depending on several factors, including the type of vehicle, rental duration, time of year, and demand. On average, you can expect to pay:

- Economy/Compact Cars: $40 to $70 per day
- Midsize/Full-Size Sedans: $50 to $90 per day
- SUVs: $70 to $120 per day
- Convertibles: $80 to $150 per day
- Jeeps: $80 to $150 per day
- Minivans: $80 to $130 per day
- Luxury Vehicles: $100 to $300 per day

Additional Costs to Consider

In addition to the base rental rate, there are several additional costs to keep in mind when renting a car in Maui:

Insurance: Rental car insurance can add $10 to $30 per day to your rental cost, depending on the coverage options you choose. While some personal auto insurance policies and credit cards offer rental car coverage, it's essential to verify the details and consider purchasing additional coverage for peace of mind.

Fuel: Gasoline prices in Maui are typically higher than on the mainland, with prices ranging from $5 to $6 per gallon. It's a good idea to budget for fuel costs, especially if you plan to do a lot of driving.

Taxes and Fees: Maui rental cars are subject to a variety of taxes and fees, including a rental car surcharge, general excise tax, and airport concession fees. These can add 15% to 20% to your total rental cost.

Additional Drivers: If you plan to share driving responsibilities, be aware that many rental car companies charge an additional fee for extra drivers. This fee is typically around $10 to $15 per day per driver.

Young Driver Fees: Drivers under the age of 25 may be subject to a young driver surcharge, which can range from $20 to $30 per day. Some companies also have age restrictions on certain vehicle types, such as luxury cars or Jeeps.

GPS and Additional Equipment: Rental car companies often offer optional add-ons, such as GPS navigation systems, child car seats, and roadside assistance. These can add $5 to $15 per day to your rental cost.

Tips for Saving Money on Car Rentals in Maui

Renting a car in Maui can be expensive, especially during peak travel seasons. However, there are several ways to save money on your rental:

Book in Advance: Rental car prices tend to increase as your travel dates approach, especially during busy periods. Booking your rental car several months in advance can help you secure a lower rate.

Compare Prices: Use online travel websites and rental car comparison tools to compare prices from different companies. Sometimes, smaller local agencies offer competitive rates compared to the big national brands.

Consider Off-Airport Locations: Renting from an off-airport location can sometimes save you money, as you may avoid certain airport-related fees. However, you'll need to factor in the cost of transportation to the rental office.

Use Membership Discounts: If you're a member of an organization like AAA, AARP, or Costco, check for rental car discounts. Many companies offer special rates for members.

Skip the Extras: While it might be tempting to add on GPS or other extras, consider using your smartphone for navigation or bringing your child car seat to save money.

Refuel Before Returning: Rental car companies often charge a premium for refueling the vehicle if you return it with less than a full tank. To avoid this, fill up the tank at a nearby gas station before returning the car.

Driving in Maui: What to Expect

Driving in Maui is generally a pleasant experience, with well-maintained roads and stunning scenery. However, there are a few things to keep in mind to ensure a safe and enjoyable journey:

Road Conditions: Most of Maui's roads are in good condition, but some areas, like the Road to Hana, have narrow, winding sections that require careful driving. Be prepared for one-lane bridges and occasional potholes, especially in more remote areas.

Speed Limits: The speed limits in Maui are lower than what you might be used to on the mainland, with most roads having limits between 25 and 45 mph.

It's important to adhere to these limits, especially in residential areas and near schools.

Traffic: While traffic in Maui is generally light, it can get congested in popular tourist areas, such as Lahaina, Kaanapali, and Kihei, especially during peak hours. Plan your driving routes accordingly and be patient during busy times.

Parking: Parking is usually easy to find in most parts of Maui, but some popular beaches and attractions can get crowded. Arrive early to secure a spot, especially at places like Haleakalā National Park or the start of the Road to Hana.

Weather Considerations: Weather in Maui can change quickly, particularly in higher elevations or along the coast. Be cautious when driving in rain or fog, and avoid unpaved roads if they are muddy or slippery.

Returning Your Rental Car

When your Maui adventure comes to an end, make sure to return your rental car on time to avoid late fees. Most rental companies have a grace period of 30 minutes to an hour, but it's best to confirm this when you pick up the vehicle. Before returning the car:

Clean Out the Car: Remove all personal belongings, trash, and sand from the vehicle. Some rental companies charge cleaning fees if the car is excessively dirty.

Refuel the Tank: As mentioned earlier, refuel the car before returning it to avoid high refueling charges. Keep your gas receipt as proof, just in case.

Inspect the Car: Do a final walk-around inspection to ensure there are no new dents, scratches, or other damage. If you notice any issues, report them to the rental company immediately.

Public Transportation: Maui Bus

Overview of the Maui Bus System

The Maui Bus is operated by the County of Maui Department of Transportation, serving both locals and visitors with a reliable network of routes that connect major towns, commercial centers, and some tourist destinations. While it doesn't reach the more isolated parts of the island, such as the Hana Highway or Haleakalā National Park, it provides an affordable and eco-friendly alternative for traveling within more populated areas.

Key Routes

The Maui Bus system consists of several fixed routes that cover the most popular parts of the island. These routes can be divided into two main categories: county routes and resort routes.

County Routes: These routes are the backbone of the Maui Bus system, connecting the island's major towns and commercial areas. Examples include the Kahului Loop, the Wailuku Loop, the Lahaina Islander, and the Kihei Islander.

Resort Routes: These are designed primarily for tourists, providing service to major resort areas such as Kaanapali, Wailea, and Kapalua.

Each route is designed to provide comprehensive coverage within its designated area, allowing riders to access key locations such as shopping centers, government offices, beaches, and recreational areas. The bus routes are numbered, making it easy to identify and navigate.

Detailed Description of Key Routes

Kahului Loop (Route 5):

This route is essential for anyone staying in or around the main town of Kahului. The Kahului Loop circles the town, stopping at important locations such as the Queen Ka'ahumanu Center (the island's largest shopping mall), Maui Mall, and the University of Hawaii Maui College.

Key Stops: Queen Ka'ahumanu Center, Kahului Airport, University of Hawaii Maui College, Maui Mall.

Frequency: The Kahului Loop operates every 60 minutes during the day.

Best For: Visitors needing to shop, access services, or catch a flight from Kahului Airport.

Wailuku Loop (Route 1):

The Wailuku Loop serves the administrative and historical heart of Maui. It connects key locations in Wailuku, including government offices, courts, and historical sites, with major bus transfer points in Kahului.

Key Stops: Maui Memorial Medical Center, Wailuku Civic Center, Queen Ka'ahumanu Center.

Frequency: Buses on this route typically run every 60 minutes.

Best For: Exploring Wailuku's cultural and historical sites or accessing government services.

Lahaina Islander (Route 20):

This route provides service between Lahaina and other parts of West Maui. It's perfect for tourists staying in Lahaina who want to explore further afield or for locals commuting to work.

Key Stops: Lahaina Cannery Mall, Lahaina Wharf Cinema Center, Whalers Village.

Frequency: Every 90 minutes.

Best For Visitors staying in Lahaina who want to explore nearby attractions without a car.

Kihei Islander (Route 10):

The Kihei Islander connects the south coast area of Kihei with Kahului and other parts of Maui. This route is popular with tourists staying in Kihei or Wailea who want to travel to Kahului or Central Maui.

Key Stops: Kihei Aquatic Center, Azeka Shopping Center, Maui Nui Golf Club.

Frequency: Every 90 minutes.

Best For: Travelers staying in the Kihei or Wailea areas.

Upcountry Islander (Route 40):

The Upcountry Islander is one of the few bus routes that serves the Upcountry area, including Pukalani, Makawao, and Kula. It's essential for residents and visitors who need to reach these higher-elevation areas.

Key Stops: Pukalani Terrace Shopping Center, Makawao Town, Kulamalu Town Center.

Frequency: Approximately every 2 hours.

Best For: Exploring Maui's Upcountry, including visits to farms, botanical gardens, and the quaint towns of Makawao and Pukalani.

Schedule and Frequency

The Maui Bus operates on a fixed schedule, with most routes running from early morning until the early evening. The frequency of buses varies depending on the route and the time of day. For example, more popular routes such as the Kahului Loop and the Wailuku Loop typically have buses arriving every 60 minutes, while less trafficked routes like the Upcountry Islander might only operate every two hours.

Weekday Service: Most routes operate more frequently on weekdays, with the first buses starting as early as 5:30 AM and the last ones departing around 8:30 PM.

Weekend and Holiday Service: Service on weekends and holidays is usually less frequent, with fewer buses running and some routes having reduced hours.

To plan your trip effectively, it's essential to check the Maui Bus website or use a real-time transit app to get up-to-date schedules and avoid long waits at bus stops.

Fares and Payment Options

The Maui Bus is known for its affordability, making it an attractive option for budget-conscious travelers. The fare structure is simple, with a flat rate for single rides and options for day passes.

Single Ride Fare: $2.00 per adult, regardless of distance traveled.

Day Pass: $4.00 for unlimited rides on all routes for the entire day. This is an excellent option if you plan on using the bus multiple times throughout the day.

Monthly Pass: $45.00, offering unlimited rides for the entire month. This is more suitable for long-term visitors or residents.

Children under 5 years old ride for free when accompanied by a paying adult, and discounts are available for seniors and individuals with disabilities.

Payment Methods: Payment is made directly to the driver when boarding the bus. You can pay with cash (exact change is required) or use a pre-purchased pass. Some buses are equipped with electronic payment systems, but it's always best to have cash on hand.

Advantages of Using the Maui Bus

Affordability: One of the biggest advantages of using the Maui Bus is its cost-effectiveness. With fares at just $2 per ride or $4 for a day pass, it's one of the most affordable ways to get around the island, especially when compared to renting a car or taking taxis.

Eco-Friendly: Opting for public transportation is an environmentally friendly choice, helping to reduce the number of cars on the road and lower your carbon footprint during your visit.

Convenience: The Maui Bus provides a reliable way to travel between major towns and commercial areas, making it a convenient option for shopping, dining, and attending events without the hassle of parking.

Stress-Free: For those who prefer not to drive, particularly on Maui's sometimes narrow and winding roads, the bus offers a stress-free alternative. You can sit back, relax, and enjoy the scenery without worrying about navigating unfamiliar territory.

No Parking Hassles: Parking can be challenging in popular areas like Lahaina or Kihei, especially during peak tourist seasons. Taking the bus eliminates the need to search for parking or pay high parking fees.

Limitations and Challenges

While the Maui Bus offers numerous benefits, there are some limitations to be aware of, particularly for tourists who want to explore the island more extensively.

Limited Coverage: The bus routes primarily serve populated areas and major towns, leaving out more remote attractions like the Road to Hana, Haleakalā National Park, and many of the island's most scenic beaches. If your itinerary includes these locations, you'll need to arrange alternative transportation.

Infrequent Service: Some routes have limited service, with buses running every 60 to 120 minutes. This can be inconvenient if you're on a tight schedule or if you miss a bus and have to wait for the next one.

Long Travel Times: While the bus is affordable, it can also be slower than driving, especially on routes with many stops. Travel times can be extended if you need to transfer between buses to reach your destination.

No Late-Night Service: The Maui Bus does not operate late at night, which can be a drawback for those who want to enjoy evening activities such as dining out or attending events. You'll need to arrange for a taxi, rideshare, or other transport options if you're out late.

Crowding: During peak tourist seasons, the buses can become crowded, particularly on popular routes. This might result in standing-room-only conditions or having to wait for the next bus if it's full.

Tips for Using the Maui Bus

Plan Ahead: Before you start your journey, review the bus routes and schedules on the Maui Bus website or a transit app. This will help you plan your day and avoid long waits at bus stops.

Carry Exact Change: If you're paying with cash, make sure you have the exact fare ready as the bus drivers do not provide change.

Consider a Day Pass: If you plan to take multiple bus trips in a single day, the $ 4-day pass is a great deal and can save you money.

Be Prepared for the Weather: Maui's weather can be unpredictable, so carry a light jacket or umbrella in case of rain, especially if you'll be waiting at outdoor bus stops.

Download a Transit App: Apps like Transit or Moovit can provide real-time information on bus arrivals, helping you time your trips more efficiently.

Be Patient: Given the potential for delays and long travel times, it's important to be patient and allow extra time for your journeys.

Taxis and Rideshare Services

Maui, known for its stunning landscapes, pristine beaches, and vibrant towns, offers a range of transportation options to help you navigate the island. Among these, taxis and rideshare services provide flexibility and convenience, allowing visitors to explore without the need for a rental car.

Taxis in Maui

Taxis have long been a staple of urban transportation, and Maui is no exception. While they may not be as prevalent as rideshare services, taxis remain a reliable choice for getting around, particularly if you prefer not to drive or need a quick ride from point A to point B. They are especially useful for airport transfers, trips to local attractions, or when public transportation is not an option.

Availability

Taxis are available throughout Maui, with concentrations in major towns such as Kahului, Lahaina, Kihei, and Wailea. The presence of taxis is more noticeable in tourist-heavy areas and near popular resorts, shopping centers, and entertainment venues. However, taxis can be less frequent in more remote or less populated areas.

Airport and Major Hotels: Taxis are readily available at Kahului Airport (OGG), which is the primary gateway to the island. There is a designated taxi stand at the airport where you can easily catch a cab. Additionally, many major hotels and resorts in tourist areas have taxi services or can arrange for one upon request.

Hailing a Taxi: While you can hail a taxi on the street in busy areas, it's generally more reliable to call a taxi service or use a dedicated taxi stand. For those staying at hotels, the concierge or front desk can assist with arranging a taxi.

Cost

Taxi fares in Maui start with a base fare and increase based on the distance traveled. The pricing structure includes a starting fare, plus additional charges per mile traveled and per minute of wait time. Here's a general breakdown:

Base Fare: Typically around $3.50 to $4.00.

Per Mile: Approximately $3.00 to $4.00.

Wait Time: About $0.50 to $0.75 per minute.

For example, a ride from Kahului Airport to Wailea might cost around $40 to $60, depending on traffic conditions and the exact pickup and drop-off points. Taxi fares are generally consistent, but it's always a good idea to confirm the estimated cost with the driver before starting your journey.

Tipping: Tipping is customary in Maui, and a tip of 15% to 20% of the fare is generally appreciated.

Booking and Contact Information

Phone Booking: You can call taxi services directly to book a ride. Some of the well-known taxi companies in Maui include:

Maui Taxi: +1 808-242-7171

Aloha Taxi: +1 808-874-2227

Kahului Taxi: +1 808-871-1000

Hotel Assistance: Many hotels and resorts offer taxi arrangements or can call a taxi service on your behalf. This can be particularly useful if you're traveling to or from the airport or need a ride during busy periods.

Tips for Using Taxis

Confirm Costs: Always ask the driver for an estimated fare before starting your journey to avoid surprises.

Carry Cash: While many taxis accept credit cards, it's a good idea to have some cash on hand for tipping and small fares.

Plan Ahead: During peak travel times or late at night, taxis can be in high demand. Booking in advance or arranging a pickup through your hotel can save time and hassle.

Rideshare Services

Overview

Rideshare services have become increasingly popular due to their convenience, ease of use, and often lower costs compared to traditional taxis. In Maui, major rideshare companies like Uber and Lyft operate, providing a modern alternative to hailing a cab.

Availability

Rideshare services are widely available throughout Maui, with coverage extending to most major towns, beaches, and attractions. The services are particularly useful for short trips within towns, airport transfers, and visits to popular spots like Lahaina, Kihei, and Wailea.

Airport Access: Both Uber and Lyft operate at Kahului Airport. Designated pickup areas for rideshare vehicles are located outside the terminal. Be sure to follow airport signage and instructions for rideshare pickups.

Rideshare Apps: To use a rideshare service, you need to download the app (Uber or Lyft) on your smartphone. The apps allow you to request rides, view estimated fares, and track your driver in real time. They also provide options for different types of rides, such as economy, premium, or shared rides.

Cost

Rideshare pricing is typically calculated based on a combination of distance traveled, time, and demand. The cost structure is dynamic, meaning fares can fluctuate depending on traffic, time of day, and current demand (known as surge pricing).

Base Fare: Usually starts at around $3.00 to $4.00.

Per Mile/Minute: Approximately $1.00 to $2.00 per mile and $0.15 to $0.25 per minute.

Surge Pricing: During peak times, such as holidays or rush hours, fares may increase due to high demand. The app will notify you if surge pricing is in effect.

For example, a ride from Kahului Airport to Wailea might cost between $35 to $55. The exact fare will be displayed in the app before you confirm the ride.

Tipping: Tipping is optional but appreciated. A tip of 10% to 20% of the fare is customary and can be added through the app after the ride is completed.

Booking and Contact Information

Uber: Available through the Uber app. To book a ride, enter your destination, choose your ride type, and confirm the pickup location.

Lyft: Available through the Lyft app. Similar to Uber, enter your destination, select your ride option, and confirm the pickup details.

Tips for Using Rideshare Services

Check Surge Pricing: Before confirming a ride, check if surge pricing is in effect. If possible, wait until prices normalize to save on costs.

Verify Your Ride: Always confirm that the vehicle and driver details match those provided in the app before getting in.

Keep the App Updated: Ensure your rideshare app is updated to the latest version for optimal performance and access to the latest features.

Safety Features: Utilize in-app safety features such as sharing your trip status with friends or family for added security.

Comparison: Taxis vs. Rideshare Services

Convenience: Both taxis and rideshare services offer door-to-door convenience. Rideshare services, however, provide real-time tracking, estimated fares, and a more streamlined booking process via apps.

Cost: Rideshare services are generally more affordable, especially for short to medium distances. Taxis may be more cost-effective for longer trips or when rideshare surge pricing is in effect.

Availability: Taxis are more readily available in areas with high foot traffic, like airports and major hotels, whereas rideshare services can be accessed anywhere with an internet connection and smartphone app.

Payment: Rideshare services are app-based with cashless transactions, which can be more convenient for many travelers. Taxis may accept both cash and card payments, but it's always good to confirm before starting your ride.

Final Thoughts

Whether you choose to use taxis or rideshare services during your Maui visit largely depends on your preferences, travel needs, and the specifics of your trip. Both options offer valuable services for navigating the island, each with its own set of advantages. Taxis provide a traditional, straightforward approach to getting around, while rideshare services offer modern conveniences and often lower costs.

Biking in Maui

Biking in Maui offers an exhilarating way to explore the island's stunning landscapes, diverse ecosystems, and vibrant communities. From coastal paths to mountain trails, Maui caters to bikers of all skill levels. This comprehensive guide provides a detailed look at biking options in Maui, including popular routes, essential tips, and bike rental information.

1. Scenic Coastal Paths

Maui's coastal paths are ideal for bikers seeking a mix of beautiful views and gentle terrain. These routes offer a fantastic introduction to the island's scenic beauty without the challenges of more rugged trails.

Ka'anapali Beach Path

Location: Ka'anapali, West Maui

This 2.5-mile path runs along the beautiful Ka'anapali Beach, offering stunning ocean views, palm trees, and well-maintained surfaces. It connects the Ka'anapali Resort area with the historic town of Lahaina.

Experience: The path is flat and easy to navigate, making it suitable for all skill levels. Riders can enjoy views of the Pacific Ocean, luxury resorts, and local shops and restaurants. It's a popular spot for both casual bikers and those looking for a scenic ride.

Wailea Beach Path

Location: Wailea, South Maui

The Wailea Beach Path stretches about 1.5 miles, linking the beaches and resorts in the Wailea area. The path offers breathtaking views of the coastline and easy access to several pristine beaches.

Experience: This paved path is relatively flat and ideal for a leisurely ride. Bikers can explore the luxurious Wailea Resort area, with its beautiful beaches and upscale dining options. The path is also popular for morning rides, providing a serene start to the day.

2. Mountain Trails

For those seeking a more adventurous biking experience, Maui's mountain trails offer challenging terrain and breathtaking vistas. These trails cater to experienced bikers and those looking to test their skills.

Makawao Forest Reserve

Location: Makawao, Upcountry Maui

The Makawao Forest Reserve features a network of trails through lush forests, offering a mix of singletrack and fire roads. The terrain varies from technical rocky sections to smoother, flowing trails.

Experience: This area is known for its cooler temperatures and scenic views of the surrounding countryside. Trails like the "Kamalani Trail" offer technical challenges with roots and rocks, while "The Loop" provides a smoother ride. The forest's diverse flora and fauna add to the experience, making it a favorite among mountain bikers.

Haleakalā Crater Trails

Location: Haleakalā National Park, East Maui

Haleakalā Crater offers several mountain biking trails that traverse the volcanic landscape of the island's highest peak. The terrain ranges from rocky and rugged to smoother volcanic paths.

Experience: Riding in Haleakalā provides a unique experience as bikers can explore the crater's surreal landscapes and enjoy panoramic views. The "Sliding Sands Trail" descends into the crater and offers a challenging ride with stunning views of the crater floor. Bikers should be prepared for changing weather conditions and high-altitude riding.

3. Road Cycling Routes

Maui is renowned for its road cycling routes, offering long stretches of scenic roads and challenging climbs. These routes are popular among road cyclists and offer some of the best biking experiences on the island.

The Road to Hana

Location: East Maui

The Road to Hana is a famous 64-mile route known for its winding roads, waterfalls, and lush rainforests. The ride offers a challenging experience with numerous curves and elevation changes.

Experience: Cyclists tackling the Road to Hana should be prepared for a demanding ride, with steep climbs and descents. The route provides opportunities to see breathtaking natural beauty, including waterfalls like Twin Falls and the Seven Sacred Pools.

It's essential to ride with caution due to narrow roads and limited visibility in some areas. Many cyclists choose to do the ride in sections, allowing for breaks and sightseeing.

Upcountry Loop

Location: Upcountry Maui

The Upcountry Loop is a popular road cycling route that offers a mix of rolling hills, scenic views, and agricultural landscapes. The route typically starts in the town of Makawao and loops through areas like Kula and Pukalani.

Experience: This loop offers a more relaxed ride compared to the Road to Hana, with rolling hills and moderate climbs. Bikers can enjoy views of Maui's agricultural areas, including farms and ranches. The cooler temperatures in Upcountry Maui make this ride more comfortable, and there are opportunities to stop at local markets and coffee farms along the way.

4. Bike Rentals and Services

Maui offers a range of bike rental options to suit different needs, from road bikes and mountain bikes to e-bikes and scooters. Several rental shops provide well-maintained bikes and additional services.

Rentals

Cost: Bike rentals typically range from $25 to $75 per day, depending on the type of bike and rental duration. E-bikes and high-end mountain bikes may cost more, around $75 to $100 per day.

Where to Rent: Popular rental shops include "Maui Bike Company" in Lahaina, "Bike Maui" in Kihei, and "South Maui Bikes" in Wailea. These shops offer a variety of bikes, including road bikes, mountain bikes, and e-bikes, and provide helpful maps and advice on local trails.

Services

Repairs and Maintenance: Many bike rental shops offer repair services and maintenance for rented bikes. It's advisable to check the bike's condition before setting out and to have a basic understanding of bike maintenance.

Tips: Consider renting a bike with a helmet, lock, and repair kit included. Also, check the shop's policy on bike returns and any additional fees for late returns or damages.

5. Safety and Etiquette

Safety and etiquette are crucial for a positive biking experience in Maui. Here are some essential tips:

Wear a Helmet: Helmets are mandatory for all riders in Hawaii. Ensure your helmet fits properly and is in good condition.

Stay Hydrated: Maui's warm climate can lead to dehydration, especially during strenuous rides. Carry plenty of water and take regular breaks.

Follow Traffic Laws: When riding on roads, obey traffic signals and rules. Use hand signals to indicate turns and be aware of your surroundings.

Respect Trail Etiquette: On mountain trails, yield to hikers and be cautious when approaching other bikers. Avoid skidding or creating ruts, and stay on designated trails to minimize environmental impact.

6. Guided Bike Tours

For those who prefer guided experiences, several companies offer bike tours of Maui's top attractions. These tours provide insights into the island's history, culture, and natural beauty while ensuring a safe and enjoyable ride.

Types of Tours: Guided tours may include scenic rides, historical tours, or adventure rides. Options include the "Road to Hana Bike Tour," which provides a supported ride along the scenic route, and the "Haleakalā Sunrise Bike Tour," which combines a sunrise view with a downhill bike ride from the summit.

Cost: Guided tours typically range from $100 to $200 per person, including bike rental, guide services, and sometimes meals.

7. Exploring on Your Own

If you prefer exploring Maui independently, plan your routes and bring the necessary supplies. Consider downloading trail maps or GPS apps to help navigate unfamiliar areas. Be prepared for variable weather conditions and ensure your bike is equipped for the terrain you'll be riding.

Final Thoughts Biking in Maui offers an incredible way to experience the island's diverse landscapes and natural beauty. Whether you're tackling challenging mountain trails, enjoying scenic coastal paths, or exploring road cycling routes, Maui provides biking experiences that cater to all skill levels. With the right preparation, a spirit of adventure, and respect for local rules and etiquette, your biking journey on Maui is sure to be an unforgettable part of your Hawaiian adventure.

Guided Tours

Guided tours in Maui offer a fantastic way to explore the island's diverse landscapes, rich cultural heritage, and natural wonders. With a range of options to suit different interests and activity levels, these tours provide an immersive experience that can enhance your understanding and enjoyment of the island. Below is a comprehensive guide to some of the most popular guided tours on Maui, detailed with what to expect, highlights, and practical information.

1. Road to Hana Tours

The Road to Hana is one of Maui's most iconic drives, renowned for its stunning landscapes, waterfalls, and lush rainforests. Guided tours along this scenic route provide a safe and educational way to experience its beauty without the stress of navigating the winding roads.

What to Expect:

Duration: Most tours last between 8 to 12 hours, depending on the number of stops and activities included.

Highlights: Tours typically include stops at key locations such as Twin Falls, Waianapanapa State Park (with its famous black sand beach), and the Hana Botanical Gardens. Many tours also offer guided hikes to waterfalls, and some provide opportunities to swim in natural pools.

Educational Aspect: Guides often share fascinating insights about the history, culture, and natural environment of the region. You'll learn about Hawaiian legends, the significance of various landmarks, and the unique flora and fauna of the area.

Comfort and Convenience: Most tours are conducted in comfortable, air-conditioned vans or minibusses with ample space for passengers. Some tours also offer small-group experiences for a more personalized touch.

Practical Information:

Cost: Guided Road to Hana tours generally range from $150 to $250 per person.

What to Bring: Comfortable clothing, sturdy shoes for hiking, swimwear, and a camera. Be prepared for variable weather conditions, and bring sunscreen and insect repellent.

Tip: Book tours in advance, especially during peak tourist seasons, as they can fill up quickly.

2. Haleakalā Sunrise Tours

Experiencing the sunrise at Haleakalā Crater is a breathtaking and unforgettable experience. Guided tours to Haleakalā National Park offer a hassle-free way to witness this natural spectacle and explore the park's unique landscapes.

What to Expect:

Duration: Sunrise tours typically start early in the morning and last around 6 to 8 hours, including transportation and time at the summit.

Highlights: Tours often include a pre-dawn departure to ensure you arrive at the summit before sunrise. The view from the top of Haleakalā, with its expansive crater and dramatic volcanic landscape, is truly awe-inspiring. Many tours also include a visit to the park's visitor center and short walks to scenic viewpoints.

Educational Aspect: Guides provide information about the park's geology, ecology, and cultural significance. You'll learn about the formation of the crater, the endemic species that thrive there, and the importance of Haleakalā in Hawaiian mythology.

Comfort and Convenience: Tours are usually conducted in comfortable vehicles with a focus on safety and convenience. Some tours may include breakfast or snacks.

Practical Information:

Cost: Haleakalā sunrise tours generally range from $100 to $200 per person.

What to Bring: Warm clothing (as temperatures can be quite cold at the summit), a camera, and a light breakfast. Most tours will provide refreshments.

Tip: Be prepared for early morning wake-up calls and check the weather forecast, as conditions can be variable at high elevations.

3. Snorkeling and Diving Tours

Maui's crystal-clear waters and vibrant marine life make it a prime destination for snorkeling and scuba diving. Guided tours provide access to the best snorkeling spots and ensure a safe and enjoyable experience underwater.

What to Expect:

Duration: Snorkeling tours typically last 4 to 6 hours, while diving tours can last anywhere from 4 to 8 hours, depending on the number of dives and sites visited.

Highlights: Popular snorkeling spots include Molokini Crater, a partially submerged volcanic caldera with clear waters and abundant marine life, and Turtle Town, known for its sea turtles. Diving tours might explore deeper sites with diverse marine species and underwater landscapes.

Educational Aspect: Guides offer briefings on marine life, snorkeling or diving techniques, and safety procedures. You'll learn about the various species you might encounter and the importance of marine conservation.

Comfort and Convenience: Most tours provide all necessary equipment, including masks, snorkels, fins, and wetsuits. For diving tours, professional-grade equipment and safety briefings are included.

Practical Information:

Cost: Snorkeling tours range from $75 to $150 per person, while diving tours typically cost between $150 and $250 per person.

What to Bring: Swimwear, sunscreen, and a towel. Tours generally provide equipment and refreshments.

Tip: Book tours in advance and check if they include transportation to and from your accommodation.

4. Whale Watching Tours

From December to April, Maui is one of the best places in the world to see humpback whales as they migrate through Hawaiian waters.

Whale-watching tours offer an exciting opportunity to witness these magnificent creatures up close.

What to Expect:

Duration: Whale-watching tours usually last between 2 to 4 hours.

Highlights: Tours take you to prime whale-watching locations, where you may see whales breaching, tail slapping, and engaging in other fascinating behaviors. Guides often share information about whale biology, migration patterns, and conservation efforts.

Educational Aspect: Guides provide insights into whale behavior, communication, and the conservation challenges they face. You'll learn about the significance of Maui's waters to these majestic creatures.

Comfort and Convenience: Tours are conducted on comfortable, stable boats with plenty of space for passengers. Many operators provide snacks and drinks, and some offer guaranteed whale sightings or partial refunds if no whales are spotted.

Practical Information:

Cost: Whale-watching tours range from $80 to $150 per person.

What to Bring: Light layers, sunscreen, and a camera. Consider bringing a light jacket, as it can be cooler on the water.

Tip: Whale sightings are not guaranteed, but the chance to see these incredible animals makes the tour worthwhile.

5. Cultural and Historical Tours

Maui's rich cultural heritage and history are explored through various guided tours that offer insights into Hawaiian traditions, art, and history.

What to Expect:

Duration: Cultural and historical tours typically last between 3 to 5 hours.

Highlights: Tours might include visits to historic sites like Lahaina, once the capital of the Hawaiian Kingdom, or the Alexander & Baldwin Sugar Museum.

Some tours offer cultural experiences such as traditional Hawaiian hula and craft demonstrations, or visits to local farms and cultural centers.

Educational Aspect: Guides provide detailed explanations of Hawaiian history, cultural practices, and traditional arts. You'll learn about the significance of various sites and cultural practices in contemporary Hawaiian life.

Comfort and Convenience: Tours usually include transportation and may offer refreshments or lunch. Some tours provide interactive experiences, allowing you to participate in traditional crafts or cooking.

Practical Information:

Cost: Cultural and historical tours range from $100 to $200 per person.

What to Bring: Comfortable clothing and shoes, and a camera. Check if the tour includes lunch or refreshments.

Tip: Choose a tour that matches your interests and check if it includes any interactive or hands-on components for a more engaging experience.

6. Adventure and Eco-Tours

For those seeking a more active experience, Maui offers adventure and eco-tours that combine outdoor activities with a focus on environmental conservation.

What to Expect:

Duration: Adventure tours vary widely in duration, from half-day excursions to full-day adventures.

Highlights: Activities might include zip-lining, ATV rides through rainforests, or guided hikes to hidden waterfalls. Eco-tours often focus on sustainable practices and offer insights into the island's ecosystems and conservation efforts.

Educational Aspect: Guides on eco-tours provide information about local flora and fauna, conservation issues, and sustainable practices. Adventure tours might include explanations of the local geology and environmental impact.

Comfort and Convenience: Tours typically include all necessary equipment and safety gear. Some may provide meals or snacks, depending on the length of the tour.

Practical Information:

Cost: Adventure and eco-tours range from $100 to $250 per person, depending on the activity and duration.

What to Bring: Appropriate clothing and footwear for the activity, sunscreen, and a camera. Most tours provide specific gear and safety equipment.

Tip: Choose tours based on your fitness level and interests, and check for any age or health restrictions.

7. Sunset Cruises

A sunset cruise is a relaxing and picturesque way to end your day in Maui, offering stunning views of the sunset over the Pacific Ocean.

What to Expect:

Duration: Sunset cruises typically last around 2 to 3 hours.

Highlights: Cruises often include breathtaking views of the sun setting over the ocean, with opportunities to see the island from a different perspective. Some cruises offer live music, appetizers, and drinks, creating a festive atmosphere.

Educational Aspect: While not as focused on education, guides may provide information about the local marine environment and landmarks visible from the boat.

Comfort and Convenience: Cruises are conducted on comfortable, well-equipped boats with amenities such as restrooms, seating, and refreshments.

Practical Information:

Cost: Sunset cruises range from $80 to $150 per person.

What to Bring: Light layers, sunscreen, and a camera. Most cruises provide refreshments, but you may want to check if dinner is included.

Tip: Book your cruise in advance, especially during peak seasons, to ensure availability and secure the best experience.

Shuttles and Hotel Transport

Navigating Maui can be an enjoyable part of your vacation experience, and utilizing shuttles and hotel transport can enhance your journey, offering convenience and sometimes unique experiences.

Types of Shuttle Services

1. Airport Shuttles

One of the most commonly used shuttle services in Maui is the airport shuttle. Upon arriving at Kahului Airport (OGG), you'll find several options to help you get to your accommodation without the need to rent a car immediately.

Shared Shuttle Services: These are cost-effective options where passengers share the ride to their respective destinations. Companies like SpeediShuttle and Maui Airport Shuttle offer shared services that can be a budget-friendly choice. Shared shuttles typically have fixed schedules and may make several stops before reaching your final destination, so the trip could take a bit longer compared to private services.

Private Airport Transfers: For a more direct and personalized experience, private airport transfers are available. Services such as Executive Limo, Royal Hawaiian Limousine, and Aloha Maui Transportation offer private shuttles that cater specifically to your travel group. This option provides comfort and convenience, often including amenities such as bottled water and Wi-Fi. Private transfers are more expensive, with prices generally ranging from $70 to $150 one way, depending on the distance and vehicle type.

2. Hotel Shuttles

Many hotels and resorts in Maui offer complimentary or paid shuttle services to and from the airport, as well as to popular local destinations.

Complimentary Shuttles: Some high-end resorts, like the Four Seasons Resort Maui at Wailea and the Andaz Maui at Wailea, provide complimentary shuttle services within a certain radius. These shuttles might include trips to nearby shopping areas, beaches, or attractions. It's advisable to check with the hotel beforehand to understand the shuttle's schedule and destinations.

Paid Shuttle Services: Mid-range hotels and vacation rentals might offer paid shuttle services.

The cost for these shuttles can vary widely based on the distance and the service provider. Some hotels offer fixed rates for round trips, while others may charge per ride. The rates generally range from $15 to $40 per person, depending on the distance and service level.

3. Resort Shuttles

Resorts often have dedicated shuttle services to facilitate guest travel between the hotel and popular tourist destinations. These shuttles are typically designed to cater to guests' needs and can be particularly useful if you're staying at a large resort or in a remote area.

Scheduled Resort Shuttles: Many resorts provide scheduled shuttle services that operate at specific times throughout the day. These might include trips to nearby beaches, golf courses, shopping centers, or cultural sites. For example, the Grand Wailea Resort offers a shuttle to nearby Wailea Beach and the Shops at Wailea.

On-Demand Resort Shuttles: Some upscale resorts offer on-demand shuttle services, where you can request a ride at your convenience. These services are often more flexible but can be more expensive. They offer a high level of convenience, especially for guests who need transportation outside regular shuttle hours.

4. Shuttle Tours

Shuttle tours are another option for exploring Maui, combining transportation with guided tours of the island's attractions.

Sightseeing Tours: Companies like Maui Tour Company and Roberts Hawaii provide shuttle tours that include transportation to popular sites such as Haleakalā National Park, the Road to Hana, and Lahaina. These tours often include a knowledgeable guide who provides commentary and insights about the island's history, culture, and natural beauty.

Specialty Tours: For a unique experience, consider booking specialty tours that cater to specific interests, such as whale watching, snorkeling excursions, or cultural tours. These tours often include round-trip shuttle service from your hotel, making them a convenient option for exploring Maui's diverse offerings.

What to Expect from Shuttle and Hotel Transport Services

1. Booking and Reservations

Booking your shuttle or hotel transport service in advance is highly recommended, especially during peak travel seasons. For airport shuttles and private transfers, reservations can usually be made online or through a travel agent. Most shuttle companies offer easy-to-use online booking systems where you can select your pick-up and drop-off locations, as well as the type of service you require.

Airport Shuttles: When booking an airport shuttle, provide details about your flight, including arrival times and flight numbers, to ensure timely pick-up. It's also helpful to reconfirm your reservation a day before your arrival.

Hotel Shuttles: For hotel shuttles, inquire about the service when booking your accommodation or contact the hotel directly. Confirm the shuttle schedule and any costs associated with the service.

2. Costs and Payment

The cost of shuttle and hotel transport services can vary based on factors such as distance, service type, and time of booking.

Shared Airport Shuttles: Generally, more affordable, with costs ranging from $30 to $60 per person for a one-way trip.

Private Transfers: Higher-end options that can range from $70 to $150 one way, depending on the vehicle and level of service.

Hotel Shuttles: Complimentary services are often included in your hotel stay, but paid shuttles can range from $15 to $40 per person.

Payment methods typically include credit cards, and some services may accept cash or mobile payments. Always check the payment options when booking and be aware of any additional fees or gratuities that might apply.

3. Comfort and Amenities

The level of comfort and amenities provided by shuttle and hotel transport services can vary:

Airport Shuttles: Shared shuttles might be less spacious but are generally clean and comfortable. Private transfers offer more luxury, including features like leather seats, air conditioning, and refreshments.

Hotel Shuttles: The comfort level can range from basic shuttle vans to more upscale vehicles, depending on the hotel. Some resorts offer luxury shuttles with added amenities for their guests.

Resort Shuttles: These services often use comfortable vehicles designed to accommodate multiple passengers and may offer additional amenities like Wi-Fi or refreshments.

4. Practical Tips for Using Shuttles and Hotel Transport

Plan: Always plan your transportation needs. Knowing your options and booking early can help ensure you get the service you need, especially during busy travel times.

Confirm Schedules: Verify the schedule for shuttle services, especially if you have specific plans or excursions. Some services may require advanced notice for scheduling or changes.

Check Reviews: Look for reviews or recommendations for shuttle and hotel transport services. This can give you insights into the quality of service and reliability.

Have Contact Information: Keep the contact information for your shuttle or hotel transport service handy in case you need to make last-minute changes or confirm details.

Scooter and Moped Rentals

Renting a scooter or moped in Maui is an exciting way to explore the island, offering a mix of freedom and practicality. With its beautiful landscapes, warm weather, and scenic roads, Maui provides an ideal backdrop for this mode of transportation.

Understanding Scooters and Mopeds

Scooters and mopeds are similar in many ways but differ in some key aspects. Both are lightweight, fuel-efficient, and easy to maneuver, making them perfect for exploring Maui's towns and scenic spots. Here's a brief overview of each:

Scooters: Generally equipped with a larger engine (50cc to 250cc), scooters can reach higher speeds and offer more power than mopeds. They typically have a step-through frame and automatic transmission, which makes them easier to ride, especially for beginners. Many scooters come with storage compartments under the seat or in the front.

Mopeds: Mopeds usually have smaller engines (less than 50cc) and are more limited in terms of speed and power. They often have pedals (though not always) and a simpler design. Mopeds are ideal for short trips and urban commuting but might not be suitable for longer journeys or highway travel.

Choosing the Right Rental

When renting a scooter or moped in Maui, consider the following factors to find the right vehicle for your needs:

Engine Size: Choose based on how you plan to use the vehicle. For short trips around town, a moped or small scooter should suffice. For longer journeys or exploring more varied terrain, a larger scooter with more power might be more comfortable.

Rental Duration: Rentals are available by the hour, day, week, or month. If you plan to use the scooter or moped frequently, longer rental periods often come with discounted rates.

Insurance and Safety Gear: Ensure that your rental includes basic insurance and that you're provided with essential safety gear like helmets. Some rental companies also offer optional insurance for additional coverage.

Storage: Consider if you need extra storage for carrying personal items or shopping. Many scooters come with under-seat storage, but if you need more space, check if the rental company offers additional storage options.

Top Rental Companies in Maui

Several rental companies on Maui offer scooters and mopeds, each with its own set of features and services. Here's a selection of top providers:

Maui Scooter Shack

Location: 79 Hana Hwy, Kahului, HI 96732

Services: Offers a wide range of scooters and mopeds, including 50cc models ideal for city exploration and larger models for more powerful rides. They provide helmets and basic insurance for each rental.

Pricing: Starts at $40 per day for a basic 50cc scooter, with discounts for weekly rentals.

Website: Maui Scooter Shack

Aloha Scooter Rentals

Location: 1325 S Kihei Rd, Kihei, HI 96753

Services: Known for its well-maintained fleet and friendly service, Aloha Scooter Rentals offers both scooters and mopeds. They provide helmets, and some models come with GPS units for an additional fee.

Pricing: Starting at $45 per day for scooters, with competitive weekly rates.

Website: Aloha Scooter Rentals

Maui Moped Rentals

Location: 21 N Market St, Wailuku, HI 96793

Services: Specializes in mopeds and scooters, providing options for different budgets and needs. They offer free helmets and basic insurance. Additionally, they have a selection of electric scooters for eco-friendly transportation.

Pricing: Rates start at $35 per day for mopeds.

Website: Maui Moped Rentals

Island Scooter Rentals

Location: 2395 S Kihei Rd, Kihei, HI 96753

Services: Offers a variety of scooter and moped models, including high-performance options. They also provide guided tours and additional rental gear upon request.

Pricing: $50 per day for standard scooters, with options for premium models at higher rates.

Website: Island Scooter Rentals

Rental Process and Tips

Booking: It's advisable to book your scooter or moped in advance, especially during peak tourist seasons. Online reservations often come with discounts and ensure availability upon your arrival.

Licensing: You will need a valid driver's license to rent a scooter or moped. In Hawaii, a regular driver's license is sufficient for scooters up to 50cc. For larger engines or if you plan to ride on highways, you may need a motorcycle license or endorsement.

Safety: Always wear a helmet, even if it's not legally required. Helmets are provided by rental companies, but you can bring your own if preferred. Additionally, familiarize yourself with local traffic laws and scooter/moped regulations.

Inspection: Before accepting the scooter or moped, thoroughly inspect it for any existing damage and ensure that it's in good working condition. Report any issues to the rental company to avoid being held responsible for pre-existing damage.

Navigation: Maui's roads are generally well-maintained, but be cautious of narrow, winding routes, especially when traveling in mountainous areas. Use a map or GPS for navigation and plan your routes accordingly.

Parking: Pay attention to parking regulations and always park in designated areas. Some tourist spots have limited parking, so plan to avoid fines or towing.

Fuel: Scooters and mopeds typically have small fuel tanks, so you may need to refuel frequently. Gas stations are available throughout Maui, but in more remote areas, they can be sparse.

Weather Considerations: Maui's weather is generally pleasant, but sudden rain showers can occur. Ensure that your rental scooter or moped is equipped with a rain cover or bring your rain gear if necessary.

Returning the Vehicle: When returning the scooter or moped, make sure it's in the same condition as when you received it. Follow the rental company's instructions for drop-off and return any accessories or gear provided.

Insurance: Consider purchasing additional insurance if available. While basic insurance is often included, additional coverage can provide extra peace of mind, especially if you plan to do a lot of riding.

Exploring Maui with a Scooter or Moped

Once you have your scooter or moped, you're ready to explore Maui's stunning landscapes and attractions. Here are some recommended routes and destinations to make the most of your rental:

Lahaina Town: Cruise along Front Street in Lahaina, where you'll find a mix of shops, restaurants, and historical sites. This area is pedestrian-friendly, but a scooter or moped makes it easier to explore further afield.

Kihei and Wailea: These coastal towns offer beautiful beaches and scenic views. Ride along South Kihei Road to access beaches like Kamaole Beach Park and the luxurious resorts of Wailea.

Road to Hana: While this scenic route is often traveled by car, a scooter or moped can be a thrilling way to experience it. Be prepared for narrow, winding roads and frequent stops to admire waterfalls and rainforests.

Upcountry Maui: Explore the cooler, higher elevations of Maui, including areas like Makawao and Kula. This region offers stunning views of the island and a different perspective compared to the coastal areas.

Haleakalā National Park: If you're up for an adventure, consider riding to the summit of Haleakalā for sunrise. While it's a challenging ride with steep inclines, the views from the top are breathtaking.

Renting a scooter or moped in Maui provides an exhilarating and flexible way to explore the island. With the right preparation and understanding of your options, you can enjoy the freedom of the open road while taking in Maui's diverse landscapes and attractions. Whether you're navigating scenic coastlines, bustling towns, or winding mountain roads, a scooter or moped rental can enhance your Maui experience and offer a unique perspective on this beautiful Hawaiian island.

Chapter 6: West Maui

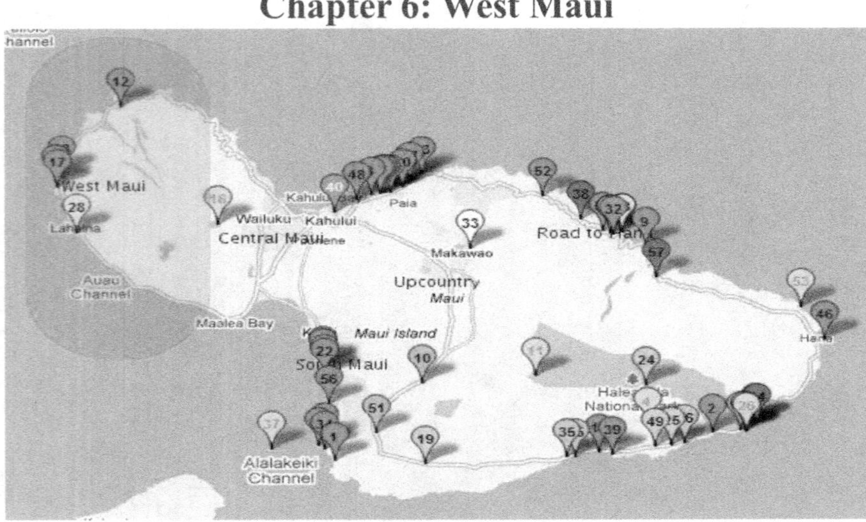

West Maui Overview

1. Geography and Landscape

West Maui is characterized by its dramatic landscapes, including the lush West Maui Mountains, picturesque beaches, and vibrant coral reefs. The region stretches from Maalaea Bay to the northern tip of the island and is home to several well-known towns and resorts.

2. Major Towns and Areas

Lahaina

Lahaina is a historic whaling village and the heart of West Maui. This bustling town is filled with shops, art galleries, restaurants, and historic sites. Front Street, Lahaina's main thoroughfare, is a popular destination for both tourists and locals. Highlights include the Banyan Tree Park, Lahaina Harbor, and the historic Baldwin Home Museum.

Kaanapali

Kaanapali is a major resort area known for its beautiful beach, luxury hotels, and golf courses. Kaanapali Beach is a three-mile stretch of white sand, perfect for swimming, snorkeling, and sunbathing. The Whalers Village shopping center offers a variety of shops, restaurants, and a whaling museum.

Kapalua

Kapalua is another upscale resort area, famous for its world-class golf courses, luxurious accommodations, and stunning beaches. Kapalua Bay is a favorite spot for snorkeling and swimming, while the Kapalua Coastal Trail offers scenic hikes along the coastline.

Napili and Honokowai

These smaller communities offer a more relaxed and local feel compared to the larger resort areas. Napili Bay is known for its calm waters and excellent snorkeling opportunities, while Honokowai has family-friendly parks and beaches.

3. Attractions and Activities

Beaches

Kaanapali Beach: Known for its golden sands and vibrant underwater life, it's perfect for snorkeling, swimming, and beachside relaxation.

Kapalua Bay: A picturesque, sheltered bay ideal for snorkeling and swimming.

Napili Bay: A quieter beach with calm waters, excellent for families and snorkeling.

Outdoor Activities

Snorkeling and Diving: The waters off West Maui are home to vibrant coral reefs and diverse marine life. Popular snorkeling spots include Black Rock, Honolua Bay, and Kapalua Bay.

Hiking: The West Maui Mountains offer scenic hiking trails, including the challenging Waihee Ridge Trail, which provides panoramic views of the island.

Golf: Kapalua and Kaanapali boast some of the best golf courses in Hawaii, attracting golf enthusiasts from around the world.

Historical and Cultural Sites

Lahaina Historic Trail: This self-guided walking tour covers important historical sites in Lahaina, including the Baldwin Home Museum, the Lahaina Courthouse, and the Masters' Reading Room.

Whalers Village Museum: Located in Kaanapali, this museum offers exhibits on the region's whaling history and marine life.

Festivals and Events

Halloween in Lahaina: Often referred to as the "Mardi Gras of the Pacific," this event features a lively parade and festivities.

Kapalua Wine and Food Festival: An annual event celebrating fine wine and gourmet cuisine.

Maui Film Festival: Held in Wailea, but often features screenings and events in West Maui.

4. Accommodations and Dining

Resorts and Hotels

West Maui is home to some of the island's most luxurious resorts and hotels, including the Ritz-Carlton Kapalua, Hyatt Regency Maui Resort and Spa, and the Westin Maui Resort & Spa.

Vacation Rentals

For a more home-like experience, there are numerous vacation rentals available, from beachfront condos to private villas.

Dining

West Maui offers a wide range of dining options, from upscale restaurants to casual beachside eateries. Highlights include:

Merriman's Kapalua: Known for its farm-to-table cuisine and stunning ocean views.

Lahaina Grill: A fine dining restaurant in Lahaina offering a blend of Hawaiian and contemporary cuisine.

Aloha Mixed Plate: A popular spot in Lahaina for traditional Hawaiian plate lunches.

5. Transportation and Accessibility

West Maui is easily accessible from the rest of the island. The main thoroughfare, Honoapiilani Highway (Route 30), connects West Maui to Central Maui and the rest of the island. Public transportation is available via Maui Bus, and many resorts offer shuttle services to popular attractions. Car rentals are recommended for the flexibility to explore at your own pace.

6. Climate and Best Time to Visit

West Maui enjoys a warm, tropical climate year-round, with temperatures typically ranging from the mid-70s to mid-80s Fahrenheit. The region's leeward location means it receives less rainfall than the windward side of the island. The best time to visit is during the spring (April to June) and fall (September to November) when the weather is pleasant, and the crowds are smaller.

Historical Sites and Cultural Attractions

West Maui is rich in historical sites and cultural attractions that reflect its unique heritage and significance in Hawaiian history. Here are some key locations to explore:

1. Lahaina Historic District

Lahaina was once the royal capital of the Hawaiian Kingdom and later a bustling whaling port. The Lahaina Historic District is a National Historic Landmark with many significant sites:

A. Baldwin Home Museum:

The Baldwin Home Museum, located in Lahaina's Historic District on Maui, stands as a testament to the missionary and social history of Hawaii. Built-in 1834, it was home to Reverend Dwight Baldwin, a prominent figure in Maui's history and the community's development. The museum showcases period furnishings, family artifacts, and exhibits that detail daily life in 19th-century Lahaina, including the impact of missionary efforts on Hawaiian culture and education. Visitors can explore the two-story wooden structure, which reflects both Western and Hawaiian architectural influences.

- **Opening Hours:** The museum is open daily from 10:00 AM to 4:00 PM.
- **Address:** 120 Dickenson Street, Lahaina, HI 96761.
- **Admission Fee:** $7.50 for adults, $5.00 for seniors (65+), $2.00 for children (ages 7-12), free for children under 7.
- **Insider Tips:** Arrive early to avoid crowds, and consider combining your visit with an exploration of other nearby historic sites like the Lahaina Banyan Court Park. The museum offers guided tours that provide deeper insights into the Baldwin family's impact on Lahaina's development.

B. Lahaina Banyan Court Park:

Lahaina Banyan Court Park, nestled in the heart of Lahaina's Historic District on Maui, is a captivating cultural and historical landmark. Planted in 1873, it features one of the largest banyan trees in the United States, sprawling across nearly an acre and providing shade over its extensive grounds.

The park's significance extends beyond its natural beauty; it serves as a gathering place for community events and hosts local artisans and musicians, embodying Lahaina's vibrant cultural heritage. Visitors can stroll through its shaded pathways, admire the tree's intricate aerial roots, and relax amidst its serene atmosphere, often dotted with local festivities.

- **Opening Hours:** Daily from 8:00 AM to 6:00 PM
- **Address:** Front Street, Lahaina, HI 96761
- **Insider Tips:** Visit early in the morning or late afternoon for quieter moments under the shade of the banyan tree. Keep an eye out for special events and performances, particularly during weekends and holidays, to experience the park at its liveliest. Parking can be limited, so consider arriving early or using public transportation if possible.

C. Lahaina Heritage Museum:

The Lahaina Heritage Museum, located within the Lahaina Historic District on Maui, offers a captivating journey into the rich history and cultural heritage of Lahaina. Housed in the historic Old Lahaina Courthouse, the museum features exhibits that chronicle Lahaina's evolution from a royal capital of Hawaii to a bustling whaling port and missionary hub. Visitors can explore artifacts, photographs, and displays that highlight the town's significance in Hawaiian history, including its cultural diversity and the impact of missionary efforts. The museum's setting itself, within a beautifully restored courthouse dating back to the mid-19th century, adds to the immersive experience.

- **Opening Hours:** Daily from 9:00 AM to 5:00 PM
- **Address:** 648 Wharf Street, Lahaina, HI 96761
- **Admission Fee:** Typically, around $5 per person
- **Insider Tips:** Plan to visit early to avoid crowds, and consider combining your visit with a stroll along Lahaina's historic Front Street. Guided tours are available and highly recommended for deeper insights into Lahaina's fascinating past.

D. Wo Hing Museum and Cookhouse:

The Wo Hing Museum and Cookhouse in the Lahaina Historic District, Maui, offers a fascinating glimpse into Maui's multicultural history. This restored Chinese social club and cookhouse, dating back to the early 20th century, showcases the contributions of Chinese immigrants to the island's sugar plantation era. Exhibits include artifacts, photographs, and displays illustrating daily life, cultural practices, and the hardships faced by early Chinese settlers. The cookhouse features a traditional kitchen and herbal medicine display, highlighting culinary traditions and medicinal practices of the time. Visitors can explore the courtyard garden and learn about Lahaina's diverse cultural heritage through guided tours and educational programs.

- **Opening Hours:** Monday to Saturday, 10:00 AM to 4:00 PM
- **Address:** 858 Front St, Lahaina, HI 96761

- **Admission Fee:** Adults $7, Children (ages 6-12) $2
- **Insider Tips:** Visit early in the day to avoid crowds. Combine your visit with nearby historic sites like the Baldwin Home Museum and Lahaina Banyan Court Park for a comprehensive cultural experience in Lahaina.

2. Hale Pa'i Printing Museum

The Hale Pa'i Printing Museum in Lahaina, Maui, stands as a testament to Hawaii's rich history of printing and journalism. Located on the grounds of Lahainaluna High School, it was here that the first Hawaiian-language newspaper, "Ka Lama Hawaii," was printed in 1834. The museum showcases original printing presses, typefaces, and exhibits detailing the evolution of printing in Hawaii, highlighting its pivotal role in cultural preservation and education during the missionary era. Visitors can explore the restored printing office and learn about the missionaries' efforts to disseminate knowledge and literacy among the Hawaiian population. This site offers a fascinating glimpse into the intersection of Western technology and Hawaiian language and culture.

- **Opening Hours:** Monday to Friday, 10:00 AM - 4:00 PM
- **Address:** Lahainaluna High School, 980 Lahainaluna Rd, Lahaina, HI 96761
- **Insider Tips:** Plan your visit early in the day to avoid crowds and engage with knowledgeable staff who can provide deeper insights into the history of

Hawaiian printing. Don't miss the opportunity to explore the picturesque Lahaina Historic District nearby, including the Baldwin Home Museum and the Lahaina Banyan Court Park.

3. Moku'ula and Mokuhinia

Moku'ula and Mokuhinia are significant cultural and historical sites located in Lahaina, Maui, within the Lahaina Historic District. Moku'ula was once a royal residence and a sacred island surrounded by Mokuhinia, a freshwater pond. It holds great spiritual and cultural importance as the ancestral homeland of Maui's ruling chiefs and a place where ceremonies and gatherings took place. Today, efforts are underway to restore and preserve these sites, which include archaeological excavations and community engagement to honor their cultural significance. Visitors can explore the site's historical artifacts and learn about Hawaiian traditions and beliefs.

- **Opening Hours:** Currently under restoration, with periodic public access for educational purposes.
- **Address:** Moku'ula and Mokuhinia are located in Lahaina, Maui, within the Lahaina Historic District.

- **Insider Tips:** Check with local cultural organizations or the Lahaina Restoration Foundation for updates on access and guided tours. Respect the site's cultural significance by following any guidelines or restrictions during visits.

4. Lahainaluna High School

Lahainaluna High School holds a significant place in Hawaiian history as the oldest operating school west of the Rockies, established in 1831. Located in Lahaina, Maui, its historical campus includes notable buildings like Hale Pa'i (House of Printing), where Hawaii's first newspaper was printed. The school's rich cultural heritage is showcased through its mission-era architecture and educational contributions to the community. Visitors can explore its grounds, which feature a monument to Henry Perrine Baldwin and a museum displaying artifacts and documents from its storied past.

- **Opening Hours**: Generally, Monday to Friday, 8:00 AM to 4:00 PM. Closed on weekends and holidays.
- **Address:** 980 Lahainaluna Road, Lahaina, HI 96761, USA.

- **Insider Tips:** Visit during school hours for a glimpse of daily life on campus and to view the historic buildings. Check for guided tours or special events that may offer deeper insights into Lahainaluna's role in Hawaiian education and history.

5. The Masters' Reading Room (Hale Halawai)

The Masters' Reading Room, also known as Hale Halawai, stands as a testament to Lahaina's rich cultural tapestry. This historical site, nestled in Lahaina's bustling Historic District, once served as a pivotal meeting place for missionaries in the early 19th century. Constructed in 1834, it hosted gatherings that shaped educational and religious discourse during Hawaii's monarchy era. Today, the restored building houses exhibits that chronicle Lahaina's missionary history, showcasing artifacts and documents that illuminate the island's transformation.

- **Opening Hours:** Open daily from 10:00 AM to 4:00 PM.
- **Address:** 525 Front St, Lahaina, HI 96761, USA.
- **Insider Tips:** Plan to visit early to avoid crowds, and consider joining a guided tour to gain deeper insights into Lahaina's missionary heritage. Parking can be limited; it's advisable to use public transportation or nearby parking lots.

6. Olowalu Petroglyphs

The Olowalu Petroglyphs, located near Lahaina on Maui's west coast, are a fascinating glimpse into Hawaii's ancient past. These rock carvings, estimated to be several centuries old, depict various symbols, shapes, and figures that hold cultural and historical significance for native Hawaiians. The site, set against a backdrop of rugged coastal terrain, offers visitors a serene setting to explore and contemplate the island's indigenous heritage. Accessible via a short hike from the main road, the petroglyphs are a reminder of the island's early inhabitants and their connection to the land.

- **Opening Hours:** Generally accessible during daylight hours.
- **Address:** Olowalu Petroglyphs, Honoapiilani Hwy, Lahaina, HI 96761.
- **Insider Tips:** Visit early in the morning or late afternoon for softer light ideal for photography. Wear sturdy shoes suitable for a short hike, and bring water and sunscreen, as there is limited shade. Respect the site's cultural significance by refraining from touching or disturbing the petroglyphs.

7. Hale Aloha (Lahaina Jodo Mission)

The Hale Aloha (Lahaina Jodo Mission) in the Lahaina Historic District, Maui, is a serene Buddhist temple that offers visitors a peaceful retreat amidst the bustling town. Established by Japanese immigrants in 1912, its architecture mirrors traditional Japanese temple styles, featuring a large bronze Buddha statue and meticulously maintained gardens. The temple grounds invite contemplation with koi ponds, stone lanterns, and a calming atmosphere, making it a cultural gem that bridges Hawaiian and Japanese heritage.

- **Opening Hours:** Open daily from 9:00 AM to 4:00 PM
- **Address:** 12 Ala Moana Street, Lahaina, HI 96761
- **Insider Tips:** Visit early in the morning for a tranquil experience and to avoid crowds. Take time to explore the gardens and learn about the history of Buddhism in Hawaii through informative displays. Respect the temple's customs, such as removing shoes before entering buildings, and consider participating in meditation sessions or cultural events when available.

Top-Rated Beaches and Outdoor Activities

West Maui is renowned for its beautiful beaches and diverse outdoor activities. Here are some of the best beaches and outdoor adventures you can enjoy in this area:

Best Beaches

1. Kaanapali Beach

Kaanapali Beach, often hailed as one of West Maui's premier beaches, captivates visitors with its golden sands and clear turquoise waters. Stretching for three miles along the coast, this beach offers an ideal setting for relaxation and recreation. The gently sloping shoreline invites swimmers and snorkelers to explore its vibrant coral reefs teeming with marine life. Spectacular sunsets paint the sky, creating a picturesque backdrop for romantic strolls or beachside dining at nearby resorts. Lined with luxury hotels, shopping centers, and restaurants along its famous Kaanapali Beachwalk, visitors can easily indulge in a blend of leisure and entertainment. Whether lounging under swaying palm trees or enjoying water sports like parasailing and jet skiing, Kaanapali Beach promises an unforgettable Hawaiian getaway.

- **Location**: Kaanapali, West Maui
- **Season:** Year-round, with peak conditions in summer and fall
- **Facilities**: Restrooms, showers, parking, beach rentals, dining options

2. Kapalua Bay

Kapalua Bay is celebrated as one of West Maui's premier beaches, renowned for its pristine white sands and crystal-clear turquoise waters. Nestled in a sheltered cove, it offers ideal conditions for swimming and snorkeling, thanks to its calm and shallow reef-protected waters. Visitors can explore vibrant coral gardens teeming with tropical fish, making it perfect for underwater enthusiasts of all ages. The beach is framed by swaying palm trees and lush vegetation, providing a picturesque backdrop for relaxation and picnicking. Its gentle slope into the sea makes it accessible and safe for families and snorkelers alike, ensuring a serene and enjoyable beach experience.

- **Location:** Kapalua Bay is located in the resort area of Kapalua on the northwest coast of Maui, Hawaii.
- **Season:** The beach is enjoyable year-round, with optimal snorkeling conditions typically from spring through fall when waters are calmer.
- **Facilities:** The bay offers amenities such as restrooms, showers, picnic tables, and shaded areas, enhancing visitors' comfort and convenience during their stay.

3. Napili Bay

Napili Bay is celebrated for its pristine crescent-shaped beach and tranquil turquoise waters, making it one of West Maui's hidden gems. Nestled between two rocky points, this family-friendly beach offers excellent swimming and snorkeling opportunities due to its clear visibility and gentle waves. Its soft, golden sands invite visitors to relax and soak in the picturesque views of Molokai and Lanai islands on the horizon. The bay's intimate size creates a sense of seclusion, perfect for a peaceful day by the ocean. Surrounded by lush tropical foliage, Napili Bay embodies Maui's natural beauty and charm.

- **Location:** Napili Bay is located in the Napili-Honokowai area of West Maui, just north of Kaanapali.
- **Season:** The beach is enjoyable year-round, with calmer conditions typically during the summer months.
- **Facilities:** Visitors can find restroom facilities, showers, and beach rentals nearby. Limited parking is available, so arriving early is recommended for a more convenient experience.

4. Honolua Bay

Honolua Bay is renowned as one of the best beaches in West Maui, celebrated for its pristine waters and exceptional snorkeling opportunities. Nestled within a marine reserve, its vibrant coral reefs teem with diverse marine life, including colorful fish and occasional green sea turtles. The bay's clear visibility makes it ideal for both snorkelers and scuba divers seeking encounters with tropical species amidst underwater lava formations. Its secluded location and lack of extensive beach facilities contribute to its natural charm, appealing to those seeking a more serene coastal experience.

- **Location:** Honolua Bay is located on the northwest coast of Maui, near Kapalua.
- **Season:** The best time to visit Honolua Bay for snorkeling and diving is during the summer months (May to September) when the ocean conditions are typically calm and clear.
- **Facilities:** Limited facilities are available at Honolua Bay, including parking areas and portable toilets. Visitors are advised to bring their snorkeling gear and supplies, as there are no concessions or rentals on-site.

5. D.T. Fleming Beach Park

D.T. Fleming Beach Park stands out as one of West Maui's premier beaches, known for its expansive golden sands and clear turquoise waters. Nestled between rocky outcrops, it offers excellent swimming and bodyboarding conditions, particularly during calmer ocean periods. The beach is fringed by ironwood trees, providing ample shade for picnics and relaxation. Its scenic beauty is complemented by views of the neighboring islands of Molokai and Lanai, making it a popular spot for both locals and tourists seeking a serene coastal retreat. D.T. Fleming Beach Park is also home to the annual Xterra World Championship triathlon, highlighting its appeal for outdoor enthusiasts and athletes alike.

- **Location:** D.T. Fleming Beach Park is located in Kapalua, West Maui.
- **Season:** Year-round, with calmer waters typically during summer months.
- **Facilities:** The park offers parking, restroom facilities, picnic tables, and showers. Lifeguards are on duty during peak times for added safety.

6 Olowalu Beach

Olowalu Beach is celebrated as one of West Maui's finest beaches, renowned for its tranquil atmosphere and vibrant marine life.

Nestled along the Honoapiilani Highway, this crescent-shaped beach offers soft golden sands and clear, shallow waters ideal for snorkeling. Its expansive coral reef teems with diverse fish species and occasional green sea turtles, making it a haven for underwater exploration and photography. The beach is framed by swaying palms and offers stunning views of the neighboring islands of Lanai and Molokai. Its secluded location lends a sense of peaceful seclusion, perfect for relaxation and enjoying Maui's natural beauty.

- **Location:** Olowalu Beach is located on the western coast of Maui, along the Honoapiilani Highway between Lahaina and Ma'alaea.
- **Season:** Year-round, with the calmest waters typically during the summer months.
- **Facilities:** Limited facilities include parking along the highway shoulder and portable toilets. Snorkeling gear is not available for rent, so visitors should bring their equipment.

Outdoor Activities

1. Snorkeling and Diving

Top Spots: Honolua Bay, Kapalua Bay, and Olowalu Beach.

Snorkeling and diving in West Maui are exceptional due to its rich marine biodiversity and crystal-clear waters. Honolua Bay and Kapalua Bay offer prime snorkeling spots with vibrant coral reefs and abundant tropical fish, while Black Rock at Kaanapali Beach provides thrilling dives near underwater cliffs and marine life. Beginners can enjoy shallow reefs close to shore, while advanced divers explore deeper waters and lava formations. Guided tours and rental equipment are readily available, ensuring safe and immersive experiences. Whether snorkeling over colorful reefs or diving alongside sea turtles and rays, West Maui’s underwater world offers unforgettable encounters with Hawaii’s marine ecosystems.

2. Surfing and Paddleboarding

Top Spots: Kaanapali Beach (for beginners), Honolua Bay (for experienced surfers).

Surfing and paddleboarding are quintessential outdoor activities in West Maui, offering enthusiasts of all levels thrilling experiences amidst stunning coastal scenery. Kaanapali Beach provides ideal conditions for beginners to learn paddleboarding in calm waters, while Honolua Bay attracts surfers with its challenging winter swells and pristine breaks. Lessons and equipment rentals are readily available, ensuring accessibility for newcomers and seasoned riders alike. Both sports allow participants to explore Maui's coastline from a unique perspective, spotting marine life like sea turtles and dolphins along the way. Whether catching waves at renowned surf spots or gliding peacefully on a paddleboard, these activities embody the island's laid-back lifestyle and deep connection to its oceanic surroundings.

3. Hiking

Kapalua Coastal Trail:

The Kapalua Coastal Trail in West Maui offers a scenic hike along the island's northwest shore, providing panoramic views of the Pacific Ocean and neighboring islands. Starting near Kapalua Bay Beach, the trail winds through lava rock formations, lush greenery, and pristine beaches. Hikers can explore secluded coves and tide pools, often spotting marine life such as sea turtles and colorful fish. The trail is well-maintained and suitable for all skill levels, making it ideal for families and casual hikers seeking a leisurely coastal stroll amidst breathtaking natural beauty.

- **Distance:** Approximately 2.6 miles (4.2 kilometers) one way

- **Duration:** 1.5 to 2 hours one way
- **Difficulty:** Easy

Mahana Ridge Trail:

The Mahana Ridge Trail in West Maui offers hikers a captivating journey through lush tropical forests and panoramic views of the Pacific Ocean. Beginning near the Kapalua Resort, the trail winds through a dense forest of Cook pines and native vegetation, providing shade and glimpses of endemic bird species. As you ascend, the trail opens up to sweeping vistas of the coastline and neighboring islands, including Molokai. The hike is renowned for its tranquility and natural beauty, offering ample opportunities for birdwatching and photography. At the end of the trail, hikers are rewarded with breathtaking views from the ridge before descending back through the forest.

- **Distance:** Approximately 5.5 miles round trip
- **Duration:** 3-4 hours
- **Difficulty:** Moderate

4. Ziplining

Kapalua Ziplines: Kapalua Ziplines offers an exhilarating adventure through the lush landscapes of West Maui.

Nestled amidst towering trees and overlooking scenic valleys, this ziplining experience provides breathtaking views of the Pacific Ocean and neighboring islands. With multiple lines varying in length and height, participants can soar through the air, experiencing the thrill of flying while immersed in Maui's natural beauty. Trained guides ensure safety and offer insights into the island's ecology and history, making it a perfect activity for both adventure seekers and nature enthusiasts. Whether gliding over waterfalls or traversing rugged terrain, Kapalua Ziplines promises an unforgettable journey through Hawaii's tropical paradise.

Jungle Zipline Maui: Jungle Zipline Maui offers an exhilarating ziplining experience amidst West Maui's lush tropical landscapes. Located in Haiku, this adventure features multiple zip lines that soar through dense jungle canopies, offering panoramic views of waterfalls and valleys below. The tour includes trained guides who ensure safety and provide insights into Maui's natural environment and conservation efforts. Participants can enjoy the thrill of soaring through the air while learning about local flora, fauna, and cultural history. Jungle Zipline Maui emphasizes eco-friendly practices and provides a memorable adventure suitable for families, groups, and thrill-seekers looking to experience Maui's beauty from a unique perspective.

5. Whale Watching

Whale watching in West Maui is a captivating outdoor activity, particularly from December to April when humpback whales migrate to Hawaiian waters. Departing from Lahaina or Ma'alaea Harbor, tours offer an intimate encounter with these majestic creatures as they breach, slap their tails, and sing their haunting songs. Knowledgeable guides provide insights into whale behavior and conservation efforts, enhancing the experience with educational commentary. Witnessing these massive mammals in their natural habitat against the backdrop of Maui's coastline is a breathtaking sight, making whale watching a must-do activity for nature enthusiasts and families alike. The tours prioritize respectful viewing distances to minimize disturbance to the whales, ensuring a responsible and memorable wildlife encounter.

- **Season:** December to April.

6. Golfing

Golfing in West Maui offers enthusiasts a blend of scenic beauty and challenging courses set against the backdrop of lush mountains and ocean views.

Renowned for its world-class facilities, the area boasts top-rated courses such as Kapalua Golf's Plantation Course, famous for hosting the PGA Tour's Tournament of Champions. Golfers can tee off amidst panoramic vistas and rolling fairways, navigating through natural hazards and enjoying immaculately groomed greens. Ka'anapali Golf Courses provide additional options with oceanfront holes that showcase stunning sunsets over the Pacific. Royal Ka'anapali Golf Course offers a challenging layout with views of the West Maui Mountains, ensuring a memorable round in a paradise setting. Whether you're a novice or a seasoned player, West Maui's golf courses promise an exceptional golfing experience amidst Hawaii's natural beauty.

Top Courses in West Maui:

- **Plantation Course at Kapalua Golf:** Known for its challenging layout and spectacular views.
- **Bay Course at Kapalua Golf:** Offers scenic ocean views and strategic holes.
- **Royal Ka'anapali Golf Course:** Features panoramic views of the West Maui Mountains and the Pacific Ocean.
- **Kaanapali Golf Courses:** Includes two courses with oceanfront holes and challenging fairways.
- **The Dunes at Maui Lani Golf Course:** Located in Central Maui, offering a unique links-style experience with views of Haleakala.

7. Kayaking and Canoeing

Kayaking and canoeing in West Maui offer adventurous ways to explore its pristine coastline and marine life. Paddle through clear waters, discovering secluded beaches, sea caves, and vibrant coral reefs perfect for snorkeling. Many rental shops provide equipment and guided tours, ensuring safety and enhancing the experience with local knowledge. Whether navigating the calm waters of Napili Bay or exploring the hidden coves near Kaanapali Beach, kayaking and canoeing offer unforgettable views of Maui's lush landscapes and crystal-clear ocean. Ideal for families and adventure enthusiasts alike, these activities provide opportunities for leisurely exploration or thrilling adventures on the water.

Top Spots:

- **Kaanapali Beach:** Rent kayaks and explore the nearby reefs and coves.
- **Napili Bay:** Enjoy calm waters ideal for both kayaking and snorkeling.
- **Honolua Bay:** Paddle along the coastline and discover its diverse marine life.

8. Sailing and Catamaran Tours

Sailing and catamaran tours offer an unforgettable way to explore the beauty of West Maui's coastline. Glide over clear turquoise waters, passing lush landscapes and iconic landmarks like Molokini Crater and the neighboring islands of Lanai and Molokai. These tours provide opportunities for snorkeling in vibrant coral reefs, swimming in secluded coves, and spotting marine life such as dolphins and humpback whales (seasonal). Sunset cruises offer a romantic setting to enjoy panoramic views and witness the sun dip below the horizon. Whether you're seeking adventure or relaxation, sailing and catamaran tours in West Maui promise a serene and immersive experience in Hawaii's tropical paradise.

Top Operators:

- **Trilogy Excursions:** Known for eco-friendly practices and expert crew, offering snorkel sails and sunset cruises.
- **Sail Maui:** Provides luxury catamaran experiences with gourmet cuisine and personalized service.
- **Pacific Whale Foundation:** Focuses on marine conservation with educational tours and whale-watching excursions.
- **Teralani Sailing:** Offers snorkeling and sailing adventures with family-friendly options and attentive staff.

9. Fishing

Fishing in West Maui offers enthusiasts diverse opportunities in both deep-sea and shore fishing. Anglers can target a variety of prized species, including mahi-mahi, tuna, marlin, and ono (wahoo) in the deep waters offshore. Shore fishing along rocky coastlines or from beaches allows for catching reef fish like Papio (jack), ulua (trevally), and bonefish. Charters depart from Lahaina and Ma'alaea harbors, offering half-day to full-day excursions with experienced captains who know the best spots. They provide all the necessary equipment and local knowledge to maximize your chances of landing a big catch while enjoying panoramic views of Maui's coastline and possibly encountering marine wildlife like sea turtles and dolphins.

Top Charters:

- **Start Me Up Sportfishing:** Known for its professional crew and successful fishing trips targeting big game fish.

- **Maui Fun Charters:** Offers customizable fishing experiences, including shared and private charters, with a focus on customer satisfaction and marine conservation.

Recommended Resorts and Accommodations

West Maui is home to some of the most luxurious and beautiful resorts in Hawaii, offering world-class amenities, stunning views, and top-notch service. Here are some of the top resorts and accommodations in the area:

1. The Ritz-Carlton, Kapalua

Nestled within 54 acres of pristine oceanfront property, The Ritz-Carlton, Kapalua offers a luxurious escape in West Maui. The resort features beautifully appointed rooms and suites with private lanais offering breathtaking views of the Pacific Ocean or lush gardens. Guests can enjoy six dining venues, two golf courses, a full-service spa, and a three-tiered pool. The resort's location near the Kapalua Coastal Trail and DT Fleming Beach makes it ideal for outdoor enthusiasts. Perfect for those seeking a blend of relaxation and adventure, this resort delivers top-notch service in an exquisite setting.

- **Star Rating:** ★★★★★
- **Location:** 1 Ritz Carlton Dr, Kapalua, HI 96761, USA
- **Phone Number:** +1 808-669-6200

2. Montage Kapalua Bay

Montage Kapalua Bay is a five-star luxury resort known for its spacious residential-style accommodations, each featuring a fully equipped kitchen, large living area, and private lanai. Situated on 24 acres of lush tropical landscape, the resort offers stunning views of the Pacific Ocean and the neighboring islands. Guests can enjoy the multi-tiered lagoon pool, a world-class spa, and exceptional dining experiences. The resort's location near Kapalua Bay Beach, one of Maui's best snorkeling spots, adds to its allure. Ideal for families, couples, and groups, Montage Kapalua Bay promises a serene and upscale Hawaiian getaway.

- **Star Rating:** ★★★★★
- **Location:** 1 Bay Dr, Lahaina, HI 96761, USA
- **Phone Number:** +1 808-662-6600

3. Hyatt Regency Maui Resort and Spa

Set on 40 oceanfront acres along Ka'anapali Beach, the Hyatt Regency Maui Resort and Spa offers a blend of luxury and family-friendly amenities. The resort features spacious rooms with private lanais, a half-acre pool with a 150-foot water slide, a rooftop astronomy program, and daily cultural activities. Guests can indulge in treatments at the award-winning Kamaha'o Spa or dine at one of the resort's five on-site restaurants. With its lush gardens, waterfalls, and wildlife, including flamingos and swans, the resort provides a unique and enchanting setting for all ages.

- **Star Rating:** ★★★★½
- **Location:** 200 Nohea Kai Dr, Lahaina, HI 96761, USA
- **Phone Number:** +1 808-661-1234

4. Sheraton Maui Resort & Spa

Perched on the iconic Black Rock on Ka'anapali Beach, the Sheraton Maui Resort & Spa is renowned for its prime location and scenic views. The resort offers a range of accommodations, from garden view rooms to oceanfront suites, all with private lanais. Guests can relax by the lagoon-style pool, enjoy beachfront dining, or partake in the nightly cliff diving ceremony, a tribute to Hawaiian culture. The resort's proximity to Whalers Village and various water activities makes it a great choice for both relaxation and adventure seekers.

- **Star Rating:** ★★★★½
- **Location:** 2605 Ka'anapali Pkwy, Lahaina, HI 96761, USA
- **Phone Number:** +1 808-661-0031

5. The Westin Maui Resort & Spa, Ka'anapali

Overlooking Ka'anapali Beach, The Westin Maui Resort & Spa offers a luxurious retreat with an emphasis on wellness and relaxation. The resort boasts newly renovated rooms with modern amenities and private balconies. Guests can unwind at the Heavenly Spa, enjoy the five outdoor pools, including an adults-only infinity pool, or savor a meal at one of the resort's restaurants. The resort's location near championship golf courses and shopping at Whalers Village adds to its appeal, making it an ideal destination for both leisure and activity-filled vacations.

- **Star Rating:** ★★★★½

- **Location:** 2365 Ka'anapali Pkwy, Lahaina, HI 96761, USA
- **Phone Number:** +1 808-667-2525

6. Aston Kaanapali Shores

Aston Kaanapali Shores is a beachfront resort offering spacious condo-style accommodations with fully equipped kitchens, private lanais, and beautiful ocean or garden views. Located on the serene shores of Kaanapali Beach, this resort features two outdoor pools, a whirlpool, a fitness center, and an on-site restaurant. The lush tropical gardens and laid-back atmosphere make it an ideal choice for families and couples seeking a more home-like environment while still enjoying upscale amenities. The resort's proximity to local shops and dining options adds convenience to its guests' stay.

- **Star Rating:** ★★★★
- **Location:** 3445 Lower Honoapiilani Rd, Lahaina, HI 96761, USA
- **Phone Number:** +1 808-667-2281

7. The Westin Nanea Ocean Villas, Ka'anapali

The Westin Nanea Ocean Villas offers a luxurious, villa-style experience with modern Hawaiian elegance. The resort features spacious villas with fully equipped kitchens, private balconies, and ocean views. Guests can enjoy the beachfront location, a large lagoon-style pool, and a range of dining options. The resort emphasizes wellness and relaxation with its full-service spa and fitness center. Its proximity to local attractions and outdoor activities makes it a versatile choice for both relaxation and exploration, catering to couples, families, and groups alike.

- **Star Rating:** ★★★★★
- **Location:** 130 Kai Malina Pkwy, Lahaina, HI 96761, USA
- **Phone Number:** +1 808-662-3000

8. Napili Kai Beach Resort

Located on the tranquil Napili Bay, Napili Kai Beach Resort offers a charming, intimate retreat with a focus on traditional Hawaiian hospitality. The resort features spacious studio and one-bedroom suites with full kitchens and private lanais overlooking the ocean or lush gardens. Guests can enjoy the calm waters of Napili Bay, perfect for swimming and snorkeling, as well as two swimming pools, a golf course, and a restaurant offering fresh local cuisine. The resort's relaxed ambiance and prime beach location make it ideal for a peaceful getaway.

- **Star Rating:** ★★★★
- **Location:** 5920 Lower Honoapiilani Rd, Lahaina, HI 96761, USA
- **Phone Number:** +1 808-669-6271

9. Kapalua Villas Maui

Kapalua Villas Maui offers a blend of luxury and tranquility with its spacious villas set amid lush tropical landscapes. Each villa features a fully equipped kitchen, private lanai, and panoramic views of the ocean or golf courses. The resort includes access to Kapalua Bay Beach, a variety of outdoor pools, and tennis courts. The property is renowned for its proximity to world-class golf courses and the scenic Kapalua Coastal Trail. This resort provides a serene setting with a focus on comfort and convenience, making it a popular choice for both long stays and short getaways.

- **Star Rating:** ★★★★
- **Location:** 300 Kapalua Dr, Lahaina, HI 96761, USA
- **Phone Number:** +1 808-665-5000

10. Kaanapali Beach Club

Kaanapali Beach Club is a beachfront resort known for its expansive ocean views and family-friendly amenities. The resort offers spacious suites with kitchenettes, private balconies, and beautiful views of the Pacific Ocean. Facilities include a large outdoor pool with a cascading waterfall, a full-service spa, and an array of dining options. The resort's prime location on Kaanapali Beach provides easy access to snorkeling, swimming, and local attractions. With its relaxed atmosphere and wide range of activities, it's an excellent choice for both families and couples seeking a comfortable and enjoyable Hawaiian experience.

- **Star Rating:** ★★★★
- **Location:** 104 Kaanapali Shores Pl, Lahaina, HI 96761, USA
- **Phone Number:** +1 808-661-8000

Chapter 7: South Maui

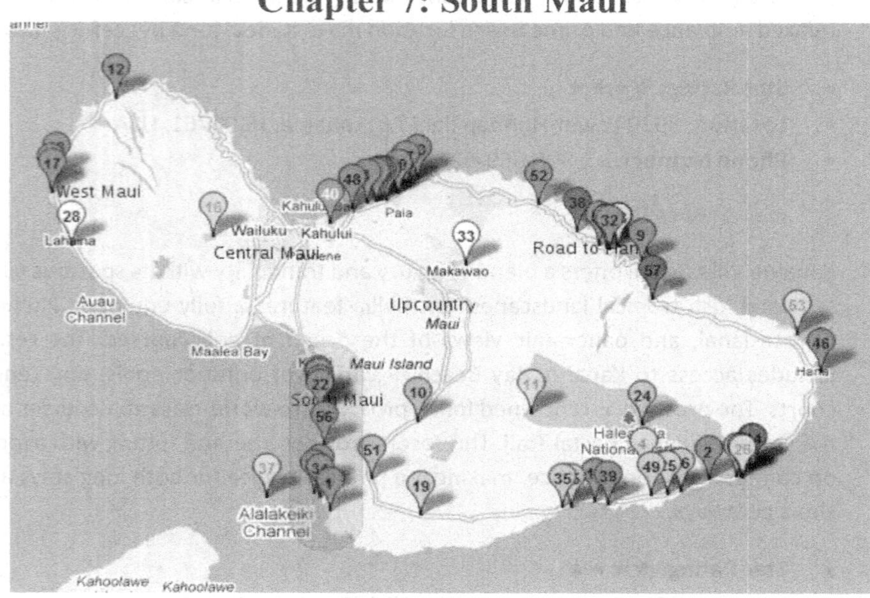

Overview of South Maui

Geography and Climate

South Maui encompasses the coastal areas of Kihei, Wailea, and Makena. This region is known for its warm, sunny weather, making it an ideal location for beach activities and outdoor adventures. The climate is typically dry and sunny, with temperatures ranging from the mid-70s to mid-80s Fahrenheit year-round.

Beaches

South Maui is home to some of the most beautiful and accessible beaches on the island.

Kamaole Beach Parks (I, II, and III): These three adjacent beaches in Kihei are popular for swimming, snorkeling, and family-friendly activities. They offer lifeguards, picnic areas, and grassy lawns.

Wailea Beach: Located in the upscale resort area of Wailea, this beach is known for its golden sands and calm waters, making it perfect for swimming and sunbathing. It's also a great spot for whale watching during the winter months.

Makena Beach State Park (Big Beach): Famous for its expansive sandy shore and stunning views, Big Beach is a favorite among both locals and visitors. Its strong shore break can make for exciting bodyboarding, but swimmers should exercise caution.

Little Beach: Located just over a small hill from Big Beach, Little Beach is known for its more relaxed, clothing-optional atmosphere and is a popular spot for sunset gatherings and drum circles.

Resorts and Accommodations

South Maui is dotted with luxurious resorts, particularly in Wailea, which is known for its world-class hospitality.

Grand Wailea: A Waldorf Astoria Resort, offering opulent accommodations, a stunning pool area, and direct beach access.

Four Seasons Resort Maui at Wailea: Known for its exceptional service, beautiful grounds, and oceanfront setting.

Andaz Maui at Wailea Resort: A contemporary resort offering sleek, modern design and a focus on local culture and sustainability.

Dining and Cuisine

South Maui offers a diverse dining scene, from casual beachside eateries to fine dining restaurants.

Mama's Fish House: Although technically in North Shore, this iconic restaurant is a must-visit for its fresh seafood and stunning ocean views.

Monkeypod Kitchen: Located in Wailea, this popular spot offers a casual yet upscale atmosphere with a focus on locally sourced ingredients and craft cocktails.

Sarento's on the Beach: An elegant restaurant located in Kihei, offering Mediterranean cuisine with a Hawaiian twist and breathtaking sunset views.

Activities and Attractions

There is no shortage of activities to enjoy in South Maui, whether you're looking for relaxation or adventure.

Snorkeling and Scuba Diving: The clear waters of South Maui are ideal for snorkeling and diving, with popular spots including Molokini Crater and Turtle Town.

Golf: South Maui is home to some of Hawaii's best golf courses, including the Wailea Golf Club, which offers three championship courses with stunning ocean views.

Shopping: The Shops at Wailea offer a range of high-end boutiques, art galleries, and restaurants, providing a luxurious shopping experience.

Spas: Many of the resorts in Wailea feature world-class spas offering a range of treatments inspired by Hawaiian healing traditions.

Culture and Events

South Maui hosts a variety of cultural events and activities throughout the year.

Wailea Film Festival: An annual event showcasing independent films, often attended by filmmakers and celebrities.

Maui Whale Festival: Held in February, this festival celebrates the annual migration of humpback whales with events, educational activities, and whale-watching tours.

Hawaiian Luaus: Several resorts in South Maui offer traditional Hawaiian luaus, complete with hula performances, live music, and a feast of local dishes.

Natural Attractions

La Perouse Bay: Located at the southern end of Makena, this bay is part of the Ahihi-Kinau Natural Area Reserve. The area features a rugged lava rock coastline and excellent snorkeling opportunities.

Keawakapu Beach: A quieter alternative to some of the more crowded beaches, Keawakapu offers a tranquil setting and beautiful sunset views.

Historical Sites and Cultural Attractions

In South Maui, while it's mostly known for its beaches and resorts, there are a few historical sites and cultural attractions worth exploring:

1. Pi'ilanihale Heiau:

Pi'ilanihale Heiau is an ancient Hawaiian temple located near Makena Beach in South Maui, renowned for its historical significance and impressive architecture. Believed to have been built in the 13th century, it stands as one of Hawaii's largest heiaus, showcasing intricate stonework and a massive lava-rock platform. The site served as a place of worship and cultural center, honoring Pi'ilani, a legendary chief credited with uniting Maui. The temple's size and complexity reflect the importance of Pi'ilani's reign in Hawaiian history, offering visitors a glimpse into ancient Hawaiian spirituality and society.

- **Opening Hours:** Typically open during daylight hours; exact hours can vary.
- **Address:** Near Makena Beach, South Maui, Hawaii.
- **Insider Tips:** Wear comfortable shoes for walking on uneven terrain. Bring sunscreen, water, and insect repellent, as facilities are limited on-site. Consider visiting early in the morning or late afternoon for quieter times and better lighting for photography.

2. Kealia Pond National Wildlife Refuge:

Kealia Pond National Wildlife Refuge in South Maui is a vital habitat for endangered Hawaiian waterbirds and migratory species. This 700-acre wetland preserve features a diverse ecosystem of ponds, marshes, and grasslands, offering visitors a glimpse into Hawaii's natural biodiversity. The refuge serves as a critical resting and feeding area for native birds such as the Hawaiian stilt and coot, alongside migratory species like the Pacific golden plover. Educational exhibits provide insight into the refuge's ecological importance and cultural relevance, highlighting its role in traditional Hawaiian practices and conservation efforts. Kealia Pond offers walking trails and observation platforms for birdwatching and nature photography, making it an ideal destination for wildlife enthusiasts and families alike.

- **Opening Hours:** Daily, 7:30 AM - 4:00 PM
- **Address:** Mokulele Hwy, Kihei, HI 96753
- **Insider Tips:** Bring binoculars for better birdwatching views. Visit early morning or late afternoon for optimal bird activity. Check for ranger-led tours and educational programs for a deeper understanding of the refuge's significance.

3. Moku'ula:

Moku'ula, located in Lahaina, near South Maui, holds significant historical and cultural importance as the former residence of Hawaiian royalty. Once a sacred site and the political center of Maui, it housed the royal compound and the Mokuhinia pond, revered for its spiritual significance. Today, efforts are underway to restore Moku'ula and its surrounding area, allowing visitors to explore its archaeological remains and learn about its rich cultural heritage through guided tours and exhibits. The site offers a glimpse into traditional Hawaiian governance, rituals, and daily life before Western influence.

- **Opening Hours:** Currently undergoing restoration; check for updates on visiting hours.
- **Address:** Moku'ula, Lahaina, Maui, Hawaii, USA.
- **Insider Tips:** Plan your visit during daylight hours as the site may not be lit for evening visits. Guided tours provide deeper insights into the site's history; check availability and book in advance if possible. Parking can be limited; consider visiting early in the day for easier access.

4. Alexander & Baldwin Sugar Museum:

The Alexander & Baldwin Sugar Museum in Puunene, Maui, offers a fascinating glimpse into the history of sugar production in Hawaii, a pivotal industry that shaped the island's economy and cultural landscape. Housed in a former plantation superintendent's residence, the museum features exhibits on the plantation era, showcasing artifacts, photographs, and interactive displays that detail the process of sugar cultivation, harvesting, and processing. Visitors can explore the labor conditions, multicultural workforce, and technological advancements that defined Maui's sugar industry from the 1800s until its decline in the late 20th century. The museum also highlights the impact of sugar on Hawaii's environment and communities.

- **Opening Hours:** Monday to Saturday, 9:30 AM to 4:00 PM
- **Address:** 3957 Hansen Road, Puunene, HI 96784
- **Entry Fee:** Adults $10, Seniors (60+) $7, Children (6-12) $2
- **Insider Tips:** Plan to visit in the morning for a quieter experience. Guided tours are available and provide deeper insights into Maui's sugar heritage. Don't miss the outdoor displays, including vintage machinery and plantation-era buildings.

Top-Rated Beaches and Outdoor Activities

In South Maui, you ll find some of Hawaii's most renowned beaches and plenty of outdoor activities to enjoy. Here are some of the best beaches and activities to consider:

Beaches:

1. Wailea Beach:

Wailea Beach in South Maui epitomizes tropical paradise with its soft, golden sands and crystal-clear waters ideal for swimming and snorkeling. Nestled in the upscale Wailea Resort area, this picturesque crescent-shaped beach offers stunning views of neighboring islands and vibrant sunsets. Its gentle surf and well-maintained facilities, including showers, restrooms, and beach equipment rentals, cater to families and sunbathers alike. The beachfront path provides easy access to nearby resorts and restaurants, enhancing its convenience and charm. Wailea Beach's calm waters make it perfect for relaxing dips and aquatic adventures, while its proximity to luxurious accommodations and fine dining establishments ensures a luxurious beach experience year-round.

- **Location:** Wailea Beach is located in the Wailea Resort area in South Maui, Hawaii.

- **Seasons:** The beach is enjoyable year-round, with peak tourist seasons typically during the winter months (December to February) and summer (June to August).
- **Facilities:** Amenities include showers, restrooms, beach equipment rentals, and nearby resorts and restaurants accessible via a beachfront path.

2. Makena Beach (Big Beach):

Makena Beach, also known as Big Beach, is renowned for its expansive stretch of golden sand flanked by dramatic lava rock formations. Located in South Maui near the town of Makena, it offers a picturesque setting with turquoise waters ideal for swimming and bodyboarding, though caution is advised due to strong shore breaks. This beach is popular among both locals and tourists seeking a more natural and less crowded alternative to nearby resort beaches. Its size allows for plenty of space to spread out and enjoy the sun, making it perfect for picnics and beach games. The backdrop of Haleakalā's slopes adds to its scenic allure, creating a stunning contrast against the azure ocean waters.

- **Location:** Makena Beach is located in South Maui near the town of Makena.
- **Seasons:** Best visited during the drier months from April to September when the ocean conditions are usually calmer.

- **Facilities:** The beach offers basic facilities such as restrooms, showers, and picnic tables, but amenities are limited compared to more developed beaches.

3. Keawakapu Beach:

Keawakapu Beach in South Maui is celebrated for its tranquil atmosphere and pristine sands, making it a favorite among locals and visitors alike. Stretching half a mile along the coast, this beach boasts soft golden sands and clear, shallow waters ideal for swimming and snorkeling. Its gentle surf and gradual slope into the ocean make it accessible for families and beginners. The beach is bordered by luxury homes and resorts, providing a picturesque backdrop of palm trees and tropical foliage. Keawakapu Beach offers stunning sunset views and is less crowded compared to some of its neighboring beaches, making it perfect for a relaxing day by the sea.

- **Location:** Kihei, South Maui, Hawaii
- **Seasons:** Year-round, with peak visitation during the dry season from April to October
- **Facilities:** Limited parking available, restrooms, showers, picnic tables, and nearby dining options

4. Kamaole Beach Parks:

Kamaole Beach Parks, located in Kihei, South Maui, consists of three adjacent beaches: Kamaole I, Kamaole II, and Kamaole III. These beaches are renowned for their fine, golden sand and clear waters, making them perfect for swimming, snorkeling, and sunbathing. Kamaole I is smaller and generally quieter, ideal for families and picnics. Kamaole II offers good snorkeling opportunities with coral reefs close to shore, while Kamaole III is the largest and has the most extensive facilities, including lifeguards, restrooms, showers, and picnic areas. These parks are popular year-round, though conditions are typically calmest during the summer months. Visitors can enjoy stunning sunset views and often spot sea turtles swimming near the shore. Whether relaxing on the sand or exploring the vibrant marine life, Kamaole Beach Parks provide a quintessential South Maui beach experience.

- **Location:** Kihei, South Maui, Hawaii
- **Seasons:** Best conditions typically from late spring through early fall
- **Facilities:** Lifeguards, restrooms, showers, picnic areas

Outdoor Activities:

1. Snorkeling:

Snorkeling in South Maui offers an immersive experience in its crystal-clear waters teeming with vibrant marine life and colorful coral reefs. The region's calm, warm waters make it ideal for both beginners and experienced snorkelers. You can explore diverse underwater ecosystems just a short swim from the shore, encountering sea turtles, tropical fish like parrotfish and butterflyfish, and even occasional sightings of manta rays and octopuses. Many beaches provide easy access to snorkeling spots, where you can enjoy the serene beauty of underwater gardens and encounter Hawaii's endemic species up close.

Top Spots for Snorkeling in South Maui:

- **Molokini Crater:** A volcanic caldera with clear waters and abundant marine life, accessible by boat tours from Kihei and Wailea.
- **Ahihi-Kinau Natural Area Reserve:** Known for its lava rock formations and rich biodiversity, including colorful fish and coral.
- **Turtle Town:** Off the coast of Makena, known for its frequent encounters with Hawaiian green sea turtles (honu) and other marine species.

2. Whale Watching:

Whale watching in South Maui is a captivating outdoor activity, especially from December to April when humpback whales migrate to Hawaiian waters. These majestic creatures come to the warm Pacific to breed and nurse their calves, creating prime opportunities for sightings. The waters off Maui's coast offer ideal conditions for observing these gentle giants as they breach, slap their tails, and sing underwater. Numerous whale-watching tours depart from Ma'alaea Harbor and Lahaina, providing educational experiences with expert naturalists who share insights into whale behavior and conservation efforts. Witnessing these massive mammals in their natural habitat amidst Maui's stunning backdrop of ocean and islands is an unforgettable adventure, perfect for nature enthusiasts and families alike.

- **Season:** December to April

3. Hiking:

Take a hike on the coastal trails: Take a hike on the coastal trails in South Maui for a breathtaking adventure along rugged cliffs and pristine beaches. These trails offer panoramic views of the Pacific Ocean, with opportunities to spot marine life and seabirds. Begin at Wailea Beach and follow the shoreline towards Makena, where the landscape transitions from sandy shores to lava formations. Along the way, discover hidden coves and tide pools perfect for exploration.

- **Distance:** Approximately 5 miles one-way from Wailea Beach to Makena Beach.
- **Duration:** Plan for about 2-3 hours each way, depending on pace and stops.
- **Difficulty:** Moderate, with some rocky sections and elevation changes.

Venture into Haleakalā National Park: Venture into Haleakalā National Park for a transformative outdoor experience in South Maui. This volcanic wonderland offers dramatic landscapes of barren cinder cones, lush valleys, and surreal sunrises above the clouds from the summit at 10,023 feet. Explore its diverse ecosystems, from the subalpine shrubland to the tropical rainforest, home to unique flora and fauna like the silversword plant.

Hiking trails range from leisurely walks to challenging treks, such as the Sliding Sands Trail descending into the crater, revealing otherworldly vistas. Witness breathtaking sunsets or stargazing under some of the clearest skies in the world.

- **Distance:** Varies by trail
- **Duration:** Varies by trail
- **Difficulty:** Easy to Strenuous

4. Golfing:

Golfing in South Maui offers enthusiasts an exceptional experience amidst stunning tropical landscapes. Renowned for its world-class courses, such as those in Wailea and Makena, South Maui attracts golfers of all levels with meticulously designed fairways that showcase panoramic ocean views and volcanic terrain. Courses like the Wailea Golf Club feature multiple championship layouts, blending challenging holes with lush greenery and impeccable course maintenance. Golfers can enjoy year-round play thanks to Maui's mild climate, with opportunities to spot local wildlife like humpback whales offshore during the winter months.

Whether teeing off at sunrise or enjoying twilight rounds against a backdrop of vibrant sunsets, golfing in South Maui combines sport with unparalleled natural beauty, making it a highlight for visitors seeking both relaxation and recreation.

5. Stand-Up Paddleboarding and Kayaking:

Stand-up paddleboarding (SUP) and kayaking are popular outdoor activities in South Maui, offering serene ways to explore its coastal beauty. SUP provides a unique perspective, allowing paddlers to glide over clear waters while enjoying views of marine life below. Kayaking offers a more traditional experience, ideal for exploring secluded coves and observing coastal landscapes. Both activities are accessible to all skill levels, with equipment rentals widely available along South Maui's beaches.

Top Spots:

- **Makena Landing:** Known for calm waters and sea turtle sightings, perfect for SUP and kayaking adventures.
- **Wailea Beach:** Offers easy launching for SUP and kayaks, with opportunities to paddle along the scenic coastline.
- **Kealia Pond National Wildlife Refuge:** Ideal for kayaking, and exploring the serene waters surrounded by diverse birdlife and scenic views.

Recommended Resorts and Accommodations

In South Maui, you'll find a range of luxurious resorts and accommodations that offer beautiful settings, excellent amenities, and easy access to the area's attractions. Here are some of the top resorts to consider:

1. Wailea Beach Resort - Marriott, Maui

Nestled on 22 acres of oceanfront property, Wailea Beach Resort - Marriott, Maui offers luxurious accommodations with stunning views of the Pacific Ocean. The resort features multiple outdoor pools, a full-service spa, and direct access to Wailea Beach. Guests can enjoy a variety of dining options, including a seafood restaurant and a poolside bar. The resort's elegant rooms and suites are equipped with modern amenities, private balconies, and stylish decor, making it a perfect retreat for both relaxation and adventure.

- **Phone Number:** +1 808-879-1922
- **Star Rating:** ★★★★★

2. Four Seasons Resort Maui at Wailea

Renowned for its exceptional service and elegance, Four Seasons Resort Maui at Wailea is a premier destination for luxury travelers. The resort boasts three saltwater pools, including an adults-only infinity pool, and offers a world-class spa experience. Dining options include award-winning restaurants with diverse cuisines and stunning ocean views. Rooms and suites are designed with sophisticated décor, offering spacious layouts, private lanais, and breathtaking views of the coastline. The resort is renowned for its impeccable attention to detail and personalized service.

- **Phone Number:** +1 808-874-8000
- **Star Rating:** ★★★★★

3. Grand Wailea, A Waldorf Astoria Resort

Grand Wailea, A Waldorf Astoria Resort is an expansive luxury resort known for its opulent ambiance and impressive amenities. The property features a 50,000-square-foot spa, an elaborate pool area with a water park, and lush tropical gardens. Guests can enjoy a variety of dining options, from casual beachside meals to fine dining experiences. The rooms and suites are elegantly furnished, offering private balconies or patios with ocean or garden views. The resort's exceptional service and extensive recreational facilities ensure a memorable stay.

- **Phone Number:** +1 808-875-1234
- **Star Rating:** ★★★★★

4. Hotel Wailea, Relais & Châteaux

Hotel Wailea, Relais & Châteaux is an intimate, adults-only resort offering a serene and romantic escape. Set on a hillside with panoramic ocean views, the resort features beautifully appointed suites with private lanais and luxurious amenities. The property includes a sophisticated restaurant, a poolside bar, and a well-equipped fitness center. The tranquil atmosphere, personalized service, and exclusive ambiance make it an ideal choice for couples seeking privacy and relaxation in a picturesque setting.

- **Phone Number:** +1 808-879-2222
- **Star Rating:** ★★★★★

5. Andaz Maui at Wailea Resort

Andaz Maui at Wailea Resort is a chic and contemporary resort that seamlessly blends modern luxury with traditional Hawaiian charm. Located on 15 beachfront acres, the resort offers three ocean-view pools, a full-service spa, and a variety of dining options. The spacious rooms and suites feature floor-to-ceiling windows, private balconies, and stylish furnishings. The resort's design emphasizes open spaces and natural light, creating a refreshing and inviting atmosphere for guests seeking a contemporary yet relaxing Hawaiian getaway.

- **Phone Number:** +1 808-879-1234
- **Star Rating:** ★★★★★

6. Makena Beach & Golf Resort

Makena Beach & Golf Resort is a charming beachfront property offering a relaxed and inviting atmosphere. Set on 180 acres, the resort features direct access to Makena Beach, a golf course, and lush tropical gardens. Guests can enjoy an array of activities, including snorkeling and kayaking, or unwind at the outdoor pool and spa. The resort's rooms and suites provide stunning ocean or garden views, private lanais, and comfortable furnishings, making it a great choice for a laid-back yet luxurious Hawaiian retreat.

- **Phone Number:** +1 808-891-6200
- **Star Rating:** ★★★★

7. The Fairmont Kea Lani

The Fairmont Kea Lani is an all-suite and villa resort located on the stunning Wailea coastline. This upscale property features spacious suites with private balconies or patios, along with luxurious villas with private pools. The resort offers a range of dining options, including a fine dining restaurant and a casual beachside eatery. Guests can enjoy three swimming pools, a wellness center, and a full-service spa. The Fairmont Kea Lani combines elegance and comfort, providing a perfect base for exploring South Maui.

- **Phone Number:** +1 808-875-4100
- **Star Rating:** ★★★★★

8. Wailea Elua Village

Wailea Elua Village is an upscale condo resort offering a more home-like experience with the benefits of resort amenities. Located on the beachfront, the property features spacious, fully-equipped condos with ocean views, private lanais, and elegant furnishings. The resort provides direct access to Ulua Beach, two swimming pools, and a tennis court. The relaxed, low-rise design and well-maintained grounds create a tranquil environment ideal for families and couples seeking a longer stay with all the comforts of home.

- **Phone Number:** +1 808-879-4888
- **Star Rating:** ★★★★

9. Maui Coast Hotel

Maui Coast Hotel is a modern, mid-range hotel situated in the heart of Kihei, just a short walk from several beaches. The hotel offers comfortable rooms with contemporary decor, private balconies, and convenient amenities like a mini-fridge and microwave. Guests can relax by the outdoor pool, enjoy a meal at the on-site restaurant, or explore nearby shops and dining options. The hotel's central location and affordable rates make it a popular choice for travelers looking for a well-rounded experience in South Maui.

- **Phone Number:** +1 808-879-8888
- **Star Rating:** ★★★★

10. Residence Inn by Marriott Maui Wailea

Residence Inn by Marriott Maui Wailea offers a blend of home comforts and resort amenities, perfect for extended stays and families. The hotel features spacious suites with full kitchens, separate living areas, and private balconies. Guests can take advantage of the outdoor pool, fitness center, and complimentary breakfast buffet. The hotel's convenient location in Wailea provides easy access to beaches, shopping, and dining, making it an ideal choice for a practical and comfortable stay in South Maui.

- **Phone Number:** +1 808-875-0911
- **Star Rating:** ★★★★

Chapter 8: Central Maui

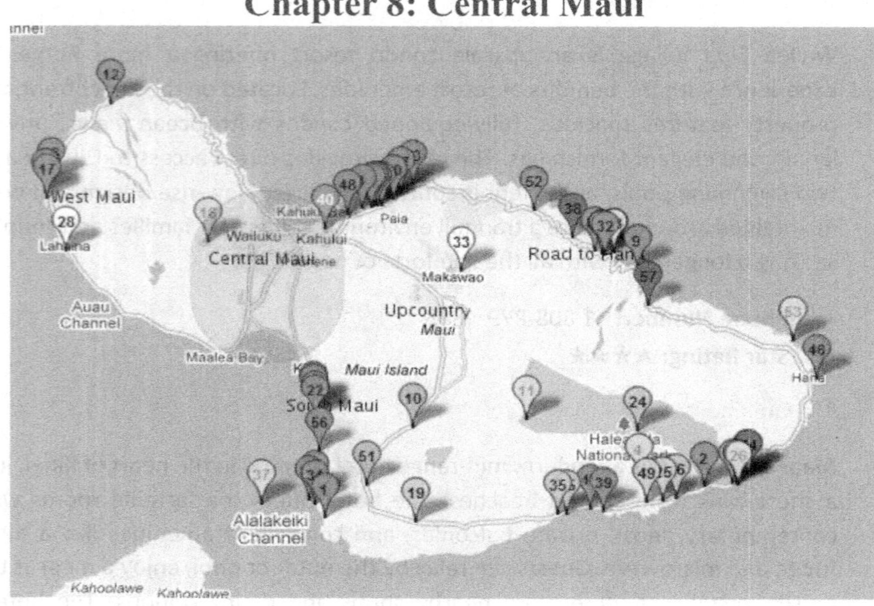

Overview of Central Maui

Geography and Location

Central Maui is located between the West Maui Mountains and Haleakala, the island's dormant volcano. It encompasses the flat isthmus between these two prominent geographic features, making it a pivotal area for transportation and commerce on Maui.

Key Towns and Areas

Kahului: As the largest town in Central Maui, Kahului is home to Maui's main airport, Kahului Airport (OGG), making it a gateway for visitors arriving on the island. It also hosts major shopping centers like Queen Ka'ahumanu Center, where locals and tourists alike can shop for both everyday items and unique Hawaiian products.

Wailuku: The historic town of Wailuku serves as the county seat of Maui and offers a glimpse into the island's past with its well-preserved buildings and cultural sites. Highlights include the Bailey House Museum, showcasing Hawaiian artifacts and history, and the Iao Valley State Park, known for its iconic Iao Needle and lush landscapes.

Iao Valley: Located just outside Wailuku, Iao Valley is a serene and picturesque valley known for its towering emerald peaks and historical significance. It's a popular spot for hiking, picnicking, and learning about Hawaiian culture and history.

Attractions and Points of Interest

Iao Valley State Park: This lush park features the iconic Iao Needle, a natural rock formation surrounded by verdant rainforest. Visitors can explore hiking trails, learn about Hawaiian history at the visitor center, and enjoy scenic views of the valley.

Bailey House Museum: Managed by the Maui Historical Society, this museum in Wailuku showcases artifacts and exhibits related to Hawaiian history, culture, and art. It offers guided tours and educational programs for visitors interested in Maui's heritage.

Maui Arts & Cultural Center (MACC): Located in Kahului, MACC is a hub for arts and entertainment on the island, hosting concerts, theatrical performances, art exhibitions, and cultural events year-round. It also includes a gallery featuring works by local and international artists.

Kanaha Beach Park: Known for its windsurfing and kiteboarding conditions, Kanaha Beach Park in Kahului attracts water sports enthusiasts from around the world. The park also offers picnic areas, volleyball courts, and opportunities for beachcombing and wildlife viewing.

Shopping and Dining

Central Maui is dotted with diverse dining options ranging from local eateries serving traditional Hawaiian cuisine to international restaurants offering a variety of flavors. Shopping centers like Queen Ka'ahumanu Center in Kahului provide a mix of retail stores, dining venues, and entertainment options for both residents and visitors.

Transportation

Central Maui is well-connected by roadways, with major highways such as Hana Highway (Route 36) and Maui Veterans Highway (Route 311) facilitating travel to other parts of the island. Public transportation, including Maui Bus routes, serves the area, offering an affordable way to explore nearby attractions and towns.

Cultural and Historical Significance

Central Maui holds significant historical importance as the seat of government and commerce on the island. Wailuku, in particular, preserves its plantation-era architecture and serves as a cultural center with events and festivals celebrating Hawaiian traditions throughout the year.

Historical Sites and Cultural Attractions

Central Maui has a rich cultural heritage and many historical sites and cultural attractions worth exploring. Here's a closer look at some of them:

Historical Sites

1. Iao Valley State Park

Iao Valley State Park is a lush, green oasis located in Central Maui, renowned for its natural beauty and historical significance. The park is home to the iconic Iao Needle, a towering 1,200-foot rock pinnacle that rises from the valley floor. This serene valley was the site of the Battle of Kepaniwai in 1790, where King Kamehameha I defeated Maui's forces in his quest to unite the Hawaiian Islands. Visitors can explore the Ethnobotanical Loop and other trails that wind through the park, offering stunning views, native flora, and informative exhibits about the valley's cultural and historical importance.

The park's tranquil streams, dense vegetation, and misty atmosphere make it a perfect spot for nature walks and photography.

- **Opening Hours:** Daily from 7:00 AM to 6:00 PM
- **Address:** 54 S High St, Wailuku, HI 96793
- **Entry Fee:** $5 per person for non-residents; $10 per vehicle
- **Insider Tips:** Arrive early to avoid crowds and secure parking. Wear sturdy shoes for the trails, and bring insect repellent. Check the weather, as the park can be misty and slippery after rain.

2. Bailey House Museum (Hale Ho'ike'ike)

The Bailey House Museum, also known as Hale Ho'ike'ike, is a significant historical site in Wailuku, Central Maui. Originally built in 1833 as the residence of missionary Edward Bailey, the museum now showcases a rich collection of Hawaiian artifacts, missionary-era artifacts, and local artwork. Visitors can explore exhibits featuring traditional Hawaiian tools, weapons, and implements, as well as photographs and paintings that document Maui's history. The museum is set in lush gardens, which include native Hawaiian plants and an ancient canoe. The Bailey House Museum provides a glimpse into Maui's past, offering insights into the island's cultural and historical evolution.

- **Opening Hours:** Monday to Saturday, 10:00 AM - 4:00 PM (Closed on Sundays and major holidays)
- **Address:** 2375 Main Street, Wailuku, HI 96793
- **Entry Fee:** Adults $10, Seniors (60+) $8, Children (7-12) $4, Children under 6 free

Insider Tips:

- Take advantage of the guided tours to gain deeper insights into the exhibits.
- Visit the gift shop for unique, locally-made souvenirs.
- Allocate time to explore the beautiful gardens and the historic canoe on the property.

3. Ka'ahumanu Church

Ka'ahumanu Church, located in Wailuku, Central Maui, stands as a testament to Hawaiian history and culture. Built in 1876 and named after Queen Ka'ahumanu, a key figure in Hawaiian royalty and the early adoption of Christianity in Hawaii, the church embodies both architectural elegance and historical significance.

Its Gothic architecture and stained-glass windows reflect the influence of missionary work during the 19th century. Ka'ahumanu Church remains an active place of worship, preserving its role as a spiritual center for the local community while offering visitors a glimpse into Hawaii's Christian heritage.

- **Opening Hours:** Open for services and special events; check local listings or contact for specific times.
- **Address:** 103 S High St, Wailuku, HI 96793, USA.

Insider Tips:

- Visit during a service or event to experience the church's vibrant community spirit.
- Take time to appreciate the historic gravestones in the churchyard, some dating back to the 19th century.

Cultural Attractions

1. Maui Nui Botanical Gardens

Maui Nui Botanical Gardens in Central Maui is a vibrant cultural attraction dedicated to preserving and showcasing Hawaiian flora. Situated in Kahului, this botanical garden educates visitors about native Hawaiian plants and their cultural significance.

The garden features a diverse collection, including traditional canoe plants and Polynesian-introduced species, highlighting their roles in Hawaiian history, food, medicine, and crafts. Visitors can explore themed gardens, learn from educational programs, and enjoy guided tours that emphasize the ecological and cultural importance of these plants. The gardens provide a serene environment for relaxation and learning, making it a valuable stop for both tourists and locals interested in Hawaiian culture and biodiversity.

- **Opening Hours:** Monday to Saturday, 8:00 AM - 4:00 PM
- **Address:** 150 Kanaloa Avenue, Kahului, HI 96732
- **Insider Tips:** Visit in the morning for cooler temperatures and fewer crowds. Check their website for special events or guided tours to enhance your experience.

2. Maui Arts & Cultural Center (MACC)

The Maui Arts & Cultural Center (MACC) in Kahului is a vibrant hub for arts and culture in Maui. It hosts a diverse range of performances, exhibitions, and community events, showcasing local Hawaiian culture as well as international talent.

The center includes the Castle Theater, McCoy Studio Theater, and Yokouchi Pavilion, offering venues for concerts, theater productions, dance performances, and visual arts displays. MACC's commitment to cultural enrichment is evident through its educational programs and workshops, fostering creativity and appreciation for the arts among residents and visitors alike.

- **Opening Hours:** Vary by event; generally, opens in the morning and closes after evening events.
- **Address:** 1 Cameron Way, Kahului, HI 96732, USA
- **Insider Tips:** Check the MACC website for upcoming events and performances. Arrive early to explore the Schaefer International Gallery's exhibitions. Parking can fill up quickly; consider carpooling or using rideshare services.

3. King Kamehameha Golf Club

The King Kamehameha Golf Club in Wailuku, Central Maui, is not just a premier golfing destination but also a significant cultural attraction. Designed by Frank Lloyd Wright, the club's architecture blends Hawaiian motifs with Wright's signature style, creating a unique ambiance. Inside, the club features a collection of artifacts and artworks that celebrate the legacy of King Kamehameha I, the Hawaiian monarch who unified the islands.

The clubhouse offers panoramic views of the West Maui Mountains and the ocean, enhancing the golfing experience with its scenic beauty and historical depth.

- **Opening Hours:** Daily, from early morning to late afternoon.
- **Address:** 2500 Honoapiilani Hwy, Wailuku, HI 96793, USA.
- **Insider Tips:** Explore the clubhouse to see artifacts related to King Kamehameha I. Enjoy lunch or dinner at the club's restaurant, featuring local Hawaiian cuisine. Book tee times in advance to secure preferred playing times, especially during peak seasons.

4. Wailuku Town

Wailuku Town, nestled in Central Maui, is a charming cultural hub rich in history and local flavor. Its quaint streets are lined with historic buildings dating back to the 19th century, offering a glimpse into Maui's past as a center of sugar cane production and missionary activity. Visitors can explore attractions such as the Bailey House Museum, showcasing Hawaiian artifacts, or the historic Ka'ahumanu Church. Art galleries, boutique shops, and eateries provide opportunities to immerse oneself in local art and cuisine. Wailuku's bustling market scene and occasional cultural festivals add to its vibrant atmosphere, making it a must-visit for those interested in Maui's cultural heritage.

- **Opening Hours:** Varies by establishment; typically, 9 AM to 5 PM
- **Address:** Wailuku, Maui, Hawaii, USA
- **Insider Tips:** Visit on the First Friday of the month for local food, art, and music; explore on foot to discover hidden gems like small cafes and historical markers.

Top-Rated Beaches and Outdoor Activities

Best Beaches

1. Kanaha Beach Park

Kanaha Beach Park stands out as one of Central Maui's premier beaches, renowned particularly among water sports enthusiasts. Located near Kahului Airport, its appeal lies in consistent trade winds ideal for windsurfing and kiteboarding, drawing enthusiasts from around the world. The expansive beach also offers calmer areas for swimming and snorkeling, making it suitable for families and beginners. Surrounded by scenic views of the West Maui Mountains and neighboring islands, Kanaha Beach Park provides a picturesque setting for both relaxation and adventure. Its facilities include restrooms, showers, picnic areas, and barbecue pits, ensuring comfort and convenience for visitors year-round.

- **Location:** Near Kahului Airport

- **Seasons:** Year-round, best conditions typically from May to September for wind sports
- **Facilities:** Restrooms, showers, picnic areas, barbecue pits

2. Waihee Beach

Waihee Beach, nestled north of Wailuku in Central Maui, offers a serene escape from the bustling coastal spots on the island. Its secluded charm and tranquil atmosphere make it a hidden gem for visitors seeking a quieter beach experience. The beach boasts soft golden sands perfect for leisurely walks and quiet contemplation. Encircled by lush greenery and backed by gently sloping hills, Waihee Beach provides a picturesque backdrop for relaxation. Its calm waters are inviting for swimming, though caution is advised as currents can vary.

- **Location:** Waihee Beach is located north of Wailuku in Central Maui, accessible via Highway 340.
- **Seasons:** Waihee Beach enjoys pleasant conditions year-round, though weather patterns can affect water clarity and currents. Summer typically offers calmer seas ideal for swimming.
- **Facilities:** Facilities at Waihee Beach are limited, so visitors should bring essentials like food, water, and beach gear. Parking is available nearby, and restroom facilities are basic.

3. Kahului Harbor Beach

Kahului Harbor Beach, often overlooked amidst Maui's more famed beaches, offers a unique coastal experience. Located adjacent to Kahului Harbor, it provides a glimpse into the island's maritime activities. This beach isn't ideal for typical sunbathing or swimming due to its proximity to the harbor and industrial areas, but it's excellent for observing boats and enjoying a peaceful stroll along the shoreline. Visitors can witness local fishermen at work, watch surfers catching waves beyond the harbor, or simply enjoy the coastal breeze with views of neighboring islands.

- **Location:** Adjacent to Kahului Harbor in Central Maui, easily accessible from Kahului town.
- **Seasons:** The beach is accessible year-round, but water activities may vary based on weather conditions.
- **Facilities:** Limited facilities on-site, nearby amenities include restaurants and shops.

4. Sugar Beach

Sugar Beach, stretching from Maalaea to Kihei in Central Maui, is renowned for its expansive stretch of golden sand, making it one of the longest beaches on Maui. This beach is ideal for strolls, sunset views, and various water activities.

Its calm waters offer excellent conditions for kayaking and stand-up paddleboarding, while its soft sands invite visitors to relax and enjoy the tranquil surroundings. Sugar Beach is perfect for families, couples, and individuals seeking a peaceful beach experience away from the more crowded tourist areas.

- **Location:** Located conveniently near Kihei
- **Seasons:** It enjoys a sunny climate throughout the year, with slightly warmer temperatures in summer and refreshing breezes in winter.
- **Facilities:** Facilities include restrooms, showers, and picnic areas, ensuring comfort for all beachgoers.

5. Baldwin Beach Park

Baldwin Beach Park is celebrated for its expansive sandy shores and family-friendly atmosphere in Central Maui. Located just north of Paia town, it stretches along the coastline with soft golden sands ideal for sunbathing, picnicking, and beach games. The park offers a mix of shaded areas and open spaces, perfect for relaxation and enjoying views of the turquoise waters. Baldwin Beach Park is also renowned for its safe swimming conditions, especially in the protected lagoon area, making it suitable for families with children. The beach's consistent trade winds make it a favorite spot for windsurfing and kiteboarding enthusiasts.

Facilities include lifeguard stations, restrooms, showers, picnic tables, and barbecue pits, ensuring visitors have everything they need for a comfortable day at the beach. Baldwin Beach Park is popular year-round, with slightly calmer conditions in the summer months for swimming and more favorable winds in winter for water sports.

- **Location:** North of Paia, Central Maui
- **Seasons:** Ideal for swimming in summer; best for windsurfing and kiteboarding in winter
- **Facilities:** Lifeguards, restrooms, showers, picnic tables, barbecue pits

Outdoor Activities

1. Hiking in Iao Valley State Park:

Hiking in Iao Valley State Park offers a captivating blend of natural beauty and historical significance. The park is renowned for its lush tropical landscape, highlighted by the iconic Iao Needle, a 1,200-foot volcanic pinnacle. Trails like the Iao Needle Lookout Trail and Ethnobotanical Loop provide stunning views of the needle and the verdant valley below. Explorers can immerse themselves in Hawaiian history and culture while enjoying moderate hikes suitable for all skill levels. Distances vary from short, easy walks to more challenging treks, accommodating both casual strolls and immersive adventures.

- **Distance:** Trails range from 0.6 miles (Ethnobotanical Loop) to 1.6 miles (Iao Needle Lookout Trail).
- **Duration:** Approximately 30 minutes to 1.5 hours, depending on the trail and pace.
- **Difficulty:** Easy to moderate, with some steep sections on certain trails.

2. Windsurfing and Kiteboarding at Kanaha Beach Park

Kanaha Beach Park in Central Maui is renowned worldwide for its exceptional conditions for windsurfing and kiteboarding. Located near Kahului Airport, its consistent trade winds and expansive, shallow waters make it an ideal spot for both beginners and experienced enthusiasts. The park offers ample space for launching and maneuvering, with designated areas for each sport to ensure safety and enjoyment. Its accessibility and facilities, including showers and picnic areas, enhance the experience. Kanaha Beach Park not only attracts water sports enthusiasts but also provides stunning views of the West Maui Mountains and nearby Molokai, making it a quintessential destination for wind-driven water activities in Maui.

3. Snorkeling and Swimming at Baldwin Beach Park

Baldwin Beach Park, nestled near Paia in Central Maui, offers fantastic opportunities for snorkeling and swimming. Its long stretch of soft sand and clear waters makes it ideal for both beginners and enthusiasts. The beach features a protected lagoon area, perfect for calm swimming conditions and observing marine life. Snorkelers can explore vibrant coral reefs close to the shore, encountering various fish species and possibly sea turtles. With amenities like lifeguards, restrooms, and showers, Baldwin Beach Park ensures a safe and comfortable experience for visitors. Whether enjoying a leisurely swim, snorkeling adventure, or simply relaxing on the beach, Baldwin Beach Park provides a picturesque setting with ample opportunities for aquatic exploration in Central Maui.

4. Golfing at King Kamehameha Golf Club

Golfing at King Kamehameha Golf Club in Wailuku offers a premier outdoor experience in Central Maui. Designed by golf legend Ted Robinson, the course provides panoramic views of the West Maui Mountains and the Pacific Ocean. The club's clubhouse, influenced by Frank Lloyd Wright's architecture, enhances the cultural ambiance with Hawaiian artifacts and artworks. Golfers can enjoy challenging play across meticulously maintained fairways and greens, offering a blend of scenic beauty and historical resonance. Whether for a leisurely round or competitive play, King Kamehameha Golf Club combines natural splendor with cultural richness, making it a standout destination for golf enthusiasts visiting Maui.

5. Kayaking and Stand-Up Paddleboarding at Sugar Beach

Kayaking and stand-up paddleboarding at Sugar Beach in Central Maui offer serene experiences on calm waters, ideal for both beginners and enthusiasts. This long stretch of sandy shoreline provides ample space for launching watercraft and enjoying coastal views. Adventurers can explore the coastline, spotting marine life like sea turtles and colorful fish beneath the clear waters. The beach's gentle waves and shallow depths make it perfect for leisurely paddling and family-friendly activities. Facilities such as restrooms and showers ensure convenience, while nearby rental shops provide equipment for those looking to try these water sports. Sugar Beach's peaceful ambiance and accessibility make it a favored spot for relaxing outings and scenic paddling adventures in Maui's central region.

6. Biking and Walking on the Northshore Greenway

The Northshore Greenway in Central Maui is a scenic, paved path ideal for biking, walking, and running. Spanning from Kahului to Paia, it offers breathtaking coastal views and a tranquil environment away from traffic. This greenway is perfect for both strolls and vigorous workouts, accommodating all fitness levels. Key highlights include views of sugarcane fields, ocean vistas, and the chance to spot native wildlife. It's a great spot for outdoor enthusiasts looking to enjoy Maui's natural beauty while staying active. Whether you're cycling, jogging, or simply walking, the Northshore Greenway provides a refreshing escape with easy access to local attractions and beaches.

7. Exploring Wailuku Town

Exploring Wailuku Town in Central Maui offers a charming blend of history, culture, and local flavor. This walkable town features historic buildings, boutique shops, art galleries, and diverse dining options. Visitors can stroll through the town's picturesque streets lined with 19th-century architecture, including the iconic Ka'ahumanu Church. Cultural highlights include the Bailey House Museum, showcasing Hawaiian artifacts and missionary history. Wailuku also hosts lively events like First Friday, a monthly street party with food trucks, live music, and art displays. It's an ideal outdoor activity for those interested in Hawaiian heritage and seeking a relaxed, authentic Maui experience away from the island's more touristy spots.

Recommended Resorts and Accommodations

1. The Westin Maui Resort & Spa

Located in the heart of Central Maui, The Westin Maui Resort & Spa offers a luxurious escape with stunning ocean views and a variety of activities. The resort features a full-service spa, multiple dining options, and spacious rooms equipped with modern amenities. Enjoy the beautiful pools, direct beach access, and the picturesque surroundings of this top-rated resort.

- **Phone:** +1 808-661-2588
- **Star Rating:** 4.5 stars

2. Fairmont Kea Lani, Maui

This elegant resort in Wailea provides a sophisticated blend of comfort and style. Fairmont Kea Lani, Maui offers spacious all-suite accommodations, beautiful beachfront locations, and exceptional service. Guests can relax in the resort's three swimming pools, indulge in world-class dining, or rejuvenate at the award-winning Willow Stream Spa. The resort is ideal for both families and couples looking for a serene retreat.

- **Phone:** +1 808-875-4100
- **Star Rating:** 5 stars

3. Maui Beach Hotel

Situated conveniently in Central Maui, Maui Beach Hotel offers a more budget-friendly option with comfortable accommodations and easy access to local attractions. The hotel features a relaxed atmosphere, an outdoor pool, and dining options that highlight local cuisine. Its proximity to the airport and downtown Maui makes it a practical choice for both short and extended stays.

- **Phone:** +1 808-877-0051
- **Star Rating:** 3 stars

4. The Ritz-Carlton, Kapalua

Nestled in the scenic Kapalua area, The Ritz-Carlton is a luxurious resort offering breathtaking ocean views and a range of premium amenities. The resort boasts a spa, several dining venues, and elegant rooms with private balconies. Guests can enjoy the golf courses, tennis courts, and the stunning beaches nearby.

It's an excellent choice for those seeking top-notch service and exclusive experiences.

- **Phone:** +1 808-669-6200
- **Star Rating:** 5 stars

5. Andaz Maui at Wailea Resort

This contemporary resort offers a chic, modern retreat with a focus on personalized service and luxurious accommodations. Andaz Maui features spacious rooms and suites, multiple infinity pools, and various dining options that cater to a range of tastes. The resort's commitment to sustainability and its stunning beachfront location enhance the overall experience, making it a perfect choice for a relaxing getaway.

- **Phone:** +1 808-879-1234
- **Star Rating:** 5 stars

6. Sheraton Maui Resort & Spa

Located at the base of the iconic Black Rock on Kaanapali Beach, Sheraton Maui Resort & Spa is a popular choice for those seeking a classic Hawaiian experience. The resort offers comfortable rooms, a large lagoon-style pool, and direct access to a beautiful sandy beach. Enjoy dining at the resort's restaurants, participate in various water sports, or relax at the on-site spa.

- **Phone:** +1 808-661-0031
- **Star Rating:** 4 stars

7. Residence Inn by Marriott Maui Wailea

This family-friendly hotel provides a home-away-from-home experience with spacious suites equipped with kitchenettes. Located in Wailea, the Residence Inn offers convenient amenities such as a complimentary breakfast, an outdoor pool, and easy access to nearby shopping and dining options. It's a great choice for extended stays or families looking for comfortable and practical accommodation.

- **Phone:** +1 808-879-4300
- **Star Rating:** 3.5 stars

8. Wailea Beach Resort – Marriott, Maui

Set on 22 acres of lush tropical gardens, Wailea Beach Resort offers a blend of luxury and relaxation. The resort features elegant rooms, multiple swimming pools, and a stunning beachfront location. Guests can enjoy a variety of dining options, a full-service spa, and activities such as snorkeling and paddleboarding. The resort's ambiance and amenities make it an excellent choice for both couples and families.

- **Phone:** +1 808-879-1922
- **Star Rating:** 4.5 stars

9. Maui Seaside Hotel

For a more budget-conscious stay, Maui Seaside Hotel offers a convenient location in Kahului, with easy access to shopping and dining. The hotel features clean, comfortable rooms, a pool, and a casual atmosphere. It's a great option for travelers looking for a straightforward and affordable place to stay while exploring Central Maui.

- **Phone:** +1 808-877-3311
- **Star Rating:** 3 stars

10. Grand Wailea, A Waldorf Astoria Resort

One of Maui's premier luxury resorts, Grand Wailea offers an opulent experience with exceptional amenities. The resort boasts a vast pool complex with water slides, a renowned spa, and several dining options. Guests can relax in elegantly appointed rooms and take advantage of the resort's beautiful beachfront location and extensive recreational facilities.

- **Phone:** +1 808-875-1234
- **Star Rating:** 5 stars

Chapter 9: North Shore, Maui

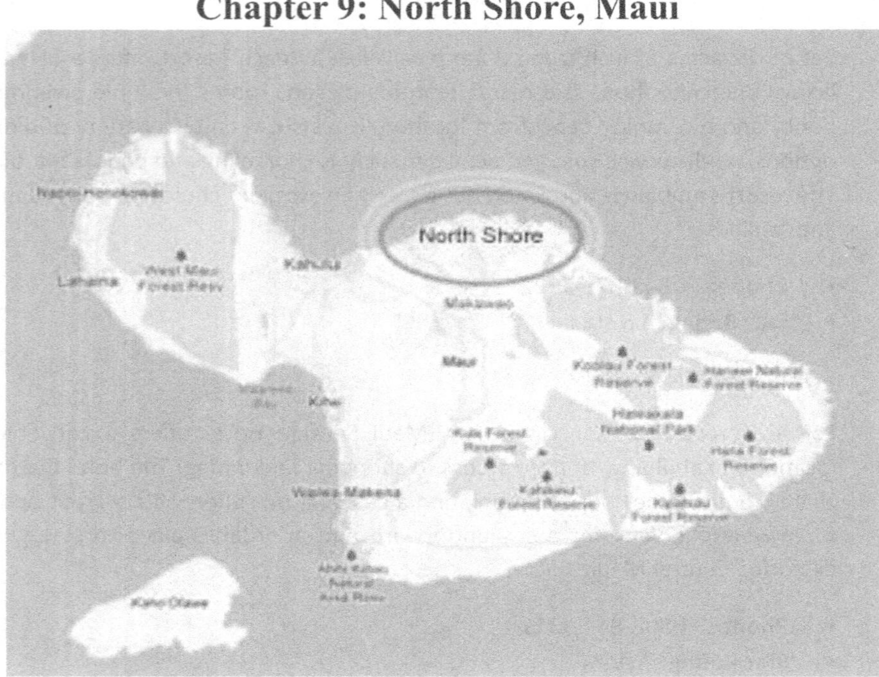

Overview of North Shore, Maui

Geography and Scenery

The North Shore of Maui stretches from Paia town to the lush and remote coastline beyond Haiku. It's characterized by dramatic cliffs, lush valleys, and a rugged shoreline pounded by powerful winter waves. This region is less developed compared to other parts of Maui, maintaining a rustic charm and a strong connection to its natural surroundings.

Highlights and Attractions

Ho'okipa Beach Park: Famous for its powerful surf breaks and as a gathering place for expert windsurfers and kiteboarders. It's also a great spot for watching sea turtles and enjoying stunning sunsets.

Paia Town: A vibrant, eclectic town known for its bohemian atmosphere, art galleries, boutiques, and diverse dining options. It serves as the gateway to the Road to Hana and attracts both locals and visitors seeking a more relaxed vibe.

Road to Hana: While technically starting from Paia, the North Shore is often considered the starting point for this iconic drive due to its proximity. The journey takes travelers through lush rainforests, cascading waterfalls, and breathtaking coastal views.

Twin Falls: Located along the Road to Hana, these picturesque waterfalls are easily accessible and offer a refreshing stop for a swim or photo opportunity.

Haiku: A rural community known for its lush landscapes, organic farms, and artistic community. It provides a glimpse into Maui's agricultural heritage and offers peaceful retreats away from tourist crowds.

Makawao: Though slightly inland, Makawao is often included in discussions of the North Shore due to its proximity and cultural relevance. It's a charming town known for its paniolo (cowboy) history, art galleries, and the annual Makawao Rodeo.

Activities and Adventures

Surfing: The North Shore is a mecca for surfers, with legendary breaks such as Jaws (Peahi) drawing big-wave riders during the winter months. Ho'okipa Beach Park offers more accessible surf spots for intermediate and advanced surfers.

Hiking: Explore the trails leading to waterfalls and through bamboo forests along the Road to Hana or venture into the lush valleys of Haiku and beyond.

Shopping and Dining: Paia and nearby towns like Makawao offer unique shopping experiences, from local boutiques to art galleries and farm-to-table dining options that highlight Maui's agricultural bounty.

Local Culture and Community

The North Shore of Maui maintains a strong sense of community and connection to Hawaiian culture. Residents include artists, farmers, surfers, and longtime families who cherish the area's natural beauty and relaxed lifestyle.

Tips for Visitors

Timing: Visit in the morning to avoid traffic on the Road to Hana and to experience Ho'okipa Beach Park at its best for surfing and turtle watching.

Respect Nature: Take care to preserve fragile ecosystems, respect private property, and heed local advisories regarding ocean conditions, especially during high surf.

Explore Off the Beaten Path: While popular spots like Ho'okipa and Paia are must-visits, consider exploring lesser-known areas and taking time to appreciate the quiet beauty of North Shore's landscapes.

Historical Sites and Cultural Attractions

On the North Shore of Oahu, you can explore several historical sites and cultural attractions that reflect Hawaii's rich heritage:

1. Polynesian Cultural Center:

The Polynesian Cultural Center on the North Shore of Oahu is a living museum that offers visitors a deep dive into the diverse cultures of Polynesia. Spread across 42 acres, it features authentic village replicas representing Hawaii, Samoa, Tahiti, Fiji, Tonga, and Aotearoa (New Zealand). Each village showcases traditional arts, crafts, and performances, allowing guests to immerse themselves in Polynesian traditions. Highlights include canoe rides, a spectacular evening show called "Ha: Breath of Life," and hands-on activities like coconut tree climbing and fire-making demonstrations.

The center's mission extends beyond entertainment, aiming to preserve and share Polynesian cultures with visitors from around the world.

- **Opening Hours:** Daily from 12:00 PM to 9:00 PM (closed Sundays)
- **Address:** 55-370 Kamehameha Hwy, Laie, HI 96762
- **Entry Fee:** Prices vary depending on the package, typically ranging from $79 to $149 for adults, with discounts for children and seniors.
- **Insider Tips:** Arrive early to explore all villages, enjoy cultural presentations, and participate in activities. Consider booking a package that includes dinner and the evening show for a complete Polynesian experience.

2. Waimea Valley:

Waimea Valley, located on the North Shore of Oahu, is a culturally and historically significant site. This lush valley was once a sacred place and center of religious activity for ancient Hawaiians. It features Waimea Falls, a picturesque waterfall surrounded by botanical gardens showcasing native Hawaiian plants. The valley holds archaeological sites, including a heiau (temple), offering insights into Hawaiian spirituality and culture. Visitors can explore the valley through guided walks or enjoy a swim in the pool at the base of Waimea Falls, making it a perfect blend of natural beauty and cultural exploration.

- **Opening Hours:** Waimea Valley is open daily from 9:00 AM to 5:00 PM.
- **Address:** 59-864 Kamehameha Hwy, Haleiwa, HI 96712, USA.
- **Insider Tips:** Arrive early to beat the crowds and enjoy a more peaceful experience. Wear comfortable walking shoes as the trails can be uneven. Don't forget your swimsuit if you plan to take a dip in Waimea Falls. Lastly, consider joining a guided tour to learn more about the valley's cultural significance and natural history firsthand.

3. Pu'u o Mahuka Heiau:

Pu'u o Mahuka Heiau, meaning "Hill of Escape," is the largest heiau (Hawaiian temple) on Oahu, located on a ridge overlooking Waimea Bay. This sacred site dates back to the 17th century and served as a religious and ceremonial center. The heiau played a significant role in the island's spiritual life, possibly dedicated to the war god Ku. The site consists of three adjoining enclosures made of stacked stone, reflecting ancient Hawaiian engineering skills. Visitors can explore the remnants of this significant structure and enjoy panoramic views of the North Shore, enhancing their understanding of Hawaii's pre-contact history and cultural practices.

- **Opening Hours:** Daily from sunrise to sunset
- **Address:** Pupukea Homestead Rd, Haleiwa, HI 96712, USA

- **Insider Tips:** Wear sturdy shoes for the uneven terrain. Visit early in the morning or late afternoon to avoid the heat and enjoy the best lighting for photos. Take some time to learn about the site's history before visiting to fully appreciate its significance. Respect the site as it is a sacred place; do not climb on the stones or disturb the area. Bring water and sunscreen, as there are no facilities on-site.

4. Bishop Museum:

The Bishop Museum, officially known as the Bernice Pauahi Bishop Museum, is the premier natural and cultural history institution in Hawaii. Although not located directly on the North Shore, it is an essential visit for anyone interested in the history and culture of the Hawaiian Islands. Established in 1889, the museum was founded in honor of Princess Bernice Pauahi Bishop, the last descendant of the Kamehameha dynasty. The museum houses an extensive collection of Hawaiian artifacts, royal regalia, and historical documents. Exhibits cover topics from ancient Hawaiian culture to contemporary issues, providing a comprehensive view of Hawaii's rich heritage. The museum also features a planetarium, interactive science exhibits, and a beautifully landscaped campus.

- **Opening Hours:** Daily, 9:00 AM to 5:00 PM (closed on Tuesdays and Christmas Day)

- **Address:** 1525 Bernice Street, Honolulu, HI 96817
- **Entry Fee:** Adults: $25, Seniors (65+): $22, Youth (4-17): $17, Children under 4: Free

Insider Tips:

- Visit early in the day to avoid crowds.
- Check the schedule for planetarium shows and cultural demonstrations.
- The museum café offers a selection of local snacks and meals.
- Allocate at least 2-3 hours to explore the exhibits fully.

5. Haleiwa Town:

Haleiwa Town is the cultural and historical heart of Oahu's North Shore. Originally a hub for the sugar industry in the 19th century, Haleiwa has preserved its plantation-era charm with a mix of historic buildings, boutique shops, art galleries, and local eateries. The town's laid-back atmosphere and picturesque setting make it a perfect place to explore on foot. Key attractions include the North Shore Surf and Cultural Museum, which highlights the area's surfing heritage, and Matsumoto Shave Ice, a beloved local treat. Stroll through the streets to admire the rustic architecture and immerse yourself in the rich history and vibrant community spirit that defines Haleiwa.

- **Opening Hours:** Generally, 9 AM to 6 PM (varies by shop and attraction)
- **Address:** Haleiwa, HI 96712, USA

Insider Tips:

- Visit early in the day to avoid crowds and get parking.
- Try Matsumoto Shave Ice for a classic Hawaiian treat.
- Check out the local farmers' market for fresh produce and handmade crafts.

Top-Rated Beaches and Outdoor Activities

The North Shore of Oahu is renowned for its stunning beaches and abundant outdoor activities. Here are some of the best beaches and activities you can enjoy:

Beaches:

1. Sunset Beach:

Sunset Beach is one of the most iconic beaches on the North Shore of Oahu, renowned for its impressive surf breaks and stunning sunsets. During the winter months, the beach becomes a hotspot for professional surfers, as the waves can reach heights of over 30 feet, making it one of the premier surf destinations in the world. In contrast, the summer brings calmer waters, transforming Sunset Beach into an ideal spot for swimming and snorkeling.

The beach's long stretch of golden sand is perfect for sunbathing, beachcombing, and leisurely walks. The breathtaking views of the horizon at sunset make it a picturesque location for photographers and romantics alike.

- **Location:** Sunset Beach is located along Kamehameha Highway, about 6 miles northeast of Haleiwa town on Oahu's North Shore.
- **Season:** Winter (November to February) is prime for surfing with massive waves, while summer (May to September) offers calmer seas suitable for swimming and snorkeling.
- **Facilities:** Sunset Beach Park provides parking, restrooms, and showers. Lifeguards are on duty, ensuring the safety of swimmers and surfers. There are also picnic tables and shaded areas for relaxation, making it a convenient spot for families and beachgoers.

2. Waimea Bay:

Waimea Bay is one of the most iconic beaches on Oahu's North Shore, known for its crystal-clear waters and dramatic waves. During the winter months, the bay transforms into a world-famous surfing destination, hosting the prestigious Eddie Aikau Big Wave Invitational, where waves can reach up to 30 feet. In contrast, the summer months offer calm waters perfect for swimming, snorkeling, and cliff jumping from the famous Waimea Rock.

The beach's scenic beauty, framed by lush cliffs and a wide sandy shore, makes it a favorite for both relaxation and adventure.

- **Location:** Waimea Bay is located on the North Shore of Oahu, about an hour's drive from Honolulu. It is situated along the Kamehameha Highway between Haleiwa and Pupukea.
- **Season:** Winter (November to February) is ideal for watching big wave surfing, while summer (May to September) is perfect for swimming and snorkeling. Spring and fall offer a mix of both experiences.
- **Facilities:** Waimea Bay provides ample parking, restrooms, and showers. There are lifeguards on duty year-round, making it a safe spot for families. Picnic tables and shaded areas are available for beachgoers to enjoy a day out.

3. Laniakea Beach (Turtle Beach):

Laniakea Beach, popularly known as Turtle Beach, is a gem on the North Shore of Oahu. It's famous for the Hawaiian green sea turtles (honu) that frequently bask on its sandy shores. These gentle giants can often be seen lounging on the beach or swimming near the shore, providing a unique wildlife experience. The beach offers a mix of sandy stretches and rocky areas, making it ideal for both relaxing and exploring marine life. Visitors are encouraged to maintain a respectful distance from the turtles, as they are a protected species. The serene atmosphere and the opportunity to observe these magnificent creatures up close make Laniakea Beach a must-visit.

- **Location:** Laniakea Beach is located on the North Shore of Oahu, just off Kamehameha Highway, near Haleiwa. It's easily accessible by car, with parking available along the highway.
- **Season:** The beach can be visited year-round, but the best time to see the turtles is during the summer months when the waters are calmer. Winter months bring higher surf, which is better suited for experienced surfers rather than casual swimmers.
- **Facilities:** There are limited facilities at Laniakea Beach. No restrooms or showers are available, and parking can be challenging, especially during peak times. Visitors should come prepared with water, snacks, and sun protection.

4. Sharks Cove:

Sharks Cove is one of the premier snorkeling and diving spots on the North Shore of Oahu. Despite its name, the cove is not typically frequented by sharks but is teeming with diverse marine life. The rocky coastline creates numerous tide pools and underwater caves, providing a haven for colorful fish, sea turtles, and other ocean creatures. The water is clear and calm during the summer months, making it ideal for snorkeling. The rocky terrain and underwater visibility make it a favorite spot for underwater photography and exploration.

- **Location:** Sharks Cove is located in Pupukea, along the Kamehameha Highway, between Waimea Bay and the Banzai Pipeline. It's easily accessible and well-signposted from the main road.

- **Season:** The best time to visit Sharks Cove is during the summer months (May to September) when the waters are calmer and safer for snorkeling and diving. During the winter, the waves can be rough, making it less suitable for water activities.
- **Facilities:** Facilities at Sharks Cove include a parking area, restrooms, and showers. There are also nearby food trucks and small stores where you can grab snacks and drinks. Equipment rentals for snorkeling and diving are available from local shops.

Outdoor Activities:

1. Surfing:

Surfing on the North Shore of Oahu is legendary, attracting surfers from around the globe for its powerful winter swells and iconic breaks. Known as the "Seven Mile Miracle," this stretch of coastline hosts some of the world's most famous surf spots. During winter, waves at spots like Pipeline, Sunset Beach, and Waimea Bay can reach heights of 20 feet or more, challenging even the most experienced surfers. The atmosphere is electrifying, with competitions like the Vans Triple Crown of Surfing drawing top athletes and spectators alike. For beginners, summer offers gentler waves at places like Chun's Reef and Haleiwa Beach Park, ideal for learning or honing skills. Surf culture permeates every aspect of life here, from surf shops in Haleiwa to the laid-back vibe of beachfront cafes. Whether you're a seasoned pro or a curious novice, the North Shore offers an unparalleled surfing experience.

Top Spots:

- **Pipeline:** Renowned for its barreling waves and challenging conditions, Pipeline is a mecca for advanced surfers seeking adrenaline-pumping rides.
- **Sunset Beach:** This expansive beach offers a variety of breaks suitable for different skill levels, with powerful winter swells and calmer summer waves.
- **Waimea Bay:** Known for its massive waves in winter, Waimea Bay also offers gentler conditions in summer, attracting both surfers and swimmers.

2. Snorkeling:

Snorkeling on the North Shore of Oahu offers an immersive experience in its vibrant underwater world. Crystal-clear waters teem with colorful fish, sea turtles, and fascinating coral formations.

During summer, spots like Sharks Cove provide calm conditions ideal for snorkeling, where you can explore diverse marine life in a protected cove setting. Beginners and experienced snorkelers alike enjoy the accessibility and beauty of these underwater environments, making it a popular activity for families and adventurers seeking aquatic exploration.

Top Spots for Snorkeling:

- **Sharks Cove:** Known for its clear waters and abundant marine life, Sharks Cove offers excellent snorkeling opportunities with easy access from the shore. Explore rocky formations and swim alongside schools of tropical fish in this natural pool.
- **Waimea Bay:** During the summer months, Waimea Bay transforms into a tranquil snorkeling spot with its calm waters and occasional sea turtle sightings. It's a picturesque location for snorkelers looking to enjoy Hawaii's marine biodiversity.

3. Hiking:

Ehukai Pillbox Hike:

The Ehukai Pillbox Hike on Oahu's North Shore offers a scenic adventure with rewarding views. Beginning near Sunset Beach, the trail winds through lush tropical vegetation and provides glimpses of the coastline along the way. The highlight of the hike is reaching the World War II-era pillboxes (bunkers), offering panoramic views of the North Shore's famous surf breaks and pristine beaches below.

This moderate hike is popular among both locals and tourists for its accessibility and stunning vistas, especially during sunrise or sunset. It's a great way to immerse yourself in the natural beauty of Oahu's rugged northwestern coast.

- **Distance:** Approximately 2 miles round-trip.
- **Duration:** Allow about 1.5 to 2 hours for the hike, depending on your pace and time spent enjoying the views.
- **Difficulty:** Moderate. The trail includes some steep sections and uneven terrain, requiring sturdy footwear and moderate fitness levels.

Pu'u o Mahuka Heiau:

Pu'u o Mahuka Heiau is a significant cultural site nestled on Oahu's North Shore, offering both historical intrigue and breathtaking views. This ancient Hawaiian temple complex overlooks Waimea Bay and spans over 2 acres, serving as a sacred place for religious ceremonies and community gatherings in ancient times. Visitors can hike up a gentle trail surrounded by native flora to reach the heiau, where they're rewarded with panoramic vistas of the coastline and lush landscapes below. The site provides a serene atmosphere for reflection on Hawaiian history and spirituality, making it a cultural gem amidst the North Shore's natural beauty.

- **Distance:** The trail to Pu'u o Mahuka Heiau is approximately 0.5 miles (0.8 km) round trip.
- **Duration:** It typically takes about 30 minutes to 1 hour to hike to the heiau and explore the site.
- **Difficulty:** The hike is considered easy to moderate, with a gradual ascent and well-maintained trail suitable for most fitness levels.

4. Stand-Up Paddleboarding (SUP):

Stand-up paddleboarding (SUP) is a popular outdoor activity on the North Shore of Oahu, offering a unique way to explore its coastal waters. Participants stand on a large, stable board and use a single paddle to propel themselves across the ocean. Beginners can enjoy calm conditions in protected areas like Haleiwa Harbor, where the water is typically clear and tranquil. More experienced paddlers can venture out to spots like Sunset Beach or Waimea Bay, where they can paddle along the coastline and admire stunning views of the island's rugged shoreline and lush landscapes. SUP provides not only a great workout but also a peaceful way to connect with nature, as paddlers often encounter marine life such as sea turtles and tropical fish along the way.

Top Spots for SUP on the North Shore:

- **Haleiwa Harbor:** Ideal for beginners due to its calm waters and scenic surroundings, offering a peaceful paddling experience.
- **Sunset Beach:** Experienced paddlers can enjoy paddling along this iconic beach, especially during calmer summer months, taking in views of surfers and natural beauty.
- **Waimea Bay:** Offers a mix of calm waters in summer and more challenging conditions in winter, providing a diverse SUP experience with breathtaking coastal scenery.

5. Camping:

Camping on the North Shore of Oahu offers a unique opportunity to immerse yourself in the island's natural beauty. Several beach parks, such as Malaekahana State Recreation Area and Camp Erdman, provide designated camping areas with facilities like restrooms and showers. Camping permits are required and can be obtained in advance. Fall asleep to the sound of crashing waves and wake up to stunning sunrises over the Pacific Ocean.

It's a fantastic way to experience Hawaii's laid-back atmosphere and connect with nature, whether you're with family, friends, or solo.

Top Spots for Camping on the North Shore:

- **Malaekahana State Recreation Area:** Located between Laie and Kahuku, this beach park offers beautiful stretches of sand and well-maintained camping facilities. It's popular for its peaceful atmosphere and oceanfront campsites.
- **Camp Erdman**: Operated by the YMCA, Camp Erdman offers a rustic camping experience amidst lush tropical surroundings. It's ideal for families and groups looking to unplug and enjoy activities like hiking and beachcombing.

Recommended Resorts and Accommodations

1. Lahaina Shores Beach Resort

Located in Lahaina, Lahaina Shores Beach Resort offers beachfront access and stunning ocean views. This resort features spacious rooms with kitchenettes, a pool, and a BBQ area. Guests can enjoy easy access to nearby shopping and dining options in Lahaina Town. The resort's location also provides convenient access to various outdoor activities and attractions.

- **Phone Number:** +1 808-661-6000
- **Star Rating:** ★★★★

2. The Westin Maui Resort & Spa, Ka'anapali

Situated on the scenic Ka'anapali Beach, The Westin Maui Resort & Spa features beautifully appointed rooms with private lanais, multiple outdoor pools, a luxurious spa, and various dining options. The resort's prime location offers easy access to water sports, shopping, and dining. The lush gardens and stunning ocean views make it a popular choice for a relaxing stay.

- **Phone Number:** +1 808-661-2588
- **Star Rating:** ★★★★★

3. Napili Kai Beach Resort

Napili Kai Beach Resort is a charming, low-rise resort located on Napili Bay. It offers a relaxed atmosphere with spacious suites and studios, a beachfront location, and lush tropical gardens.

The resort features a golf course, tennis courts, and an on-site restaurant. Its prime location provides easy access to snorkeling, swimming, and other outdoor activities.

- **Phone Number:** +1 808-669-6271
- **Star Rating:** ★★★★

4. Honua Kai Resort & Spa

This upscale resort on Kaanapali Beach offers modern, spacious suites with full kitchens and private lanais. Honua Kai features multiple pools, a spa, and various dining options, including a beachside restaurant. The resort is well-suited for families and couples seeking a luxury experience with direct beach access and proximity to local attractions.

- **Phone Number:** +1 808-662-2800
- **Star Rating:** ★★★★★

5. Maui Seaside Hotel

Located in Kahului, Maui Seaside Hotel provides a more budget-friendly option with comfortable, basic accommodations. The hotel offers easy access to the airport and nearby shopping centers. With its simple amenities, including a pool and restaurant, it's a practical choice for travelers seeking convenience and value.

- **Phone Number:** +1 808-877-3311
- **Star Rating:** ★★★

6. Ka'anapali Beach Hotel

Known for its authentic Hawaiian experience, Ka'anapali Beach Hotel offers traditional Hawaiian hospitality and beachfront accommodations. The hotel features a range of room types, cultural activities, and oceanfront dining options. Located on Ka'anapali Beach, it provides easy access to water sports and scenic views, making it a great choice for those looking to immerse themselves in local culture.

- **Phone Number:** +1 808-661-0011
- **Star Rating:** ★★★★

7. The Ritz-Carlton, Kapalua

Set amidst 54 acres of lush gardens, The Ritz-Carlton, Kapalua offers luxurious rooms and suites with private balconies overlooking the ocean or golf courses. The resort features a world-class spa, fine dining, and multiple swimming pools. Its location on the Kapalua coast allows guests to enjoy stunning sunsets and easy access to nearby golf courses and hiking trails.

- **Phone Number:** +1 808-669-6200
- **Star Rating:** ★★★★★

8. Aston Kaanapali Shores

Aston Kaanapali Shores provides a family-friendly atmosphere with spacious suites featuring kitchenettes and private lanais. The resort offers direct beach access, two swimming pools, and a variety of recreational activities. Its location on Kaanapali Beach makes it convenient for exploring nearby shops and dining options.

- **Phone Number:** +1 808-667-7711
- **Star Rating:** ★★★★

9. Maui Oceanfront Inn

Situated in Ma'alaea, Maui Oceanfront Inn offers a more intimate and budget-friendly beachfront experience. The property features comfortable rooms with ocean views, a small pool, and direct beach access. Its location provides easy access to Ma'alaea Harbor for whale watching and other water excursions.

- **Phone Number:** +1 808-243-6411
- **Star Rating:** ★★★

10. Turtle Bay Resort

While located on the North Shore of Oahu rather than Maui, Turtle Bay Resort is a renowned destination worth considering if your plans include Oahu. The resort boasts a variety of accommodations, from ocean-view rooms to private villas, along with multiple dining options, a world-class spa, and numerous outdoor activities. The scenic location offers a more remote, tranquil experience compared to other resorts.

- **Phone Number:** +1 808-293-6000

Chapter 10: Upcountry Maui

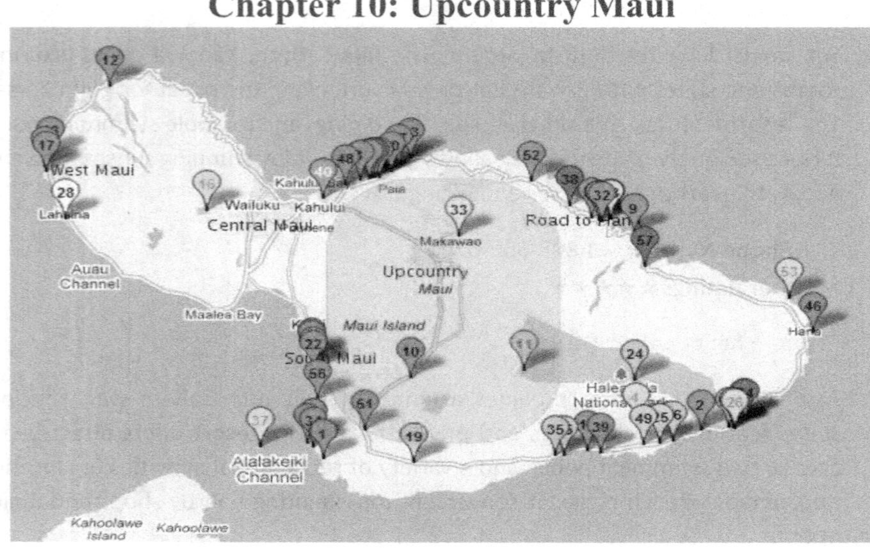

Overview of Upcountry Maui

Geography and Climate

Upcountry Maui spans the elevated terrain from approximately 1,000 to 4,000 feet above sea level, encompassing towns such as Makawao, Kula, Pukalani, and Ulupalakua. The region's higher elevation contributes to a cooler climate compared to the coastal areas, with temperatures often dipping into the 60s Fahrenheit (15-20°C) at night, making it a refreshing escape from the heat of the beach towns.

Cultural and Historical Significance

Upcountry Maui is deeply rooted in Hawaiian culture and history. It was traditionally the center of agriculture and ranching on the island, a heritage that continues to shape its identity today. Visitors can explore historic sites like the Makawao History Museum, which offers insights into the area's paniolo (cowboy) culture and the legacy of sugar plantations.

Attractions and Points of Interest

Ali'i Kula Lavender Farm: Known for its fragrant fields of lavender and panoramic views of the island's central valley, this farm offers guided tours, workshops, and a gift shop featuring lavender-based products.

Surfing Goat Dairy: A family-owned goat dairy farm where visitors can tour the facility, learn about the cheese-making process, and even participate in goat milking and cheese tastings.

Ulupalakua Ranch and MauiWine: Established in 1845, Ulupalakua Ranch is one of the oldest cattle ranches in Hawaii. It's also home to MauiWine, where visitors can enjoy wine tastings, tours of the vineyards, and scenic views of the West Maui Mountains and neighboring islands.

Pukalani Country Club: A popular golf course offering challenging play amid stunning views of Maui's north shore and the Haleakala Crater.

Kula Botanical Garden: A lush garden featuring a diverse collection of tropical plants, flowers, and native Hawaiian species, with scenic views overlooking the island's southern coastline.

Outdoor Activities

Upcountry Maui is a haven for outdoor enthusiasts. Visitors can embark on scenic hikes in areas like the Hosmer Grove Trail in Haleakala National Park or the Polipoli Spring State Recreation Area, known for its forested trails and camping facilities. The region also offers opportunities for horseback riding, zip-lining, and paragliding adventures.

Dining and Shopping

The towns of Makawao and Kula are known for their quaint boutiques, art galleries showcasing local artists, and farm-to-table dining experiences. Fresh produce markets, roadside stands, and the Saturday Upcountry Farmers Market in Pukalani offer opportunities to taste and purchase locally grown fruits, vegetables, and artisanal products.

Events and Festivals

Upcountry Maui hosts various events throughout the year, celebrating Hawaiian culture, agriculture, and community spirit. Highlights include the annual Makawao Rodeo, featuring traditional rodeo events and parades, and the Maui Onion Festival in May, showcasing the island's famous sweet onions with culinary demonstrations and live entertainment.

Practical Tips for Visitors

Driving: Roads in Upcountry Maui can be narrow and winding, so drive cautiously and be prepared for changing weather conditions, especially at higher elevations.

Weather: Bring layers of clothing, as temperatures can vary significantly between daytime warmth and cooler evenings.

Timing: Plan visits to attractions and restaurants in advance, as some establishments may have limited operating hours or require reservations.

Local Etiquette: Respect the rural environment and local communities by following designated trails, disposing of trash properly, and being mindful of private property.

Historical Sites and Cultural Attractions

In Upcountry Maui, you can find several historical sites and cultural attractions that offer insights into the area's rich heritage and local traditions. Here are some notable ones:

1. Makawao History Museum:

The Makawao History Museum in Upcountry Maui showcases the area's rich cultural heritage, focusing on its plantation era and cowboy history.

Housed in a historic building, the museum features exhibits, artifacts, and photographs that offer insights into Makawao's evolution from a small agricultural community to a vibrant cultural hub. Visitors can learn about local traditions, including the paniolo (cowboy) culture that still thrives in the region today.

- **Opening Hours:** Wednesday to Saturday: 10:00 AM - 4:00 PM and Closed Sunday to Tuesday
- **Address:** 3643 Baldwin Ave, Makawao, HI 96768

Insider Tips:

- Plan your visit during the morning or early afternoon to avoid crowds.
- Check for special events or guided tours to enhance your experience.
- Combine your visit with exploring Makawao town for art galleries and local shops.

2. Hui No'eau Visual Arts Center:

The Hui No'eau Visual Arts Center, nestled in the town of Makawao on Maui, occupies a historic estate with a rich plantation-era legacy. Originally built in 1917 by a prominent local businessman, the center now serves as a hub for artistic expression and cultural enrichment.

Its mission includes fostering creativity through workshops, exhibitions, and community events. Visitors can explore the center's galleries showcasing diverse artworks and participate in classes ranging from painting to ceramics, all set against the backdrop of lush gardens and scenic views. The Hui No'eau Visual Arts Center stands out not only for its cultural significance but also for its dedication to preserving and promoting Maui's artistic heritage.

- **Opening Hours:** Monday to Saturday, 9:00 AM - 4:00 PM
- **Address:** 2841 Baldwin Ave, Makawao, HI 96768
- **Insider Tips:** Check the center's calendar for workshops and events; the grounds offer beautiful spots for picnics with panoramic views of the surrounding countryside.

3. Holy Ghost Catholic Church:

The Holy Ghost Catholic Church in Upcountry Maui holds historical significance dating back to the late 19th century, reflecting the area's Portuguese immigrant community. Nestled in Kula, the church's architecture blends traditional styles with elements unique to Maui, such as its vibrant community murals and serene surroundings. Visitors can appreciate its cultural importance through guided tours, exploring its intricate stained-glass windows, and learning about its religious and social impact on the local community.

The church remains an active place of worship, hosting occasional events that celebrate its heritage and invite community participation.

- **Opening Hours:** Typically open during daylight hours; specific times for tours may vary.
- **Address:** 4300 Lower Kula Rd, Kula, HI 96790, USA
- **Insider Tips:** Check ahead for tour availability, as church activities may affect accessibility. Respect the church's sacred nature and enjoy the serene garden area adjacent to the building.

4. Alexander & Baldwin Sugar Museum:

The Alexander & Baldwin Sugar Museum in Puunene, near Upcountry Maui, offers a fascinating glimpse into the island's sugar industry, a pivotal part of its history. Housed in a former plantation superintendent's residence, the museum showcases an exhibit on sugar cane cultivation, processing, and its impact on Maui's economy and culture. Visitors can explore vintage machinery, photographs, and artifacts illustrating the lives of plantation workers and the evolution of the industry. The museum also highlights the multicultural heritage of Maui's sugar era, celebrating the contributions of diverse immigrant communities.

- **Opening Hours:** Tuesday to Saturday, 9:30 AM - 4:00 PM
- **Address:** 3957 Hansen Road, Puunene, HI 96784

- **Entry Fee:** Adults $7, Seniors (60+) $5, Children (6-12) $2, Children under 6 free
- **Insider Tips:** Check for guided tours or special events to enhance your visit. Plan to visit in the morning to avoid crowds and have time to explore the exhibits thoroughly.

5. Ulupalakua Ranch:

Ulupalakua Ranch, situated in Upcountry Maui, holds significant historical and cultural value as one of the oldest cattle ranches in Hawaii, dating back to the early 19th century. Originally a sugar plantation, it later transitioned to ranching under King Kamehameha III. Today, Ulupalakua Ranch encompasses over 18,000 acres and is known not only for its cattle operations but also for its scenic vineyard, MauiWine. Visitors can tour the ranch, learn about its rich history, and enjoy wine tastings at MauiWine, which produces a variety of wines from locally grown grapes. The ranch offers stunning views of the surrounding countryside and Haleakalā volcano, providing a serene escape into Maui's pastoral past.

- **Opening Hours:** Daily, 10:00 AM - 5:30 PM
- **Address:** 14815 Piilani Highway, Kula, HI 96790
- **Insider Tips:** Arrive early to enjoy the tranquility and beautiful views; consider pairing a visit with a hike in nearby Haleakalā National Park for a full day of outdoor exploration.

Top-Rated Beaches and Outdoor Activities

Upcountry Maui is not typically known for its beaches, as it's located on the slopes of Haleakalā away from the coastline. However, it offers a wide range of outdoor activities amidst its scenic landscapes and cooler climate. Here are some of the best outdoor activities you can enjoy in Upcountry Maui:

1. Hiking:

Halemau'u Trail:

The Halemau'u Trail in Upcountry Maui offers hikers a captivating journey through diverse landscapes within Haleakalā National Park. Beginning near the park's summit, the trail descends into the Halemau'u Crater, revealing ancient lava formations, vibrant silversword plants, and panoramic views of Maui's volcanic terrain. The trail's rugged path winds through alpine desert and patches of lush vegetation, providing a stark contrast to the island's coastal scenery. Hikers can witness Haleakalā's unique ecology and may encounter native wildlife like the nēnē (Hawaiian goose). This challenging hike rewards adventurers with an immersive experience of Hawaii's natural beauty.

- **Distance:** Approximately 7 miles (11.3 km) round trip.
- **Duration:** 4 to 6 hours, depending on hiking pace and stops.
- **Difficulty:** Moderate to strenuous, due to elevation changes and rocky terrain.

The Sliding Sands Trail:

The Sliding Sands Trail in Upcountry Maui is a mesmerizing hiking experience renowned for its stark volcanic landscapes and sweeping views of Haleakalā Crater. Beginning at the Haleakalā Visitor Center, the trail descends into the crater, revealing otherworldly terrain dotted with cinder cones and colorful mineral deposits. Hikers traverse through a range of ecosystems, from alpine deserts to sub-tropical rainforests, encountering endemic plant species like the silversword. This challenging trail spans approximately 11 miles round-trip, typically taking 5-7 hours to complete. Its difficulty lies in the steep descent and strenuous return ascent, making it suitable for experienced hikers seeking a rewarding adventure amidst Maui's natural wonders.

- **Distance:** Approximately 11 miles round-trip
- **Duration:** 5-7 hours
- **Difficulty:** Strenuous

2. Horseback Riding:

Horseback riding in Upcountry Maui offers a unique way to explore its scenic landscapes and connect with its rich cowboy heritage. Visitors can ride through lush pastures, eucalyptus forests, and panoramic ridges with views of Haleakalā and the Pacific Ocean. Guided tours at places like Piiholo Ranch and Thompson Ranch provide opportunities for all experience levels, from beginner to advanced riders.

This activity not only showcases Maui's natural beauty but also offers insights into its agricultural history and the traditions of paniolo (Hawaiian cowboys). Horseback riding in Upcountry Maui blends adventure with cultural immersion, making it a memorable experience for outdoor enthusiasts and those seeking a deeper connection to the island's rural charm.

3. Zip Lining:

Zip lining in Upcountry Maui offers an exhilarating outdoor adventure amidst lush landscapes and scenic views. Visitors can soar through forested valleys and across gulches, experiencing the thrill of flight while enjoying panoramic vistas of Maui's countryside. Popular zip-lining locations like Skyline Eco-Adventures provide safe, guided tours with multiple zip lines of varying lengths and speeds, suitable for both beginners and adrenaline seekers. This activity not only offers an adrenaline rush but also an opportunity to appreciate Maui's natural beauty from a unique perspective, making it a memorable addition to any itinerary in Upcountry Maui.

4. Cycling

Cycling in Upcountry Maui offers a scenic and exhilarating way to explore the region's lush landscapes and charming countryside. Cyclists can ride through rolling hills, pastures, and quaint towns like Makawao, immersing themselves in the area's cool climate and rich cultural heritage. Popular routes include the winding roads around Haleakalā, offering stunning views of the volcanic terrain and occasional glimpses of the Pacific Ocean. Whether biking independently or on guided tours, cyclists can enjoy encounters with local flora and fauna, stop at lavender farms or botanical gardens, and experience the relaxed pace and beauty that define Upcountry Maui.

5. Lavender Farm Tours:

Lavender Farm Tours in Upcountry Maui offer a serene and aromatic escape amidst the island's lush landscapes. Ali'i Kula Lavender Farm, a notable destination, invites visitors to explore its expansive fields of lavender and other botanicals. Guided tours provide insights into lavender cultivation, essential oil production, and sustainable farming practices. Visitors can stroll through vibrant gardens, enjoy panoramic views of Maui's countryside, and participate in workshops or tastings featuring lavender-infused products. These tours not only showcase the farm's natural beauty but also offer a relaxing and educational experience, making them a popular outdoor activity for those seeking tranquility and connection with Maui's agricultural heritage.

6. Botanical Gardens:

In Upcountry Maui, Botanical Gardens offer serene outdoor experiences amidst diverse plant life. Kula Botanical Garden, for instance, showcases native Hawaiian flora alongside exotic species, creating a botanical haven with scenic views. Visitors can stroll through lush pathways, discovering vibrant flowers, towering trees, and unique gardens. These gardens not only serve as educational venues but also as peaceful retreats where guests can learn about Maui's biodiversity and conservation efforts. Whether exploring on guided tours or self-guided walks, Botanical Gardens in Upcountry Maui provide a tranquil setting to appreciate the island's natural beauty and cultural significance in a leisurely outdoor activity.

7. Farm Tours and Tastings:

Farm tours and tastings in Upcountry Maui offer a hands-on experience of the island's agricultural traditions and local flavors. Visitors can explore working farms like Surfing Goat Dairy, where they learn about goat farming practices and sample artisanal cheeses. These tours often include insights into sustainable farming methods and the opportunity to interact with farm animals. Additionally, places like MauiWine at Ulupalakua Ranch provide wine tastings amidst picturesque vineyards, showcasing Maui's unique viticultural history. Such experiences not only educate about Maui's agricultural heritage but also allow visitors to taste fresh, locally produced goods while enjoying the serene rural landscapes of Upcountry Maui.

Recommended Resorts and Accommodations

1. Hotel Wailea, Relais & Châteaux

Nestled in the hills of Wailea, Hotel Wailea offers a serene retreat with stunning views of the Pacific Ocean and lush tropical gardens. This adults-only resort features elegant suites with private lanais, a world-class spa, and an on-site restaurant serving farm-to-table cuisine. The peaceful ambiance and personalized service make it a perfect getaway for relaxation and rejuvenation.

- **Phone Number:** +1 808-879-2222
- **Star Rating:** 5 stars

2. Maui Upcountry Lodge

This charming lodge provides a cozy and intimate experience with its rustic decor and picturesque surroundings. Located near Makawao, it offers comfortable rooms with stunning views of the island's rolling hills. Guests can enjoy a hearty breakfast made with locally sourced ingredients and take advantage of the proximity to nearby hiking trails and cultural attractions.

- **Phone Number:** +1 808-572-1246
- **Star Rating:** 4 stars

3. Lumeria Maui

Lumeria Maui is a unique retreat that focuses on wellness and tranquility. Set in a historic estate surrounded by gardens and fruit orchards, it provides spacious rooms and suites, each thoughtfully designed for relaxation. The property features a range of wellness programs, including yoga classes, meditation, and spa treatments. It's an ideal choice for those seeking a holistic vacation experience.

- **Phone Number:** +1 808-579-8877
- **Star Rating:** 4 stars

4. Hale Ho'olei Resort

Located within the Grand Wailea Resort, Hale Ho'olei offers luxurious villa-style accommodations with beautiful views of the ocean and golf course. Each villa features multiple bedrooms, a fully equipped kitchen, and a private lanai. The resort provides access to the Grand Wailea's extensive amenities, including its renowned pools, restaurants, and spa facilities.

- **Phone Number:** +1 808-875-1234
- **Star Rating:** 5 stars

5. The Ritz-Carlton, Kapalua

Although slightly outside Upcountry, The Ritz-Carlton, Kapalua offers a luxurious escape with its spacious rooms and stunning ocean views. The resort is set amidst 54 acres of tropical gardens and features several dining options, a world-class spa, and championship golf courses. Its commitment to providing top-notch service and amenities makes it a standout choice for a high-end stay.

- **Phone Number:** +1 808-669-6200
- **Star Rating:** 5 stars

6. Maui Country Inn

The Maui Country Inn offers a quaint and charming experience with its rustic design and cozy accommodations. Located in the heart of Upcountry, it provides easy access to local farms, markets, and hiking trails. The inn features comfortable rooms with classic decor, and guests can enjoy a complimentary breakfast made from locally sourced ingredients. Its relaxed atmosphere is ideal for those seeking a peaceful retreat.

- **Phone Number:** +1 808-876-1234
- **Star Rating:** 3 stars

7. Hale Pua Villa

Hale Pua Villa is a boutique property offering a personalized and intimate stay with stunning views of the surrounding landscape. Each villa is elegantly designed with modern amenities and features private outdoor spaces, including gardens and pools. Guests can enjoy personalized services and a tranquil setting that combines comfort with luxury, perfect for a romantic getaway or a private retreat.

- **Phone Number:** +1 808-575-5678
- **Star Rating:** 4 stars

8. The Montage Kapalua Bay

Situated a short drive from Upcountry, The Montage Kapalua Bay offers luxurious oceanfront accommodations with expansive suites and villas. The resort features a variety of dining options, a full-service spa, and a range of recreational activities, including golf and water sports. Its commitment to excellence and breathtaking views make it a top choice for those seeking a high-end Maui experience.

- **Phone Number:** +1 808-662-6600
- **Star Rating:** 5 stars

9. Makawao Mansion

Makawao Mansion combines historical charm with modern luxury. This beautifully restored mansion offers spacious suites with antique furnishings and modern amenities. Located in the quaint town of Makawao, it provides easy access to local attractions, shops, and restaurants. The property features lush gardens and a serene atmosphere, making it an ideal choice for a relaxing stay.

- **Phone Number:** -1 808-573-4567
- **Star Rating:** 4 stars

10. Kula Lodge & Restaurant

Perched on the slopes of Haleakalā, Kula Lodge & Restaurant provides spectacular views and a cozy atmosphere. The lodge offers comfortable rooms and a restaurant serving delicious, locally sourced cuisine. Its unique location provides guests with easy access to Haleakalā National Park and other Upcountry attractions. The lodge's blend of rustic charm and comfort makes it a favorite among visitors.

- **Phone Number:** -1 808-878-1535
- **Star Rating:** 3 stars

Chapter 11: East Maui

Overview of East Maui

East Maui, often celebrated for its lush landscapes and serene beauty, offers a stark contrast to the more developed and bustling areas of the island. This region, encompassing the famous Road to Hana and the town of Hana itself, is rich in natural wonders, cultural history, and traditional Hawaiian lifestyle. Here's an in-depth look at what East Maui has to offer:

Geography and Climate

East Maui is characterized by its dense rainforests, dramatic coastline, and abundant waterfalls. The region experiences a tropical climate, with frequent rainfall contributing to its lush greenery. The Hana Highway (HI-360) winds along the coastline, providing access to many of East Maui's attractions and scenic spots.

The Road to Hana

The journey along the Hana Highway is an adventure in itself, renowned for its winding roads, single-lane bridges, and breathtaking scenery. Key highlights along the way include:

Twin Falls: The first major waterfall stops, offering short hikes to picturesque falls and swimming holes.

Garden of Eden Arboretum: A botanical garden with panoramic views, peacocks, and diverse plant species.

Keanae Peninsula: A historic Hawaiian village with taro fields, rugged lava rock coastline, and the picturesque Keanae Congregational Church.

Wai'anapanapa State Park: Home to a stunning black sand beach, sea caves, and hiking trails with coastal views.

Hana Town

The small, isolated town of Hana serves as the heart of East Maui. Despite its remoteness, Hana is rich in culture and history, offering a glimpse into traditional Hawaiian life. Key attractions in and around Hana include:

Hana Cultural Center and Museum: Showcases the history and culture of Hana through artifacts, photographs, and exhibits.

Hana Bay: A popular spot for swimming, picnicking, and observing local fishermen.

Hana Ranch: Offers horseback riding tours and insights into local agriculture.

Natural Attractions

East Maui is home to numerous natural attractions, each offering unique experiences:

Oheo Gulch (Seven Sacred Pools): Located within Haleakala National Park, this series of cascading pools and waterfalls is a popular spot for hiking and swimming.

Pipiwai Trail: A scenic 4-mile round-trip hike that takes you through a bamboo forest to the impressive Waimoku Falls.

Hamoa Beach: A beautiful crescent-shaped beach perfect for swimming and surfing, located just a few miles south of Hana.

Cultural and Historical Sites

East Maui is steeped in Hawaiian history and culture. Some notable sites include:

St. Sophia's Church: A landmark in Hana, rebuilt after a devastating hurricane, serving as a symbol of the community's resilience.

Hana Lava Tube (Kaeleku Caverns): Offers a subterranean adventure through one of Maui's largest lava tubes, with educational tours about volcanic activity and geology.

Local Cuisine and Markets

Hana's isolation means that much of its food is locally sourced. Visitors can enjoy:

Hana Farms: A community-based farm and marketplace offering fresh produce, baked goods, and artisanal products.

Huli Huli Chicken: A local roadside stand offering delicious, traditional Hawaiian barbecue chicken.

Farmers Markets: Small markets where local farmers sell fresh fruits, vegetables, and homemade treats.

Accommodations and Lodging

Accommodations in East Maui range from luxury resorts to cozy bed-and-breakfasts and vacation rentals:

Travaasa Hana: A luxury resort offering all-inclusive packages with activities like horseback riding, spa treatments, and cultural classes.

Hana Kai Maui: Oceanfront condos provide a more independent stay with stunning views and easy access to Hana Bay.

Outdoor Activities

East Maui is a paradise for outdoor enthusiasts:

Hiking: Numerous trails offer varying levels of difficulty and scenery, from coastal paths to rainforest hikes.

Snorkeling and Swimming: Many beaches and coves provide excellent opportunities for snorkeling and swimming in clear waters.

Surfing: Hana Bay and nearby beaches are popular spots for both beginners and experienced surfers.

Hana Highway (Road to Hana)

The Hana Highway, commonly known as the Road to Hana, is a 64.4-mile scenic drive along Maui's northeastern coast. It's renowned for its breathtaking views, lush rainforests, cascading waterfalls, and numerous hiking trails. The journey begins in Kahului and ends in the small town of Hana, offering visitors a glimpse into the natural beauty and cultural history of Maui.

Key Highlights and Stops

1. Twin Falls:

Twin Falls is one of the first major stops along the Hana Highway, making it a perfect introduction to the scenic wonders of the Road to Hana. Located at Mile Marker 2, Twin Falls offers visitors a chance to explore lush tropical landscapes and swim in natural freshwater pools. The area features multiple waterfalls, with the main falls being easily accessible via a short hike from the parking area. The trail is well-maintained and suitable for families, leading to a beautiful waterfall where visitors can swim, relax, and enjoy the tranquil surroundings. The farm stand at the entrance sells fresh coconut water, fruit smoothies, and other local treats, making it a great spot to refresh and refuel. The combination of accessible trails, stunning waterfalls, and local refreshments makes Twin Falls a must-see stop on the Road to Hana.

- **Opening Hours:** 7:00 AM - 7:00 PM
- **Address:** 6300 Hana Hwy, Haiku, HI 96708

Insider Tips:

- Arrive Early: To avoid crowds and secure parking, visit early in the day.
- Footwear: Wear sturdy shoes for the hike, as the trail can be muddy and slippery.
- Swimming: Bring swimwear and towels for a refreshing dip in the pools.
- Refreshments: Try the fresh coconut water and fruit smoothies at the farm stand.

2. Garden of Eden Arboretum:

The Garden of Eden Arboretum is a must-see stop along the Hana Highway, offering 26 acres of lush botanical gardens and stunning panoramic views. Established by Alan Bradbury, Maui's first certified arborist, the arboretum features over 700 species of tropical and indigenous plants. Visitors can explore well-maintained trails leading to scenic overlooks of waterfalls, such as the Puohokamoa Falls, and breathtaking ocean vistas. The garden is designed to educate visitors about the island's diverse flora, with labeled plants and trees providing a self-guided educational experience.

The garden also includes peacocks, ducks, and other wildlife, enhancing the overall experience. The Garden of Eden is not just about plant life; it also offers art installations, picnic areas, and a small café where you can enjoy refreshments while soaking in the natural beauty.

- **Opening Hours:** 8:00 AM - 4:00 PM, daily
- **Address:** 10600 Hana Highway, Haiku, HI 96708
- **Entry Fee:** $20 per adult, $10 per child (ages 5-16), free for children under 5

Insider Tips:

- Arrive early to avoid crowds and enjoy the tranquility.
- Wear comfortable walking shoes and bring a hat and sunscreen.
- Don't miss the lookout points for some of the best photo opportunities on the Road to Hana.
- Pack a picnic to enjoy in one of the designated picnic areas.

3. Ke'anae Peninsula:

Ke'anae Peninsula is a captivating stop along the Hana Highway, offering a glimpse into traditional Hawaiian life. This picturesque peninsula is known for its lush taro fields, which have been cultivated for centuries by local farmers. The rugged coastline, with its dramatic lava rock formations and powerful waves crashing against them, creates a stunning and unique landscape.

Visitors can explore the Ke'anae Congregational Church, built in 1856, which stands as a testament to the area's rich history. The peninsula is also a great spot for fishing and picnicking, providing a peaceful retreat from the bustling highway. One of the most striking features of Ke'anae Peninsula is its sense of timelessness. Walking through the taro fields and along the rocky shore, visitors can imagine what life was like for the early Hawaiian settlers. The peninsula's natural beauty and cultural significance make it a must-visit stop on the Road to Hana, offering a serene and educational experience.

- **Opening Hours:** Always open
- **Address:** Ke'anae Rd, Haiku, HI 96708

Insider Tips:

- Visit Aunty Sandy's for delicious banana bread.
- Wear sturdy shoes for exploring the rocky shoreline.
- Bring a camera to capture the stunning coastal views.
- Respect the local community and private property.

4. Wai'anapanapa State Park:

Wai'anapanapa State Park is a must-visit gem along the Hana Highway, offering dramatic coastal scenery and natural wonders. Located near Hana on Maui's northeastern coast, this park features rugged black lava cliffs, a striking black sand beach, sea caves, and volcanic rock formations.

Visitors can explore tidal pools, ancient Hawaiian burial sites, and hiking trails that lead to panoramic ocean views. The park's lush vegetation includes hala and hau trees, adding to its mystical ambiance. Swimming is possible in certain areas, though caution is advised due to strong currents.

- **Opening Hours:** Daily, 7:00 AM to 6:00 PM
- **Address:** Hana Hwy, Hana, HI 96713
- **Entry Fee:** $10 per vehicle for non-residents
- **Insider Tips:** Arrive early to avoid crowds and enjoy the serene morning atmosphere. Wear sturdy footwear for exploring volcanic rock formations and bring swimwear for a refreshing dip in the clear waters. Respect the park's cultural significance by not disturbing any archaeological sites or native plants. Check weather conditions, as rain can create slippery trails and impact swimming conditions. Capture the stunning black sand beach and sea arches during sunrise or sunset for unforgettable photos.

5. Hana Town:

Hana Town is a serene and culturally rich destination along the Hana Highway, offering a glimpse into traditional Hawaiian life. Nestled on Maui's eastern coast, Hana is known for its lush landscapes, secluded beaches, and authentic Hawaiian atmosphere. Visitors can explore local art galleries, sample traditional Hawaiian cuisine, and visit historical sites such as the Hana Cultural Center and Museum, which showcases artifacts and exhibits depicting the area's history and culture.

The town also features charming beaches like Hana Bay, ideal for swimming and picnicking amidst tranquil surroundings. Hana's laid-back vibe and friendly locals make it a perfect stop to unwind and connect with Maui's natural beauty and heritage.

- **Opening Hours:** Generally open daily; hours may vary for specific attractions and businesses.
- **Address:** Hana, Maui, Hawaii 96713

Insider Tips:

- Early Arrival: Visit early in the day to avoid crowds and fully experience the town's peaceful ambiance.
- Local Eateries: Try roadside food stands for authentic Hawaiian treats like coconut candy and fresh fruit.
- Respect Local Culture: Embrace the relaxed pace and respect local customs; Hana is known for its warm hospitality.

6. Hamoa Beach:

Hamoa Beach is a picturesque crescent-shaped beach located along Maui's eastern coastline, celebrated for its stunning beauty and tranquil ambiance. Encircled by lush cliffs and swaying palm trees, its soft golden sands meet crystal-clear waters that are ideal for swimming, bodyboarding, and relaxing. The beach offers a peaceful retreat away from the crowds, often less crowded compared to other stops along the Hana Highway.

- **Opening Hours:** Hamoa Beach is accessible year-round from dawn to dusk.
- **Address:** Hamoa Beach, Hana Highway (Highway 360), Hana, HI 96713, USA.
- **Insider Tips:** Arrive early to secure parking as spaces can be limited. Bring snorkeling gear to explore the nearby reefs and marine life. Pack a picnic to enjoy amidst the beach's natural beauty. Be mindful of the ocean conditions, as waves can vary from calm to moderate, making it ideal for various water activities.

7. Seven Sacred Pools (Ohe'o Gulch):

Seven Sacred Pools (Ohe'o Gulch) is a series of cascading waterfalls and freshwater pools nestled within the lush landscapes of Haleakala National Park along Maui's Hana Highway. The pools, fed by the Palikea and Pipiwai streams, offer a refreshing retreat amid towering bamboo forests and volcanic cliffs. Visitors can swim in the crystal-clear waters of the pools, hike along scenic trails to majestic waterfalls, or picnic amidst serene natural surroundings.

- **Opening Hours:** Daily, from sunrise to sunset.
- **Address:** Seven Sacred Pools, Hana Hwy, Hana, HI 96713, USA.
- **Entry Fee:** $30 per vehicle (valid for three days) for Haleakala National Park entrance fee.

Insider Tips:

- Early Arrival: Visit early in the day to avoid crowds and enjoy a tranquil experience.
- Hiking Trails: Explore the Pipiwai Trail for views of towering waterfalls and bamboo forests.
- Safety First: Observe posted signs and warnings about changing water conditions, especially after heavy rainfall.
- Pack Essentials: Bring swimwear, water shoes, sunscreen, and insect repellent. Limited facilities are available, so pack snacks and drinks.
- Environmental Respect: Respect wildlife and vegetation, stay on marked trails and carry out all trash.

8. Wailua Falls:

Wailua Falls is one of the most picturesque and easily accessible waterfalls along the Hana Highway. Plunging 80 feet into a shimmering pool below, it is located near the Wailua Valley State Wayside. The falls are visible from the road, making it a popular stop for those seeking a quick and rewarding photo opportunity without a strenuous hike. Surrounded by lush greenery, Wailua Falls offers a quintessential tropical waterfall experience, and the mist from the falls provides a refreshing respite on a warm day. It's an ideal spot for a short stop to marvel at the natural beauty, take photos, and enjoy the serene ambiance of the area.

- **Opening Hours:** Always open
- **Address:** Hana Highway, Mile Marker 45, Hana, HI 96713

Insider Tips

- Arrive Early: To avoid crowds, especially during peak tourist season.
- Safety: The rocks around the falls can be slippery, so be cautious if you decide to explore close to the water.
- Parking: Limited roadside parking is available; be mindful of traffic and park safely.
- Respect Nature: Stay on designated paths and do not leave any trash behind to preserve the natural beauty of the site.

Town of Hana

Hana is a small, secluded town located on the eastern coast of Maui, known for its natural beauty, rich cultural heritage, and tranquil atmosphere. The journey to Hana via the Hana Highway is a memorable experience, but the town itself offers unique attractions and activities that make the trip worthwhile.

Key Attractions

1. Hana Bay

Hana Bay is a picturesque and serene spot in the town of Hana, known for its black sand beach and tranquil waters. The bay is an excellent location for swimming, snorkeling, and relaxing by the ocean.

Hana Bay is sheltered by a long breakwater, making its waters calm and safe for families. The Hana Pier, extending into the bay, offers a scenic spot for fishing and enjoying panoramic views of the coastline. The surrounding area features picnic facilities, making it an ideal location for a leisurely beachside lunch. The bay's black sand, created by volcanic activity, contrasts beautifully with the lush greenery and blue waters, providing a stunning natural backdrop.

- **Opening Hours:** Open 24 hours
- **Address:** 150 Keawa Pl, Hana, HI 96713

Insider Tips:

- Early Visit: Arrive early to secure a good picnic spot and avoid crowds.
- Snorkeling Gear: Bring your snorkeling gear to explore the underwater scenery.
- Safety: While the waters are generally calm, always check for local conditions and heed any posted warnings.
- Facilities: Restrooms and picnic tables are available, but there are no lifeguards on duty, so swim with caution.
- Parking: Limited parking is available; consider carpooling if visiting with a group.

2. Hana Cultural Center and Museum

The Hana Cultural Center and Museum is a small yet significant museum located in the heart of Hana, dedicated to preserving and showcasing the rich cultural heritage of the region.

The museum features a collection of artifacts, photographs, and exhibits that offer a glimpse into the history and traditions of the Hawaiian people, particularly those from Hana. Visitors can explore traditional Hawaiian tools, clothing, and household items, as well as learn about the significant events and figures that shaped Hana's history. The museum also includes a replica of a Hawaiian village, providing a hands-on experience of traditional Hawaiian life. Through its exhibits and educational programs, the Hana Cultural Center and Museum plays a vital role in keeping Hana's cultural heritage alive for both residents and visitors.

- **Opening Hours:** Monday to Friday, 10:00 AM - 4:00 PM; Saturday, 10:00 AM - 2:00 PM; Closed on Sundays.
- **Address:** 4974 Uakea Road, Hana, HI 96713

Insider Tips:

- Plan your visit to coincide with one of the museum's special events or workshops for a more immersive experience.
- The museum is small, so a visit typically takes about an hour.
- Combine your visit with a trip to nearby Hana Bay for a relaxing day exploring Hana's history and natural beauty.

3. Hamoa Beach

Hamoa Beach is a stunning crescent-shaped beach located just outside the town of Hana on Maui's eastern coast. Known for its powdery white sand and clear blue waters, it offers a picturesque and serene setting perfect for relaxation and recreation. The beach is surrounded by lush greenery and sea cliffs, creating a secluded atmosphere that feels like a hidden paradise. The gentle waves make it ideal for swimming and bodyboarding, while the tranquil environment is perfect for sunbathing and picnicking. The beach is relatively uncrowded, providing a peaceful escape from more touristy areas. Amenities include restrooms and showers, but no lifeguards are on duty, so swimming should be done cautiously.

- **Opening Hours:** Open daily, sunrise to sunset
- **Address:** Haneoo Road, Hana, HI 96713

Insider Tips:

- Parking: Limited parking is available on the road; arrive early to secure a spot.
- Facilities: Bring your snacks and drinks, as there are no food vendors nearby.
- Safety: Watch out for occasional strong currents and waves, especially during high surf conditions.
- Snorkeling: Best on calm days; bring your gear to explore the marine life near the rocks.
- Shade: Limited natural shade, so bringing an umbrella or tent is advisable.

4. Kaihalulu Red Sand Beach (Kaihalulu Beach)

Kaihalulu Red Sand Beach, located near the town of Hana, is one of Maui's most unique and picturesque spots. The beach is famous for its striking red sand, created by the erosion of the surrounding red cinder cliffs.

The secluded cove is protected by a natural lava rock wall, creating calm waters that are ideal for swimming and snorkeling. The dramatic contrast between the red sand, turquoise waters, and lush green vegetation makes it a photographer's dream. However, reaching the beach requires a short but challenging hike along a narrow, rocky trail. The trail can be slippery, especially after rain, so it's recommended to wear sturdy shoes and proceed with caution.

- **Opening Hours:** Always open, but visiting during daylight hours is recommended for safety.
- **Address:** Near Uakea Road, Hana, HI 96713 (exact location can be tricky to find; follow signs to the trailhead near the Hana Community Center).

Insider Tips:

- Footwear: Wear sturdy shoes for the hike; the trail can be slippery and uneven.
- Safety The beach is secluded; don't swim alone and be cautious of changing tides and currents.
- Respect: The area is culturally significant to Native Hawaiians; be respectful and pack out all trash.
- Parking: Limited parking is available near the trailhead, so arrive early to secure a spot.

5. Hana Lava Tube (Ka'eleku Caverns)

The Hana Lava Tube, also known as Ka'eleku Caverns, is a fascinating natural attraction in the town of Hana.

Formed by volcanic activity over 960 years ago, the lava tube extends underground, showcasing remarkable geological formations such as stalactites, stalagmites, and lava stalagmites. Visitors can embark on a self-guided tour, equipped with flashlights and informative guides, to explore this subterranean wonder. The tube is a safe, family-friendly adventure, offering a cool and unique perspective on Maui's volcanic history. The temperature inside the tube remains relatively constant, making it a refreshing escape from the tropical heat outside. Interpretive signs along the path provide educational insights into the tube's formation and the surrounding ecosystem.

- **Opening Hours:** Daily: 10:30 AM – 4:00 PM
- **Address:** Hana Lava Tube: 205 Ulaino Road, Hana, HI 96713

Entry Fee:

- Adults: $15
- Children (5-12 years): $10
- Children (under 5): Free

Insider Tips:

- Wear Sturdy Shoes: The ground can be uneven and slippery in places.
- Bring a Light Jacket: It can be cool inside the tube.
- Visit Early: To avoid crowds and ensure a more leisurely exploration.
- Camera Ready: Flash photography is allowed, so bring a camera to capture the unique formations.

6. Kahanu Garden and Pi'ilanihale Heiau

Kahanu Garden is a serene botanical garden in Hana, Maui, showcasing native Hawaiian plants and Polynesian-introduced species. The garden is part of the National Tropical Botanical Garden network and is dedicated to preserving traditional Hawaiian agricultural practices. One of the garden's main highlights is Pi'ilanihale Heiau, the largest ancient temple (heiau) in Hawaii. This sacred site, constructed from lava rock, dates back to the 14th century and is an important cultural and historical landmark. Visitors to Kahanu Garden can explore lush landscapes, see a variety of tropical plants, and learn about the significance of the heiau and Hawaiian cultural heritage. The garden also features stunning views of the Pacific Ocean and the Hana coastline, making it a peaceful and educational experience for visitors.

Opening Hours:

- Monday to Friday: 9:00 AM – 3:00 PM
- Closed on weekends and public holidays

Address: 650 Ulaino Road, Hana, HI 96713

Entry Fee:

- $15 per adult
- $10 for children (6-12 years old)
- Free for children under 6

Insider Tips:

- Wear comfortable walking shoes and bring water.
- Visit in the morning for cooler temperatures and fewer crowds.
- Respect the sacredness of Pi'ilanihale Heiau by not climbing on the structure.
- Guided tours are available and highly recommended for a deeper understanding of the site's cultural significance.

7. Wailua Falls

Wailua Falls, located near the town of Hana on Maui's eastern coast, is one of the most picturesque and accessible waterfalls on the island. This 80-foot waterfall cascades into a beautiful pool surrounded by lush tropical vegetation, making it a popular spot for both locals and tourists. The falls are easily visible from the Hana Highway, offering a perfect photo opportunity without a strenuous hike. For those looking to get closer, a short trail leads to the base of the falls, where you can feel the mist and enjoy the serene atmosphere. The sound of the rushing water and the surrounding greenery create a tranquil setting, ideal for a refreshing dip or a picnic.

- **Opening Hours:** Always open
- **Address:** Hana Highway, Mile Marker 45, Hana, HI 96713

Insider Tips

- Visit early in the morning to avoid crowds and enjoy the falls in a more peaceful setting.
- Wear water shoes if you plan to hike to the base, as the rocks can be slippery.
- Bring a waterproof camera or phone case for capturing close-up shots.
- Pack a snack and water, as there are no facilities nearby.
- Respect the natural environment by not leaving any trash behind and staying on designated paths.

8. Hana Ranch

Hana Ranch is a working cattle ranch located in the tranquil town of Hana, offering visitors a unique glimpse into traditional Hawaiian ranching life. Spanning 3,600 acres, the ranch is dedicated to sustainable agricultural practices and preserving the natural beauty of East Maui.

Visitors can participate in guided tours to learn about the history of the ranch, the local flora and fauna, and the sustainable farming methods employed. One of the highlights is the horseback riding tours, which take guests through lush pastures and provide stunning ocean views. Additionally, the ranch operates a farm-to-table restaurant where guests can savor fresh, locally sourced meals, showcasing the produce grown on the ranch.

- **Opening Hours**: Daily from 9:00 AM to 5:00 PM
- **Address:** 5670 Hana Highway, Hana, HI 96713
- **Entry Fee**: Varies by activity; guided tours and horseback riding require reservations and have associated fees.

Insider Tips:

- Reservations: Book tours and horseback rides in advance to secure your spot.
- Dress Appropriately: Wear comfortable clothing and closed-toe shoes for tours and rides.
- Local Products: Visit the ranch's store to purchase fresh produce and other local products.
- Dining: Don't miss dining at the ranch's restaurant for a true farm-to-table experience.

Dining

1 Huli Huli Chicken: Huli Huli Chicken offers mouthwatering barbecue chicken, a local specialty, near Koki Beach in Hana. Known for its smoky flavor and tender meat, it's a perfect choice for a casual meal or picnic. The food truck setting adds to the laid-back atmosphere, making it a favorite among locals and visitors alike.

- **Location:** Near Koki Beach, Hana, Maui
- **Opening:** Daily, timings vary

2. Hana Ranch Restaurant: Enjoy farm-to-table dining at Hana Ranch Restaurant, emphasizing local ingredients and flavors. Located in the heart of Hana, it offers a relaxed atmosphere with indoor and outdoor seating. Highlights include fresh seafood, grilled meats, and seasonal produce from the ranch.

- **Location:** Hana Highway, Hana, HI 96713
- **Opening:** Daily, Lunch 11:00 AM - 2:00 PM, Dinner 5:30 PM - 8:30 PM
- **Phone Number:** (808) 270-5280

3. Braddah Hutts BBQ Grill: Known for its hearty portions of barbecue and Hawaiian dishes, Braddah Hutts BBQ Grill is a favorite among locals and visitors alike in Hana. This food truck offers delicious barbecue chicken, ribs, and pulled pork, served with traditional sides like macaroni salad and rice. The casual outdoor dining experience complements its flavorful menu, making it a perfect stop after a day of exploring Hana's attractions.

- **Location:** Near Koki Beach, Hana, Maui
- **Opening Hours:** Daily, 11:00 AM - 5:00 PM
- **Phone Number:** (808) 248-7829

4. Thai Food by Pranee: Thai Food by Pranee is a popular spot in Hana, known for its authentic Thai cuisine prepared with fresh, locally sourced ingredients. The menu includes favorites like Pad Thai, green curry, and fresh spring rolls, all bursting with flavor. The casual, outdoor setting adds to the dining experience, making it a must-visit for those exploring Hana.

- **Location:** 5050 Uakea Rd, Hana, HI 96713
- **Opening Hours:** Monday to Friday, 10:00 AM - 4:00 PM
- **Phone Number:** (808) 419-1533

Haleakala National Park

Haleakala National Park, located on the island of Maui, is a vast and diverse natural wonder encompassing over 33,000 acres of wilderness. The park is divided into two distinct sections: the Summit District and the Kipahulu District, each offering unique landscapes, ecosystems, and experiences. It is renowned for its dormant volcano, stunning sunrises, unique flora and fauna, and rich cultural history.

1. Summit District

The Summit District is located in the central part of the park and is accessible via Haleakala Highway (Route 378). This area is famous for the Haleakala Crater, which offers otherworldly landscapes and panoramic views.

Key Attractions and Activities:

Haleakala Visitor Center

Provides educational exhibits, park information, and interpretive programs.

Location: Near the summit at an elevation of 9,740 feet.

Activities: Learn about the park's geology, ecology, and cultural history. Rangers offer guided talks and answer questions.

Sunrise at Haleakala

The summit provides a vantage point above the clouds, offering breathtaking views of the sunrise over the volcanic landscape.

Experience: Watching the sunrise from the summit of Haleakala is a popular and awe-inspiring experience.

Tips: Arrive early to secure a spot, dress warmly (temperatures can be very cold), and make a reservation through the National Park Service website.

Haleakala Crater

A massive depression 7 miles across, 2 miles wide, and nearly 2,600 feet deep.

Activities: Explore the crater via hiking trails that traverse its unique terrain, including cinder cones, lava fields, and rare plant species.

Notable Trails:

Sliding Sands Trail (Keonehe'ehe'e Trail): A challenging 11-mile round trip hike that descends into the crater, offering stunning views of the volcanic landscape.

Halemau'u Trail: A shorter hike that provides access to the crater floor and connects with other trails for longer hikes.

Pu'u'ula'ula (Red Hill)

Offers 360-degree views of the island, the Pacific Ocean, and on clear days, neighboring islands.

Location: The highest point in the park at 10,023 feet.

Activities: Enjoy the panoramic vistas and take in the beauty of the surrounding landscape.

Stargazing

Join a ranger-led astronomy program or bring your telescope to observe the night sky.

Experience: The high elevation and lack of light pollution make Haleakala an ideal spot for stargazing.

2. Kipahulu District

The Kipahulu District is located on the southeastern coast of Maui, accessible via the Hana Highway. This area is known for its lush rainforests, waterfalls, and cultural sites.

Key Attractions and Activities:

Kipahulu Visitor Center

Offers exhibits on the natural and cultural history of the area and provides information on trails and activities.

Location: Near the park entrance in the Kipahulu District.

Activities: Participate in ranger-led programs and learn about the district's unique ecosystem and cultural heritage.

Pipiwai Trail

A 4-mile round trip hike through a diverse and scenic landscape.

Highlights:

Bamboo Forest: Walk through a serene bamboo forest with towering stalks and the sound of rustling leaves.

Waimoku Falls: The trail culminates at a stunning 400-foot waterfall, providing a picturesque and refreshing destination.

Seven Sacred Pools (Ohe'o Gulch)

A series of tiered pools and waterfalls fed by freshwater streams.

Activities: Swim in the pools (if conditions allow), explore the area on foot, and enjoy the scenic beauty of the lush surroundings.

Safety Tips: Check for current conditions and closures, as swimming can be dangerous during heavy rains or flash floods.

Coastal Trails

Trails that offer scenic views of the rugged coastline and ocean.

Activities: Hike along the coast, explore tide pools, and observe marine life and seabirds.

Flora and Fauna

Haleakala National Park is home to a variety of unique plant and animal species, many of which are endemic to Hawaii.

Flora:

Silversword (Argyroxiphium sandwicense): A rare and striking plant found only on the slopes of Haleakala. It blooms once in its lifetime, producing a tall stalk of flowers.

Hawaiian Lobelioids: A diverse group of plants with unique adaptations to the volcanic environment.

Fauna:

Nene (Hawaiian Goose): The state bird of Hawaii, found in the park's high-elevation areas.

Hawaiian Petrel (Ua'u): An endangered seabird that nests in the park's volcanic craters.

Cultural History

Haleakala has significant cultural and historical importance to Native Hawaiians. The park contains numerous archaeological sites, including ancient trails, heiau (temples), and agricultural terraces.

Key Cultural Sites:

Kipahulu Valley: An area rich in cultural heritage, with ancient taro fields and traditional Hawaiian practices still in use.

Haleakala Summit: Considered sacred by Native Hawaiians, with historical significance in Hawaiian cosmology and mythology.

Practical Information

Entrance Fees: The park charges an entrance fee, which supports maintenance and conservation efforts. Annual passes are available for frequent visitors.

Visitor Centers: Both districts have visitor centers that provide information, maps, and educational exhibits.

Weather: Conditions can vary greatly within the park. Be prepared for cold temperatures at the summit and warm, humid conditions in the Kipahulu District.

Safety: Stay on marked trails, carry sufficient water, and be aware of rapidly changing weather conditions.

Waterfalls and Natural Wonders

1. Wailua Falls:

Wailua Falls is a breathtaking 80-foot waterfall located near Hana in East Maui. It is one of the most accessible and picturesque waterfalls on the island, often considered a must-see for visitors traveling along the Hana Highway.

The falls cascade into a beautiful pool below, surrounded by lush tropical vegetation, creating a perfect spot for photography and nature appreciation. The waterfall is easily visible from the road, making it an ideal quick stop for travelers. For those looking to get closer, a short hike down a well-trodden path provides a more immersive experience.

- **Address:** Hana Highway, Mile Marker #45, Hana, HI 96713
- **Opening Hours:** Open 24 hours

Insider Tips:

- Best Time to Visit: Early morning or late afternoon to avoid crowds and enjoy the falls in softer light.
- Safety: The path to the base can be slippery; wear sturdy footwear and be cautious.
- Photography: Bring a waterproof camera or protective gear for stunning shots from the pool area.
- Swimming: While the pool is inviting, always check conditions as water levels can change rapidly.

2. Puohokamoa Falls:

Puohokamoa Falls is one of the hidden gems along the Hana Highway, offering visitors a serene and picturesque waterfall experience in East Maui.

This stunning waterfall is divided into two sections: the Upper Puohokamoa Falls and the Lower Puohokamoa Falls. The Upper Falls is more accessible and features a short, easy hike leading to a viewing area where you can admire the 30-foot cascade plunging into a serene pool. The Lower Falls, while more challenging to reach, rewards adventurous hikers with a more secluded and equally beautiful 200-foot drop into a lush, tropical ravine. Surrounded by vibrant greenery and tropical flora, Puohokamoa Falls provides a perfect backdrop for nature photography and a peaceful escape from the more crowded attractions along the Hana Highway. The area around the falls is rich in native Hawaiian plants and wildlife, making it a great spot for nature enthusiasts.

- **Address:** Mile Marker 11 on Hana Highway (Route 360), Haiku, HI 96708
- **Opening Hours:** Open 24 hours (best visited during daylight)

Insider Tips:

- Parking: Limited roadside parking is available near the trailhead. Arrive early to secure a spot.
- Footwear: Wear sturdy, waterproof shoes as the trail can be muddy and slippery.
- Safety: Exercise caution, especially if attempting to reach the Lower Falls, as the path can be steep and challenging.
- Respect Nature: Stay on marked trails to protect the delicate ecosystem and avoid trespassing on private property.

3. Bamboo Forest:

The Bamboo Forest in East Maui is a mesmerizing natural wonder located along the famous Pipiwai Trail in Haleakala National Park. This enchanting forest features towering bamboo stalks that create a serene and otherworldly atmosphere, with sunlight filtering through the dense canopy, casting a beautiful glow. The gentle rustling of the bamboo in the breeze adds to the tranquility of the environment. The trail through the forest is well-maintained and easy to follow, making it accessible for hikers of various skill levels. As you walk through this magical forest, you'll encounter several scenic spots, including cascading waterfalls and charming streams. The highlight is the Waimoku Falls, a 400-foot waterfall that marks the end of the trail and offers a stunning reward for your efforts.

- **Address:** Pipiwai Trail, Haleakala National Park, Kipahulu District, Maui, HI
- **Opening Hours:** Daily from 9:00 AM to 5:00 PM
- **Entry Fee:** $30 per vehicle for a 3-day pass to Haleakala National Park

Insider Tips:

- Wear sturdy shoes as the trail can be muddy and slippery.
- Bring plenty of water and snacks, as the hike can take a few hours.
- Start early to avoid crowds and enjoy the serene environment.
- Don't forget your camera to capture the breathtaking scenery.

Cultural and Historical Sites

1. Ke'anae Peninsula:

Ke'anae Peninsula is a scenic and culturally rich area on Maui's northeastern coast, renowned for its rugged lava rock coastline, taro fields, and historical significance. This small Hawaiian village offers a glimpse into traditional Hawaiian life and agricultural practices. The peninsula was formed by an ancient lava flow, creating a unique and dramatic landscape. Visitors can explore the lush taro fields, which have been cultivated for centuries, and learn about their importance in Hawaiian culture. The peninsula also features a historic stone church, Ke'anae Congregational Church, built in 1856. The picturesque setting, with waves crashing against the black lava rocks, makes it a popular spot for photography and relaxation.

- **Address:** Ke'anae Rd, Haiku, HI 96708
- **Opening Hours:** Open 24 hours

Insider Tips:

- Best Time to Visit: Early morning or late afternoon for fewer crowds and softer lighting for photography.
- Facilities: There are no facilities, so plan accordingly and bring snacks and water.
- Safety: The coastline can be slippery and dangerous. Exercise caution and avoid swimming due to strong currents.
- Local Treats: Don't miss Aunty Sandy's Banana Bread, a local favorite available at a nearby stand.

2. Kaumahina State Wayside Park:

Kaumahina State Wayside Park is a scenic stop along the Hana Highway, offering stunning views and a peaceful respite amid lush tropical foliage. This 7.8-acre park is nestled on Maui's northeastern coast and provides visitors with panoramic vistas of the rugged coastline, including the Ke'anae Peninsula and the vast Pacific Ocean.

It's a perfect spot for a picnic, with several tables set amidst native Hawaiian plants and towering trees. The park is also rich in cultural significance, serving as a reminder of the area's historical importance to native Hawaiians. The name "Kaumahina" means "the moonlit place," reflecting the park's tranquil and reflective ambiance. Informative plaques around the park provide insights into the local flora and fauna, as well as the cultural and historical context of the area. Hikers can enjoy a short trail that winds through the lush landscape, offering opportunities to spot native birds and plants. The park's clean restrooms and ample parking make it a convenient and comfortable stop for those traveling the famous Road to Hana.

- **Address:** Hana Highway, Haiku, HI 96708
- **Opening Hours:** Daily, 7:00 AM – 6:00 PM

Insider Tips:

- Arrive early to avoid crowds and secure a good picnic spot.
- Bring mosquito repellent, as the park can be buggy.
- Take your time to read the informational plaques for a deeper appreciation of the area's history and ecology.

Outdoor Activities

1. Swimming and Snorkeling:

Swimming and snorkeling in East Maui offer a unique opportunity to explore the island's vibrant marine life and picturesque coastal scenery. The crystal-clear waters, diverse coral reefs, and abundant sea life make it a paradise for water enthusiasts. The region's serene and less crowded beaches provide a tranquil setting for both beginners and experienced snorkelers. While exploring East Maui's waters, you can encounter colorful fish, sea turtles, and occasionally dolphins. Always be mindful of ocean conditions and respect the delicate marine environment to ensure a safe and enjoyable experience.

Top Spots:

- **Hamoa Beach:** Known for its beautiful crescent shape and clear waters, perfect for swimming and snorkeling.
- **Waianapanapa State Park:** Offers a unique black sand beach and crystal-clear waters with fascinating underwater rock formations.
- **Koki Beach:** A stunning beach with vibrant red sand and calm waters ideal for snorkeling, especially near the rocky outcrops.
- **Hana Bay:** Provides sheltered waters, making it an excellent spot for beginner snorkelers and swimmers.

2. Hiking and Exploring:

East Maui offers a paradise for hikers and explorers, with its lush rainforests, dramatic waterfalls, and breathtaking coastal views. The diverse landscapes provide trails for all levels of hikers, from easy walks to challenging treks. The Road to Hana is a gateway to many of these trails, each offering unique experiences. Hiking in East Maui allows you to immerse yourself in the island's natural beauty, discover hidden gems, and experience the serenity of untouched nature. Many trails lead to stunning viewpoints, cascading waterfalls, and vibrant botanical gardens, making it a perfect activity for nature enthusiasts and adventure seekers alike.

Top Spots for Hiking

A. Pipiwai Trail

The Pipiwai Trail is one of the top hiking spots in East Maui, located within Haleakala National Park near the Seven Sacred Pools (Ohe'o Gulch). This 4-mile round trip trail takes hikers through lush rainforest, towering bamboo forests, and past several stunning waterfalls, including the 200-foot Makahiku Falls and the breathtaking 400-foot Waimoku Falls. The trail is well-maintained and offers several scenic viewpoints, including the iconic banyan tree.

Wooden boardwalks through the bamboo forest enhance the hiking experience, creating an otherworldly atmosphere. The Pipiwai Trail is perfect for nature enthusiasts looking to experience Maui's diverse landscapes and tranquil beauty.

- **Distance:** 4 miles round trip
- **Duration:** 2-3 hours
- **Difficulty:** Moderate

B. Wai'anapanapa State Park

Wai'anapanapa State Park is a must-visit destination in East Maui, renowned for its striking black sand beach, dramatic sea cliffs, and lush tropical landscape. The park offers a variety of hiking trails that lead visitors through scenic coastal paths, past ancient Hawaiian burial sites, and along lava rock formations. Key attractions include the freshwater caves, the natural stone arch, and the blowhole. The park also features native vegetation and provides opportunities for bird-watching. With its breathtaking views and cultural significance, Wai'anapanapa State Park offers a unique and memorable hiking experience.

- **Distance:** Varies by trail, with the most popular trail approximately 2 miles round trip.
- **Duration:** Around 1-2 hours.
- **Difficulty:** Easy to moderate, with some uneven terrain and rocky paths.

C. Twin Falls

Twin Falls, located along the Hana Highway, is one of the most accessible and popular hiking spots in East Maui. This destination features a series of picturesque waterfalls and natural pools, making it a perfect spot for swimming and photography. The hike takes you through a lush rainforest, offering views of tropical plants and vibrant flowers. There are multiple falls to explore, including the main Twin Falls, which is ideal for a refreshing dip. The trail is well-marked, and local vendors often sell fresh fruit and smoothies near the entrance, adding to the experience.

- **Distance:** 1.8 miles round trip
- **Duration:** Approximately 1-2 hours
- **Difficulty:** Easy to moderate

D. Kahanu Garden

Kahanu Garden, part of the National Tropical Botanical Garden network, is a hidden gem in East Maui, renowned for its lush landscapes and cultural significance. The garden is home to the largest ancient Hawaiian temple (heiau) in Hawaii, Pi'ilanihale Heiau. Visitors can explore a variety of tropical plants, including rare and endangered species while learning about traditional Hawaiian agriculture and culture. The garden's serene pathways offer a tranquil hiking experience, with stunning views of the coastline and the opportunity to immerse in the natural beauty and history of the area. This spot provides a perfect blend of nature, culture, and scenic beauty, making it a must-visit for hikers.

- **Distance:** 1-2 miles (various paths)
- **Duration:** 1-2 hours
- **Difficulty:** Easy

E. Haleakala National Park (Kipahulu District)

Located in East Maui, the Kipahulu District of Haleakala National Park is renowned for its lush landscapes, cascading waterfalls, and scenic hiking trails. One of the highlights is the Pipiwai Trail, which leads hikers through a lush bamboo forest and past several impressive waterfalls, including the stunning 400-foot Waimoku Falls. The trail offers breathtaking views of the surrounding rainforest and provides opportunities to explore the unique flora and fauna of the area. Additionally, visitors can enjoy the Ohe'o Gulch, also known as the Seven Sacred Pools, where a series of tiered pools and waterfalls create a serene and picturesque setting.

- **Distance:** 4 miles round trip
- **Duration:** 2-3 hours
- **Difficulty:** Moderate

Recommended Resorts and Accommodations

1. Travaasa Hana

Travaasa Hana offers a luxurious retreat surrounded by natural beauty in Hana. This resort provides a unique Hawaiian experience with its thatched-roof bungalows, lush gardens, and stunning ocean views. Guests can enjoy activities like yoga, spa treatments, and cultural classes, all designed to immerse visitors in the tranquility of Hana. The resort emphasizes sustainability and traditional Hawaiian practices, making it a perfect spot for relaxation and rejuvenation.

- **Star Rating:** 4.5 stars
- **Phone Number:** +1 808-248-8211

2. Hotel Hana-Maui

Hotel Hana-Maui is a serene hideaway located on the lush coast of Hana. The hotel offers spacious, elegantly appointed suites and cottages with private lanais, allowing guests to take in the breathtaking scenery of tropical gardens and ocean views. The property features a range of amenities including a world-class spa, fine dining options, and a variety of outdoor activities such as hiking and kayaking. It's an ideal destination for those seeking both adventure and relaxation in an unspoiled setting.

- **Star Rating:** 4 stars
- **Phone Number:** +1 808-248-8211

3. Hana Kai Maui

Hana Kai Maui provides a more intimate and home-like atmosphere with its beachfront condos. Each unit is designed with comfort and convenience in mind, featuring full kitchens, private lanais, and stunning views of the ocean or tropical gardens. The property is perfect for longer stays or families seeking a more self-sufficient accommodation option while still enjoying the beauty of Hana. The laid-back vibe and proximity to local attractions make it a favorite among repeat visitors.

- **Star Rating:** 4 stars
- **Phone Number:** +1 808-248-8311

4. Hana-Maui Resort

Hana-Maui Resort is a tranquil escape set in lush tropical gardens with breathtaking views of the Pacific Ocean. The resort's accommodations include elegantly furnished suites and private cottages, each designed to reflect the natural beauty of the surrounding landscape. Guests can enjoy fine dining at the resort's restaurant, relax at the spa, or explore nearby beaches and waterfalls. The focus on personalized service and local Hawaiian culture enhances the overall guest experience.

- **Star Rating:** 4 stars
- **Phone Number:** +1 808-248-8211

5. Kailani Suite

The Kailani Suite offers a charming and private retreat for those seeking a home-away-from-home experience in East Maui. This vacation rental features a spacious suite with modern amenities, a fully equipped kitchen, and panoramic views of the ocean and lush greenery. The property's serene setting and proximity to local attractions like Hana's famous beaches and waterfalls make it an excellent choice for a relaxing getaway. Guests can enjoy a peaceful environment while still being close to Hana's attractions.

- **Star Rating:** 4 stars
- **Phone Number:** +1 808-248-8322

6. The Plantation House by the Sea

The Plantation House by the Sea is a boutique accommodation offering a unique blend of luxury and authenticity. This property features elegantly designed rooms and suites with ocean views, private lanais, and direct access to nearby beaches. Guests can enjoy personalized service, gourmet breakfast options, and a variety of on-site activities. The property's focus on integrating local Hawaiian culture and traditions into the guest experience provides a memorable and enriching stay.

- **Star Rating:** 4.5 stars
- **Phone Number:** +1 808-248-8215

7. Haleakala Views

Haleakala Views provides a serene and picturesque setting for travelers seeking a peaceful retreat in East Maui. This vacation rental offers spacious accommodations with stunning views of Haleakala Volcano and the surrounding landscape. The property is equipped with modern amenities, including a fully equipped kitchen and private outdoor spaces. Its location allows easy access to hiking trails and local attractions, making it a great base for exploring East Maui's natural beauty.

- **Star Rating:** 4 stars
- **Phone Number:** +1 808-248-8312

Chapter 12: Cultural and Historical Experiences

Museums and Historical Sites in Maui

Maui is rich in history and culture, offering visitors a variety of museums and historical sites that provide insight into the island's past. Here are some of the most notable places to explore:

Bailey House Museum (Hale Hō'ike'ike)

The Bailey House Museum, also known as Hale Ho'ike'ike, is located in Wailuku and is operated by the Maui Historical Society. The museum is housed in a historic mission home built in 1833 and offers a comprehensive collection of Hawaiian artifacts, including pre-contact tools, weapons, and traditional crafts. The museum also features the work of Edward Bailey, an artist and missionary who lived in the home, with his paintings depicting 19th-century Hawaiian landscapes and life. The lush grounds of the museum are home to native Hawaiian plants and offer beautiful views of the Iao Valley. This site provides an in-depth look at Maui's history, from the missionary period to the early days of the Hawaiian Kingdom.

- **Opening Hours:** Monday to Saturday, 10:00 AM - 4:00 PM
- **Address:** 2375 Main St, Wailuku, HI 96793
- **How to Get There:** Located in Wailuku, the museum is easily accessible by car with parking available on-site.
- **Admission Fee:** $10 for adults, $8 for seniors, $6 for students, free for children under 6.

- **Insider Tip:** Take a guided tour to gain deeper insights into the exhibits and the history of the building.

Alexander & Baldwin Sugar Museum

The Alexander & Baldwin Sugar Museum, located near the historic sugar mill in Puunene, offers a comprehensive history of Maui's sugar industry, which was once the backbone of the island's economy. The museum is housed in the former residence of the plantation supervisor and features exhibits on the plantation lifestyle, the process of sugar production, and the impact of the sugar industry on Maui's cultural and economic development. Artifacts include plantation tools, historic photographs, and personal stories from plantation workers. The museum provides insight into the diverse immigrant communities that came to Maui to work in the sugar fields, shaping the island's multicultural identity.

- **Opening Hours:** Monday to Saturday, 10:00 AM - 2:00 PM
- **Address:** 3957 Hansen Road, Puunene, HI 96784
- **How to Get There:** The museum is located just off Highway 311, making it easy to reach by car with ample parking available.
- **Admission Fee**: $7 for adults, $5 for seniors, $2 for children (6-16), free for children under 6.

- **Insider Tip:** Don't miss the outdoor exhibits, which include large-scale equipment used in sugar production.

Lahaina Heritage Museum

The Lahaina Heritage Museum, located in the Old Lahaina Courthouse, offers a fascinating journey through Maui's history. The museum covers various aspects of Lahaina's past, including its time as the capital of the Hawaiian Kingdom, its role as a major whaling port, and its cultural significance to Native Hawaiians. Exhibits feature photographs, artifacts, and multimedia presentations that bring to life the stories of the people and events that shaped Lahaina. The museum is situated in the heart of Lahaina's historic district, making it a convenient stop for those exploring the town's many historical landmarks.

- **Opening Hours:** Daily, 9:00 AM - 5:00 PM
- **Address:** 648 Wharf St, Lahaina, HI 96761
- **How to Get There:** Centrally located in Lahaina, the museum is accessible by foot, car, or the Maui Bus with parking available nearby.
- **Insider Tip:** Combine your visit with a self-guided walking tour of historic Lahaina to see nearby sites like the Baldwin Home and the Banyan Tree.

Haleakala National Park (Kipahulu District)

The Kipahulu District of Haleakala National Park is not only a top hiking destination but also a site rich in cultural history. It features the historic Pipiwai Trail leading to Waimoku Falls and the Ohe'o Gulch (Seven Sacred Pools). The area showcases ancient Hawaiian agricultural practices and archaeological sites. Interpretive exhibits at the visitor center provide insights into the lives of the early Hawaiians who cultivated taro and lived in the Kipahulu area.

- **Opening Hours:** Daily, 9:00 AM - 5:00 PM (Kipahulu Visitor Center)
- **Address:** Hana Hwy, Kipahulu, HI 96713
- **How to Get There:** Accessible via Hana Highway, about 12 miles past Hana town; a long but scenic drive.
- **Admission Fee:** $30 per vehicle for a 3-day pass (includes Summit District).
- **Insider Tip:** Arrive early to avoid crowds and enjoy the pools at Ohe'o Gulch before they get busy.

Hale Pa'i Printing Museum

Hale Pa'i, meaning "House of Printing," is a small but historically significant museum located at Lahainaluna High School, the oldest high school west of the Rockies, founded in 1831. The museum is housed in the building where the first printing press in Hawaii was established in 1834.

It was here that the first Hawaiian language newspaper, "Ka Lama Hawaii," was printed. The museum displays the original printing press, early Hawaiian publications, and exhibits about the history of printing in Hawaii. It's an intriguing stop for those interested in Hawaiian history, language, and education.

Location: Lahainaluna High School, Lahaina

Whalers Village Museum

Located in the popular Whalers Village shopping center in Ka'anapali, the Whalers Village Museum offers an in-depth look at the whaling era that played a crucial role in Maui's history during the 19th century. The museum's exhibits include whale bones, harpoons, and other whaling equipment, as well as interactive displays that detail the life of whalers and the impact of the whaling industry on Lahaina. Visitors can also learn about the biology and conservation of whales, which continue to be a significant part of Maui's natural environment. The museum is an educational stop that provides context for understanding the island's maritime history.

- **Opening Hours:** Daily, 10:00 AM - 6:00 PM
- **Address:** 2435 Kaanapali Parkway, Lahaina, HI 96761
- **How to Get There:** Located within the Whalers Village shopping complex, easily accessible by car with parking available.
- **Insider Tip:** After visiting the museum, take a stroll along Kaanapali Beach or enjoy dining at one of the beachfront restaurants.

Wo Hing Museum and Cookhouse

The Wo Hing Museum & Cookhouse in Lahaina celebrates the contributions of Chinese immigrants to Maui's history. The museum is part of the Wo Hing Society, a Chinese fraternal organization, and is housed in a historic building that was once a social center for the Chinese community. Exhibits include photographs, artifacts, and personal stories that highlight the role of Chinese immigrants in the development of Lahaina, particularly in agriculture and trade. The adjacent cookhouse, once used for communal meals, now hosts cooking demonstrations and offers a glimpse into traditional Chinese cuisine. The museum is a testament to Maui's diverse cultural heritage and the contributions of its immigrant communities.

- **Opening Hours:** Tuesday to Saturday, 10:00 AM - 4:00 PM
- **Address:** 858 Front St, Lahaina, HI 96761
- **How to Get There:** Centrally located on Front Street, easily accessible by foot, car, or the Maui Bus with parking available nearby.
- **Admission Fee:** $7 for adults, $5 for seniors, $4 for children (7-12), free for children under 7.
- **Insider Tip:** Visit during Chinese New Year for special celebrations and cultural demonstrations.

Baldwin Home Museum

The Baldwin Home Museum is the oldest standing house on Maui, built in the early 1830s by Reverend Dwight Baldwin, a missionary who played a significant role in the community. The home served as both a residence and a medical clinic for the local population. Today, the museum offers a glimpse into 19th-century life in Lahaina, showcasing period furniture, artifacts, and medical instruments. Guided tours are available, providing detailed information about the Baldwin family and the broader history of the area. The museum is centrally located in Lahaina, making it easily accessible for visitors exploring the historic town.

- **Opening Hours:** Monday to Saturday, 10:00 AM - 4:00 PM
- **Address:** 120 Dickenson St, Lahaina, HI 96761
- **How to Get There:** Located in Lahaina's historic district, accessible by foot, car, or the Maui Bus with parking available nearby.
- **Admission Fee:** $7 for adults, $5 for seniors, $4 for children (7-12), free for children under 7.
- **Insider Tip:** Join a guided tour to learn more detailed stories about the Baldwin family and their impact on Maui.

Hana Cultural Center & Museum

The Hana Cultural Center & Museum offers a unique perspective on the history and culture of East Maui. Located in the remote town of Hana, the museum features exhibits on traditional Hawaiian life, including tools, clothing, and artifacts from the area's early inhabitants. The museum also has a replica of a Hawaiian hale (house) and a courthouse built in the early 1900s. The Hana Cultural Center provides a more intimate and localized view of Hawaiian culture, focusing on the traditions and history specific to the Hana region. It's an essential stop for those exploring the scenic and culturally rich Hana Coast.

Location: Hana

Kahanu Garden and Pi'ilanihale Heiau

Kahanu Garden, part of the National Tropical Botanical Garden network, is home to the Pi'ilanihale Heiau, the largest ancient temple in Hawaii. Located near Hana, the garden features native Hawaiian plants and cultural exhibits. The Pi'ilanihale Heiau, a National Historic Landmark, is an impressive lava-rock structure that offers insights into ancient Hawaiian religious practices and social organization. Visitors can take self-guided tours to explore the garden and learn about traditional Hawaiian agriculture and botany.

- **Opening Hours:** Monday to Friday, 10:00 AM - 2:00 PM
- **Address:** 650 Ulaino Rd, Hana, HI 96713
- **How to Get There:** Accessible via Hana Highway, with signs leading to the garden; a scenic drive from central Maui.
- **Admission Fee:** $10 for adults, free for children under 12.
- **Insider Tip:** Wear comfortable shoes and bring water as the garden covers a large area with uneven terrain.

Maui Ocean Center

The Maui Ocean Center in Maalaea is Hawaii's largest tropical aquarium, showcasing marine life native to Hawaii and the Pacific Ocean. Exhibits feature a vast array of sea creatures, including sharks, rays, turtles, and colorful reef fish. Highlights include a 750,000-gallon Open Ocean tank with a walk-through acrylic tunnel, interactive touch pools, and daily educational programs. The center's mission focuses on marine conservation and environmental stewardship, offering visitors an educational and immersive experience of Hawaii's diverse aquatic ecosystems.

- **Opening Hours:** Daily, 9:00 AM - 5:00 PM
- **Address:** 192 Maalaea Rd, Wailuku, HI 96793
- **How to Get There:** Located in Maalaea Harbor, accessible by car with ample parking available.
- **Admission Fee:** $34.95 for adults, $24.95 for children (4-12), discounts available for seniors and military.
- **Insider Tip:** Plan your visit around feeding times and educational presentations for a deeper understanding of marine life.

Haleakala National Park (Summit District)

The Summit District of Haleakala National Park encompasses the volcanic summit of Haleakala, Maui's highest peak. The park features otherworldly landscapes, unique flora and fauna, and stunning views of the crater and surrounding islands. Visitors can drive to the summit for sunrise or sunset views, hike through volcanic terrain, and explore scenic trails such as the Sliding Sands Trail and Halemauu Trail. The park's Visitor Center offers educational exhibits on geology, ecology, and Hawaiian culture, providing insights into Haleakala's natural history and significance.

- **Opening Hours:** Daily, 24 hours (Summit District Visitor Center hours vary)
- **Address:** Haleakala National Park, Kula, HI 96790
- **How to Get There:** Accessible via Haleakala Highway (Highway 378) from central Maui; approximately a 1.5-hour drive from Kahului.
- **Admission Fee:** $30 per vehicle for a 3-day pass (includes Kipahulu District).
- **Insider Tip:** Dress warmly for sunrise or sunset visits, as temperatures at the summit can be significantly colder than at sea level.

Whale Education Center (Pacific Whale Foundation)

The Whale Education Center, operated by the Pacific Whale Foundation in Maalaea, offers educational exhibits and interactive displays focused on marine conservation and whale research. Visitors can learn about humpback whales through multimedia presentations, life-size models, and hands-on activities. The center provides insights into whale behavior, migration patterns, and conservation efforts to protect these majestic creatures. Seasonally, visitors can join whale-watching tours departing from nearby Maalaea Harbor to observe humpback whales in their natural habitat, further enhancing the educational experience.

- **Opening Hours:** Monday to Sunday, 9:00 AM - 4:00 PM
- **Address:** 300 Maalaea Rd, Maalaea, HI 96793
- **How to Get There:** Located in Maalaea Harbor, accessible by car with parking available nearby.
- **Insider Tip:** Visit during whale season (December to April) for the best chance to see humpback whales and participate in whale-watching tours organized by the Pacific Whale Foundation.

Makawao History Museum

The Makawao History Museum in Maui offers a fascinating glimpse into the region's plantation and cowboy (paniolo) history. Located in the charming upcountry town of Makawao, the museum is housed in a historic building that once served as a library and courthouse.

Exhibits highlight the area's evolution from its agricultural roots to becoming a hub for paniolo culture, showcasing artifacts, photographs, and displays that depict life in upcountry Maui over the decades. Visitors can explore the impact of plantation life on the community and learn about the traditions and lifestyles of Maui's paniolo.

- **Opening Hours:** The museum is typically open from Tuesday to Saturday, 10:00 AM to 4:00 PM.
- **Address:** 3643 Baldwin Ave, Makawao, HI 96768.
- **How to Get There:** Makawao is about a 20-minute drive from Kahului Airport. From Kahului, take Route 36 (Hana Highway) and follow signs to Makawao town center.
- **Admission Fee:** Admission is usually affordable, often around $5 per person.
- **Insider Tips:** Check for special events or guided tours for deeper insights into the area's history. Combine your visit with exploring Makawao town's boutiques, galleries, and cafes, known for their local arts and crafts. Parking can be limited; consider visiting earlier in the day for easier access.

Waiola Church and Waiola Cemetery

Waiola Church and Waiola Cemetery, located in Lahaina, Maui, are significant historical sites dating back to 1823. The church, originally built of lava rock and coral mortar, is one of the oldest surviving churches in Hawaii and holds deep cultural and religious importance. It was associated with early missionary efforts and has undergone several renovations while preserving its historic charm.

Adjacent to the church is the Waiola Cemetery, where many prominent figures from Maui's history are buried, offering insights into the island's past through its grave markers and monuments.

- **Opening Hours:** The church grounds are typically open daily during daylight hours.
- **Address:** Waiola Church and Cemetery, 535 Waine'e Street, Lahaina, HI 96761.
- **How to Get There:** Located in Lahaina town, Waiola Church is easily accessible by car or on foot from most parts of Lahaina. Parking is available nearby.
- **Insider Tips:** Visit early in the morning or late afternoon for quieter moments to appreciate the historical ambiance. The church often hosts community events and occasional services, providing opportunities to experience local culture firsthand.

Traditional Hawaiian Luaus

Attending a traditional Hawaiian luau is one of the best ways to experience the rich cultural heritage of Hawaii. A luau is a festive gathering that typically includes a feast, live music, hula dancing, and storytelling. In Maui, several venues offer authentic luaus that provide a deep dive into Hawaiian traditions. Here's a look at some of the most popular luaus on the island:

Old Lahaina Lua – Lahaina

The Old Lahaina Luau is widely regarded as one of the most authentic luaus in Hawaii. Situated on the beachfront in Lahaina, this luau emphasizes traditional Hawaiian culture, with an emphasis on historical accuracy. Guests are welcomed with a fresh flower lei and can explore the beautifully landscaped grounds before the feast begins. The imu ceremony, where the pig is unearthed from the underground oven, is a highlight of the evening. The menu features traditional Hawaiian dishes, including kalua pig, poi, poke, and haupia. The evening concludes with a hula performance that traces the history of Hawaii from ancient times to the present day. The Old Lahaina Luau is known for its intimate atmosphere, attention to detail, and cultural integrity.

Feast at Lele – Lahaina

The Feast at Lele offers a more upscale and intimate luau experience, located at the same beachfront venue as the Old Lahaina Luau but with a different approach. Instead of a buffet, the Feast at Lele provides a sit-down, multi-course dinner that highlights the cuisines of Hawaii, Tahiti, Samoa, and Aotearoa (New Zealand). Each course is paired with a performance from the corresponding Polynesian culture, making the evening a culinary journey through the Pacific. The setting is elegant, with tables set right on the beach, offering stunning views of the sunset. The Feast at Lele is ideal for those looking for a refined and romantic luau experience with a strong emphasis on culinary excellence.

Drums of the Pacific Luau – Hyatt Regency Maui, Kaanapali

The Drums of the Pacific Luau, held at the Hyatt Regency in Kaanapali, is one of Maui's most popular luaus. This high-energy show features not only traditional Hawaiian performances but also dances and music from other Polynesian cultures, including Samoa, Tahiti, and Fiji. The luau begins with the traditional imu ceremony, followed by a lavish buffet that includes both Hawaiian and international dishes. The grand finale of the evening is the Samoan fire knife dance, which is always a crowd favorite. The Drums of the Pacific Luau is perfect for families and those looking for a lively, entertaining evening with a variety of cultural performances.

The Grand Luau at Honua'ula – Grand Wailea Resort, Wailea

The Grand Luau at Honua'ula, located at the luxurious Grand Wailea Resort, offers a dramatic retelling of Maui's history and mythology through song and dance. The show takes guests on a journey back in time to the days of ancient Hawaii, with performances that depict the legends of Maui, the demi-god, and the migrations of the Polynesians across the Pacific. The buffet features traditional Hawaiian dishes as well as local favorites like macadamia nut-crusted mahi-mahi and lilikoi cheesecake. The setting is stunning, with the luau grounds overlooking the ocean, making it an ideal spot for watching the sunset before the show begins. The Grand Luau at Honua'ula is a great choice for those staying in the Wailea area who want to experience a luau with a strong storytelling element.

Wailele Polynesian Luau – The Westin Maui Resort & Spa, Kaanapali

The Wailele Polynesian Luau at The Westin Maui offers a vibrant and interactive luau experience. Set against the backdrop of cascading waterfalls, the luau includes a buffet dinner with a focus on local Hawaiian cuisine, such as kalua pork, ahi poke, and tropical fruits.

The show features traditional Hawaiian hula as well as performances from other Polynesian cultures, culminating in an exhilarating fire knife dance. The Wailele Polynesian Luau is known for its intimate setting and engaging performers who often invite guests to join in the dancing. It's a family-friendly luau that offers a great balance of entertainment and cultural education.

Royal Lahaina Luau – Royal Lahaina Resort, Kaanapali

The Royal Lahaina Luau, located at the Royal Lahaina Resort, is one of Maui's longest-running luaus. The luau grounds are set right on the beach, providing stunning ocean views, especially at sunset. The evening begins with traditional Hawaiian games and crafts, followed by the imu ceremony and a buffet dinner that includes local specialties like kalua pig, teriyaki chicken, and island-style desserts. The show is a journey through Polynesian history, with performances from Hawaii, Tahiti, Samoa, and New Zealand. The Royal Lahaina Luau is a great choice for those staying in the Kaanapali area who want a classic luau experience with a picturesque setting.

Te Au Moana Luau – Wailea Beach Marriott Resort & Spa, Wailea

The Te Au Moana Luau at the Wailea Beach Marriott Resort & Spa offers a blend of traditional Hawaiian hospitality and modern entertainment. The luau's name, meaning "The Ocean Tide," reflects the deep connection between the Hawaiian people and the sea. The evening begins with cultural demonstrations, including lei making and coconut husking, followed by a buffet featuring both traditional Hawaiian and contemporary dishes. The show tells the story of the Polynesians' migration across the Pacific and their settlement in Hawaii, with hula, chants, and a thrilling fire knife dance. The Te Au Moana Luau is ideal for those staying in the Wailea area who want to experience a luau with a strong cultural and historical focus.

Art Galleries and Local Art

Maui boasts a vibrant arts scene, with a range of galleries showcasing local and regional artists. Here are some notable art galleries and places to experience local art on the island:

1. Hui No'eau Visual Arts Center

Hui No'eau Visual Arts Center, nestled in the upcountry town of Makawao, is a key cultural hub on Maui.

The center features a rotating selection of exhibitions showcasing the work of local and regional artists. In addition to gallery exhibits, Hui No'eau offers art classes and workshops for all ages. The historic estate, with its beautiful gardens and charming architecture, adds to the appeal of the center. The gallery's mission is to support and promote the visual arts in Maui, and it is a great place to find unique, locally-made artwork.

- **Location:** 2841 Baldwin Avenue, Makawao
- **Hours:** Monday to Friday, 9:00 AM - 4:00 PM; Saturday, 10:00 AM - 2:00 PM; Closed on Sundays
- **Tip:** Check their website for current exhibitions and special events, as they often host artist talks and community art events.

2. Lahaina Arts Society

Located in the heart of Lahaina, the Lahaina Arts Society showcases a diverse collection of artwork from local Maui artists. The gallery features paintings, sculptures, ceramics, and jewelry, reflecting the island's natural beauty and cultural heritage. The gallery also hosts regular art walks and workshops. It's a wonderful place to find unique souvenirs and gifts that support local artists. The space is vibrant and welcoming, making it an enjoyable stop for art enthusiasts.

- **Location:** 648 Wharf Street, Lahaina
- **Hours:** Daily, 9:00 AM - 5:00 PM
- **Tip:** Visit during the monthly Lahaina Art Night for special exhibitions and artist meet-and-greets.

3. Maui Arts & Cultural Center (MACC)

The Maui Arts & Cultural Center is more than just an art gallery; it's a comprehensive cultural venue that includes exhibition spaces, performance halls, and outdoor areas. The center hosts rotating art exhibitions featuring both local and international artists, as well as performances, concerts, and cultural events. It's a central venue for Maui's artistic and cultural community, providing a broad spectrum of artistic experiences.

- **Location:** 1 Cameron Way, Kahului
- **Hours:** Varies by event; generally open weekdays, 9:00 AM - 5:00 PM
- **Tip:** Check the MACC's calendar for current exhibitions and events to make the most of your visit.

4. The Village Gallery

Situated in the vibrant Kihei area, The Village Gallery is known for its eclectic mix of contemporary and traditional art from Maui artists. The gallery features paintings, prints, and photography, with a focus on pieces that capture the essence of the island. The gallery also hosts artist receptions and special events. It's a great spot to discover emerging local talent and enjoy a range of artistic styles.

- **Location:** 1202 N. Kihei Road, Kihei
- **Hours:** Daily, 10:00 AM - 4:00 PM
- **Tip:** Look out for local artist showcases and gallery events, which are often announced on their website and social media.

5. J. M. A. Studios

J. M. A. Studios is a working art studio and gallery run by artist Janice M. A. The gallery features a selection of Janice's paintings, which often draw inspiration from Maui's landscapes and natural beauty. The studio is located in a serene setting, offering a personal and intimate experience with the artist's work. Appointments are required for visits, making it a unique opportunity to explore art in a more personal setting.

- **Location:** 4080 Lani Rd, Lahaina
- **Hours:** By appointment only
- **Tip:** Contact the studio in advance to schedule a visit and discuss the artwork with the artist.

6. Lena's Art Studio & Gallery

Lena's Art Studio & Gallery is known for its vibrant and colorful artworks, often reflecting the beauty of Maui's landscapes and seascapes. The gallery features paintings, prints, and mixed media works by local artist Lena, whose work is celebrated for its bold use of color and texture. The studio also offers art classes and workshops. It's a charming and welcoming space for art lovers looking to experience local creativity.

- **Location:** 222 Papalaua Street, Lahaina
- **Hours:** Monday to Saturday, 10:00 AM - 5:00 PM; Closed on Sundays
- **Tip:** Visit during the first Saturday of the month for special gallery events and openings.

7. Maui Hands

Maui Hands is a cooperative gallery that features a wide range of handcrafted art and jewelry created by Maui artists. The gallery emphasizes high-quality, locally-made items, including paintings, ceramics, glass, and textiles. It's an excellent place to find unique art pieces and gifts that represent the spirit of Maui. The cooperative nature of the gallery means that you'll often meet the artists themselves, adding a personal touch to your visit.

- **Location:** 1169 Makawao Avenue, Makawao
- **Hours:** Daily, 10:00 AM - 5:00 PM
- **Tip:** Check their website for information on featured artists and special exhibitions.

Hawaiian Music and Dance

Hawaiian Music

Hawaiian music encompasses a range of styles, from ancient chants and traditional hula songs to contemporary genres influenced by jazz, rock, and reggae. Key instruments include the ukulele, slack-key guitar (ki ho'alu), and steel guitar, each contributing to the unique sounds of the islands.

Traditional Hawaiian Music:

Chants (Mele): Ancient chants, known as oli, tell stories of Hawaiian legends, genealogy, and nature. These chants are often performed at ceremonies and cultural events.

Hula Songs: Hula is not just a dance but also a storytelling art form. Hula songs, accompanied by chanting and rhythmic instruments, convey tales of love, nature, and historical events.

Contemporary Hawaiian Music:

Hawaiian Renaissance: In the 1970s, there was a revival of interest in Hawaiian culture, leading to a resurgence in traditional music styles fused with modern influences.

Genres: Contemporary Hawaiian music spans various genres, including Jawaiian (a mix of reggae and Hawaiian music), and folk rock with Hawaiian themes.

Musical Events and Festivals:

Hawaiian Music Concerts: Many resorts and venues host concerts featuring renowned Hawaiian musicians, offering visitors a chance to experience authentic Hawaiian music.

Festivals: Events like the Maui Hawaiian Steel Guitar Festival and the Ukulele Festival showcase local talent and celebrate Hawaiian musical traditions.

Hula Dance

Hula is a traditional Hawaiian dance form that combines foot movement (kaholo and 'ami) with hand gestures (ho'i and 'uwehe) to tell stories through movement and expression.

Types of Hula:

- **Hula Kahiko:** Ancient hula accompanied by chanting and traditional instruments.
- **Hula 'Auana:** Modern hula danced to contemporary music with instruments like the ukulele and guitar.

Significance and Cultural Expression:

Cultural Preservation: Hula plays a vital role in preserving Hawaiian culture, language, and history.

Spiritual Connection: Each movement and gesture in hula carries spiritual significance, connecting dancers and audiences to the natural world and ancestral spirits.

Places to Experience Hula:

Hula Shows: Many resorts and cultural centers host hula performances, providing opportunities for visitors to witness the artistry and beauty of hula.

Hula Workshops: Some venues offer hula workshops where participants can learn basic movements and gain insight into the cultural meanings behind the dance.

Cultural Significance

Hawaiian music and dance are more than entertainment—they serve as vehicles for cultural expression, storytelling, and spiritual connection. They reflect the values, history, and traditions of the Hawaiian people, making them essential elements of Maui's cultural landscape.

Enjoying Hawaiian Music and Dance on Maui

Attend Cultural Events: Check local event listings for concerts, festivals, and hula performances during your visit to Maui.

Visit Cultural Centers: Places like the Maui Arts & Cultural Center often host cultural events featuring Hawaiian music and dance.

Respect Cultural Practices: When attending hula performances or participating in cultural activities, respect cultural protocols and traditions to honor the significance of Hawaiian music and dance.

Traditional Hawaiian Festivals and Events

Maui is home to a variety of local festivals and events that celebrate its rich culture, history, and natural beauty. Here are some of the most popular festivals and events that take place throughout the year:

Maui Film Festival

The Maui Film Festival is a premier event that attracts filmmakers, celebrities, and film enthusiasts from around the world. Held in the luxurious resort area of Wailea, the festival features outdoor screenings under the stars, with the Celestial Cinema being one of the highlights. In addition to film screenings, the event includes panel discussions, filmmaker Q&A sessions, and exclusive parties. The festival focuses on uplifting, inspiring films that reflect the spirit of Maui and its connection to nature and humanity.

- **When:** June
- **Where:** Wailea

Maui Whale Festival

The Maui Whale Festival celebrates the annual return of humpback whales to the waters around Maui. Organized by the Pacific Whale Foundation, the festival includes a variety of events such as whale-watching tours, educational talks, and the popular Parade of Whales. The festival also features an Ocean Awareness Village, where visitors can learn about marine conservation and the importance of protecting the ocean. The festival culminates with the Run & Walk for Whales, a family-friendly event that raises funds for whale research and conservation.

- **When:** February
- **Where:** Kihei

Aloha Festivals Maui

Aloha Festivals is a statewide celebration of Hawaiian culture, and Maui's events are some of the most vibrant. The festival includes a variety of cultural activities, including hula performances, lei-making workshops, and traditional Hawaiian music. The Ho'olaule'a (celebration) in Lahaina is a highlight, featuring food booths, local crafts, and live entertainment. Aloha Festivals is a great opportunity to immerse yourself in Hawaiian traditions and experience the island's warm hospitality.

- **When:** September
- **Where:** Various Locations

Maui Onion Festival

The Maui Onion Festival is a unique event that celebrates the sweet Maui onion, a beloved local ingredient. Held at Whalers Village in Kaanapali, the festival features cooking demonstrations by celebrity chefs, onion-themed contests, and tastings of delicious onion-inspired dishes. The event also includes live music, hula performances, and activities for children. The Maui Onion Festival is a fun and flavorful way to experience one of Maui's most famous agricultural products.

- **When:** May
- **Where:** Whalers Village, Kaanapali

Kapalua Wine & Food Festival

The Kapalua Wine & Food Festival is one of Hawaii's most prestigious culinary events, attracting top chefs, winemakers, and food enthusiasts from around the world. Held in the beautiful resort area of Kapalua, the festival features wine tastings, cooking demonstrations, and gourmet meals prepared by world-renowned chefs.

Attendees can also participate in interactive seminars on wine pairing, mixology, and culinary trends. The festival offers a luxurious and indulgent experience for food and wine lovers.

- **When:** June
- **Where:** Kapalua

East Maui Taro Festival

The East Maui Taro Festival is a cultural celebration dedicated to taro, a staple crop in Hawaiian cuisine. Held in the remote and scenic town of Hana, the festival features a variety of taro-based dishes, cultural demonstrations, and live entertainment. Visitors can learn about the significance of taro in Hawaiian culture, participate in traditional Hawaiian games, and enjoy performances by local musicians and hula dancers. The festival also includes a farmers' market, offering fresh produce and handmade crafts.

- **When:** April
- **Where:** Hana

Maui County Fair

The Maui County Fair is the island's largest community event, attracting thousands of visitors each year. The fair features a variety of attractions, including carnival rides, games, agricultural exhibits, and food booths serving local delicacies. Highlights of the fair include the floral parade, live entertainment on multiple stages, and the popular Baby of the Year contest. The fair is a fun-filled event for families and provides a great opportunity to experience Maui's local culture and community spirit.

- **When:** October
- **Where:** Wailuku

Chinese New Year Celebration

Maui's Chinese New Year Celebration takes place in the historic town of Lahaina and honors the island's Chinese heritage. The event includes a traditional lion dance, firecrackers, cultural performances, and martial arts demonstrations. Visitors can also enjoy Chinese cuisine, calligraphy demonstrations, and children's activities. The celebration is a vibrant and colorful event that offers a unique cultural experience on the island.

- **When:** January or February (dates vary)
- **Where:** Lahaina

Hula O Na Keiki

Hula O Na Keiki is a children's hula competition held at the Ka'anapali Beach Hotel. The event aims to preserve Hawaiian culture by teaching the younger generation the art of hula. Young dancers from across Hawaii and beyond participate in the competition, showcasing their skills in traditional and modern hula. The event also includes Hawaiian arts and crafts, cultural workshops, and live music. It's a wonderful opportunity to witness the beauty of hula and support the preservation of Hawaiian traditions.

- **When:** November
- **Where:** Ka'anapali

Olukai Hoolaulea

The Olukai Hoolaulea is a watersports festival held on Maui's North Shore, celebrating the island's ocean culture. The event includes paddleboard and outrigger canoe races, as well as beach games, cultural demonstrations, and live music. Participants and spectators can enjoy the thrill of competitive racing, as well as the laid-back atmosphere of the beach festival. The event is open to all ages and skill levels, making it a fun and inclusive experience for both locals and visitors.

- **When:** May
- **Where:** North Shore

Cultural Tours and Workshops

Maui offers a variety of cultural tours and workshops that allow visitors to dive deep into the island's rich Hawaiian heritage. These experiences provide an authentic glimpse into Maui's traditions, arts, and history, offering hands-on learning and meaningful connections with local culture.

1. Maui Nei Native Expeditions

Maui Nei Native Expeditions offers immersive cultural walking tours that explore the island's rich history and traditions. The tours are led by Native Hawaiian guides who share stories passed down through generations. One of their most popular tours is the Lahaina Historical Town Tour, which takes you through significant cultural sites, including ancient Hawaiian structures and missionary buildings. The tour also covers the impact of European contact and the Hawaiian monarchy. This is an excellent way to understand the deep historical roots of Maui.

- **Location:** Lahaina, Maui, HI 96761
- **Duration:** 2 hours
- **Contact:** +1 808-661-9494

2. Hawaiian Cultural Classes at The Ritz-Carlton, Kapalua

The Ritz-Carlton, Kapalua, offers a variety of cultural classes led by local cultural advisors. These classes include lei-making, hula dancing, and Hawaiian language lessons. The lei-making class teaches participants how to create traditional Hawaiian leis using fresh flowers and leaves, while the hula dancing class introduces you to the basics of this expressive dance form. The Hawaiian language lessons cover basic phrases and the cultural significance of the Hawaiian language. These classes are designed to give participants a deeper understanding of Hawaiian customs and traditions.

- **Location:** 1 Ritz-Carlton Drive, Kapalua, Maui, HI 96761
- **Duration:** 1-2 hours per class
- **Contact:** +1 808-669-6200

3. Old Lahaina Luau

The Old Lahaina Luau is one of Maui's most renowned cultural experiences, offering an evening of traditional Hawaiian food, music, and hula. The luau is set against the backdrop of a beautiful beachfront, providing a stunning setting as you enjoy an authentic Hawaiian feast. The event begins with cultural demonstrations, including traditional Hawaiian games and crafts, followed by a spectacular hula show that tells the story of Hawaii's history through dance. This luau is a perfect blend of entertainment and cultural education.

- **Location:** 1251 Front St, Lahaina, HI 96761
- **Duration:** 3 hours
- **Contact:** +1 808-667-1998

4. Maui Craft Tours

Maui Craft Tours offers a unique experience combining local food, drink, and crafts. Their Cultural and Culinary Adventure tour takes you to local farms, distilleries, and artisans, where you can sample Maui-grown produce and learn about traditional Hawaiian farming practices. The tour also includes visits to local craft studios, where you can watch artisans create handmade goods inspired by Hawaiian culture. This tour is ideal for those interested in the intersection of culture, food, and art.

- **Location:** Varies by tour
- **Duration:** 6 hours
- **Contact:** +1 808-359-0478

5. Hui No'eau Visual Arts Center

Hui No'eau Visual Arts Center offers workshops and classes in various art forms, including Hawaiian crafts, painting, and sculpture. The center is located in a historic plantation estate and provides a peaceful environment for creativity. One of their popular workshops is the Hawaiian Quilting class, where participants learn the intricate art of making traditional Hawaiian quilts. These quilts often feature bold, symmetrical designs inspired by native plants and are a significant part of Hawaiian heritage.

- **Location:** 2841 Baldwin Ave, Makawao, HI 96768
- **Duration:** 2-3 hours per workshop
- **Contact:** +1 808-572-6560

6. Hawaiian Outrigger Canoe and Cultural Experience

This tour offers an authentic Hawaiian paddling experience aboard a traditional outrigger canoe. Led by a knowledgeable guide, you'll learn about the history of outrigger canoes in Hawaiian culture and the techniques used by ancient Hawaiians to navigate the seas. The tour also includes insights into the marine life of Maui and the significance of the ocean in Hawaiian spirituality. It's a hands-on way to engage with the island's culture while enjoying the natural beauty of Maui's coastline.

- **Location:** Kaanapali Beach, Lahaina, HI 96761
- **Duration:** 2 hours
- **Contact:** +1 808-667-7701

7. Ke'anae Peninsula Cultural and Agricultural Tour

The Ke'anae Peninsula is known for its lush taro fields and traditional Hawaiian farming practices. This tour takes you through the heart of the peninsula, where you'll learn about the significance of taro in Hawaiian culture and the sustainable farming methods used by the locals. The tour also includes a visit to a traditional Hawaiian home and a demonstration of taro cultivation and poi making. It's an excellent way to see traditional Hawaiian life in one of Maui's most picturesque settings.

- **Location:** Ke'anae Peninsula, Hana, Maui, HI 96713
- **Duration:** 4 hours
- **Contact:** +1 808-248-8300

8. Hawaiian Cultural Activities at Kaanapali Beach Hotel

Kaanapali Beach Hotel offers a range of free cultural activities for its guests, including hula lessons, ukulele classes, and Hawaiian language workshops. These activities are led by the hotel's cultural advisors and are designed to immerse guests in the traditions and practices of Hawaii. The hotel's commitment to preserving and sharing Hawaiian culture makes it a great place to learn about the island's heritage in a hands-on and engaging way.

- **Location:** 2525 Kaanapali Pkwy, Lahaina, HI 96761
- **Duration:** 1 hour per activity
- **Contact:** +1 808-661-0011

9. Pacific Whale Foundation's Cultural Eco-Tours

The Pacific Whale Foundation offers eco-tours that combine whale watching with cultural education. During these tours, naturalists and cultural experts provide information on the significance of whales in Hawaiian culture and the traditional practices of whale hunting and conservation. The tour also includes a discussion on the broader marine ecosystem and its importance to the Hawaiian people. These tours are both educational and inspiring, offering a unique perspective on the connection between Hawaiian culture and the natural world.

- **Location:** Maalaea Harbor, Wailuku, HI 96793
- **Duration:** 3-4 hours
- **Contact:** +1 808-249-8811

10. Aloha `Āina Cultural Tours

Aloha Āina Cultural Tours offers a variety of experiences focused on Hawaiian land stewardship and traditional agricultural practices. Their tours take you to sacred sites, ancient fishponds, and traditional taro patches, where you learn about the relationship between Hawaiians and their environment. The tours emphasize the importance of sustainability and respect for the land, providing a deep understanding of the Hawaiian concept of āina (land) as a source of life and spiritual connection

- **Location:** Various locations around Maui
- **Duration:** 3-5 hours
- **Contact:** +1 808-280-3957

Chapter 13: Dining and Culinary Experiences

Overview of Local Cuisine

Maui cuisine reflects the island's diverse cultural influences, blending traditional Hawaiian flavors with Asian, American, and Pacific Rim influences. Here's a comprehensive overview of Maui cuisine:

1. Traditional Hawaiian Dishes

Poke: A staple of Hawaiian cuisine, poke consists of marinated chunks of raw fish (often ahi tuna) mixed with soy sauce, sesame oil, onions, and other seasonings.

Kalua Pig: Slow-roasted pork cooked in an underground oven (imu), resulting in tender, smoky meat often served with poi (taro root paste) and lomi lomi salmon (salmon salad).

Lau Lau: Pork, fish, or chicken wrapped in taro leaves and steamed, imparting a rich, earthy flavor.

Poi: Mashed taro root that forms a starchy, mildly sweet accompaniment to many traditional Hawaiian meals.

2. Asian Influences

Loco Moco: A hearty dish featuring a hamburger patty served over rice, topped with a fried egg and brown gravy, reflecting Japanese-American culinary influences.

Malasadas: Portuguese-inspired fried doughnuts coated in sugar, often filled with flavors like custard or tropical fruit jams.

Plate Lunch: A local favorite consisting of a protein (like chicken katsu or teriyaki beef), macaroni salad, and rice, reflecting the fusion of Asian flavors with American comfort food.

3. Seafood and Pacific Rim Flavors

Fresh Fish: Maui's coastal location offers an abundance of fresh fish options, including mahi-mahi, ono, opah, and snapper, prepared grilled, blackened, or sashimi.

Shrimp Trucks: Found primarily on the North Shore, these trucks serve garlic shrimp plates influenced by Filipino and Pacific Island flavors.

Fusion Cuisine: Upscale restaurants on Maui often blend local ingredients with Pacific Rim influences, creating dishes like macadamia nut-crusted fish or pineapple-glazed ribs

4. Farm-to-Table and Local Ingredients

Farmers Markets: Maui's fertile land supports a variety of fruits and vegetables, including pineapple, mango, papaya, and taro, featured prominently in local cuisine.

Coffee: Maui's coffee farms produce specialty coffee beans, known for their smooth, rich flavor and aromatic profile.

Craft Beverages: Local breweries and distilleries offer craft beers, spirits, and cocktails incorporating tropical fruits and flavors unique to Maui.

5. Dining Experiences

Luaus: Traditional Hawaiian feasts featuring kalua pig, poi, and Hawaiian music and hula performances, providing cultural immersion along with culinary delights.

Fine Dining: Maui boasts award-winning restaurants showcasing innovative cuisine using locally sourced ingredients, often with oceanfront views.

Food Trucks and Stands: Found in towns like Lahaina and Paia, these offer casual dining with a variety of quick bites and local specialties.

6. Desserts and Sweets

Shave Ice: A refreshing treat consisting of finely shaved ice topped with flavored syrups like mango, passionfruit, or li hing mui (dried plum).

Haupia: A coconut milk-based pudding or custard, often served as a dessert or filling in pies and cakes.

Mochi: Japanese rice cakes filled with sweet fillings like azuki bean paste or tropical fruits, popular as a snack or dessert.

Must-Try Dishes in Maui

Maui's culinary scene reflects its diverse cultural heritage and abundant natural resources, offering a variety of dishes that combine traditional Hawaiian flavors with influences from Asia, Europe, and mainland America. Here are 10 must-try Maui dishes that showcase the island's unique flavors:

1. Kalua Pork:

A staple of Hawaiian cuisine, kalua pork is traditionally cooked in an underground imu (earth oven) until tender and smoky. The shredded pork is often served with steamed white rice and accompanied by poi (taro root paste).

2. Laulau:

This traditional Hawaiian dish consists of pork, fish, or chicken wrapped in taro leaves and steamed until tender. The flavors meld together, creating a savory and satisfying dish.

3. Poke:

A Hawaiian favorite, poke (pronounced poh-keh) is a raw fish salad typically made with ahi tuna or octopus. The fish is marinated in soy sauce, sesame oil, onions, and other seasonings, then served over rice or on its own as a refreshing appetizer.

4. Loco Moco:

A hearty Hawaiian comfort food, loco moco features a mound of steamed rice topped with a hamburger patty, a fried egg, and brown gravy. It's a filling dish that originated as a local favorite in diners and coffee shops.

5. Malasadas:

Introduced by Portuguese immigrants, malasadas are deep-fried doughnuts rolled in sugar and often filled with flavors like custard, guava, or haupia (coconut). They're best enjoyed fresh and warm from local bakeries.

6. Lomi Lomi Salmon:

This traditional Hawaiian side dish features diced salmon mixed with tomatoes, onions, and sometimes green onions. It's lightly seasoned with salt and sometimes chili pepper, creating a refreshing and flavorful accompaniment to meals.

7. Huli Huli Chicken:

Huli huli chicken is marinated in a sweet and tangy sauce made with soy sauce, brown sugar, ginger, and garlic, then grilled over an open flame. The name "huli huli" comes from the Hawaiian term for "turning" or "rotating," referencing the method of cooking.

8. Plate Lunch:

A local favorite, plate lunch typically includes two scoops of rice, macaroni salad, and a protein such as teriyaki beef, fried mahi-mahi, or chicken katsu (breaded and fried chicken cutlet). It's a satisfying and filling meal found at local eateries and food trucks.

9. Haupia:

A traditional Hawaiian dessert, haupia is a creamy coconut pudding made with coconut milk, sugar, and cornstarch. It's often served chilled and topped with toasted coconut flakes, offering a sweet and refreshing end to a meal.

10. Poi:

A Hawaiian staple, poi is a thick paste made from taro root (kalo). It's traditionally prepared by pounding cooked taro root until smooth and creamy, with water added as needed to achieve the desired consistency. Poi ranges in texture from thick to thin, and its flavor can vary from slightly sweet to tangy. It's often served alongside meats like kalua pork or as a standalone dish.

Fine Dining and Farm-to-Table Restaurants

Maui is home to an exceptional array of fine dining and farm-to-table restaurants that showcase the island's rich agricultural heritage and bountiful fresh ingredients. Here are some top recommendations, each offering a unique culinary experience:

1. Merriman's Kapalua

Merriman's Kapalua is one of Maui's most celebrated fine dining establishments, known for its commitment to farm-to-table cuisine and stunning oceanfront setting. Located on the scenic Kapalua Bay, this restaurant offers breathtaking views, particularly at sunset, making it a perfect spot for a romantic dinner. Chef Peter Merriman, a pioneer of Hawaii Regional Cuisine, emphasizes the use of local ingredients, with 90% of the menu sourced from Hawaiian farmers, ranchers, and fishermen. The menu features fresh seafood, such as the macadamia nut-crusted mahi-mahi and ahi poke, alongside tender meats like house-smoked pork or grass-fed beef. The wine list is extensive, featuring selections from around the world, and the cocktails are crafted with fresh island fruits. The ambiance is elegant yet relaxed, with outdoor seating that allows diners to enjoy the cool ocean breeze. Merriman's Kapalua offers a true taste of Maui's culinary landscape, blending upscale dining with the island's natural beauty.

- **Location:** 1 Bay Club Place, Kapalua, HI 96761
- **Opening Hours:** Daily, 3:00 PM - 9:00 PM
- **Phone Number:** +1 808-669-6400

2. The Mill House

The Mill House at Maui Tropical Plantation in Waikapu offers a unique dining experience that blends fine dining with a strong farm-to-table ethos. The restaurant is set amidst lush fields and gardens, from which much of the produce on the menu is harvested. Executive Chef Taylor Ponte creates innovative dishes that celebrate the island's agricultural bounty, using ingredients sourced directly from the plantation and other local farms. The menu changes frequently based on what's in season, but you can expect beautifully crafted dishes like the Kula corn risotto, locally caught fish, and house-made charcuterie. The restaurant's open-air setting allows guests to take in the breathtaking views of the West Maui Mountains, adding to the overall dining experience.

The Mill House also offers a carefully curated selection of wines, craft beers, and cocktails that pair perfectly with fresh, flavorful cuisine.

- **Location:** 1670 Honoapiilani Hwy, Waikapu, HI 96793
- **Opening Hours:** Monday to Friday, 11:00 AM - 9:00 PM; Saturday and Sunday, 10:00 AM - 9:00 PM
- **Phone Number:** +1 808-270-0333

3. Mama's Fish House

Located on the North Shore of Maui in the quaint town of Paia, Mama's Fish House is an iconic dining destination that combines fine dining with a deep appreciation for fresh, locally sourced seafood. The restaurant is housed in a Polynesian-style building set on a private beach, offering stunning ocean views that enhance the dining experience. The menu changes daily based on the catch of local fishermen, and each dish highlights the freshness of the seafood. Signature dishes include the stuffed mahi-mahi with lobster and crab, and the macadamia nut-crusted ahi. The restaurant's interior is adorned with Polynesian artifacts and tropical flowers, creating a warm, inviting atmosphere. Mama's Fish House is also known for its impeccable service, with staff who are knowledgeable about the menu and eager to share stories about the fishermen and ingredients.

- **Location:** 799 Poho Place, Paia, HI 96779
- **Opening Hours:** Daily, 11:00 AM - 9:00 PM
- **Phone Number:** +1 808-579-8488

4. Hali'imaile General Store

Hali'imaile General Store is a beloved Maui institution that offers a unique blend of Hawaiian flavors and contemporary cuisine. Located in the heart of Maui's upcountry in Hali'imaile, this charming restaurant occupies a former plantation store, adding a rustic and nostalgic ambiance to the dining experience. Executive Chef Beverly Gannon, one of the founders of Hawaii Regional Cuisine, crafts a menu that highlights fresh, local ingredients with a creative twist. Signature dishes include the Sashimi Napoleon with layers of ahi, smoked salmon, and crab, and the Asian duck tostada. The interior is cozy and welcoming, with vintage decor that reflects the restaurant's history. The service is warm and attentive, making every visit feel special. Hali'imaile General Store is perfect for those seeking a refined yet relaxed dining experience that captures the essence of Maui's upcountry charm.

- **Location:** 900 Hali'imaile Road, Makawao, HI 96768
- **Opening Hours:** Monday to Friday, 11:00 AM - 8:00 PM; Saturday, 10:30 AM - 8:00 PM; Closed on Sundays
- **Phone Number:** +1 808-572-2666

5. Ko Restaurant

Located at the Fairmont Kea Lani in Wailea, Ko Restaurant offers a refined dining experience that celebrates the multicultural culinary traditions of Maui. Ko, meaning "sugarcane" in Hawaiian, draws inspiration from the plantation era when immigrants from China, Portugal, Korea, Japan, and the Philippines brought their flavors to Hawaii. The menu features dishes that pay homage to these diverse cultures, such as the Keahole lobster tempura, macadamia nut-crusted lamb chops, and wok-seared opakapaka. The restaurant emphasizes the use of local ingredients, including fresh seafood, produce, and meats sourced from Maui farms and ranches. The ambiance is elegant and serene, with indoor and outdoor seating that offers views of the resort's lush gardens. Ko's commitment to honoring the island's history and its dedication to sustainability make it a standout dining experience in Maui.

- **Location:** 4100 Wailea Alanui Drive, Wailea, HI 96753
- **Opening Hours:** Daily, 5:00 PM - 9:00 PM
- **Phone Number:** +1 808-875-2210

6. Pacific'O Restaurant

Pacific'O Restaurant, located on the beachfront in Lahaina, is a pioneer in Maui's farm-to-table movement. The restaurant is dedicated to sourcing its ingredients from local farms, including its own O'o Farm in upcountry Maui. This commitment to fresh, organic produce is reflected in every dish, from the pan-seared fish to the farm-fresh salads. The menu is seasonal, showcasing the best of what Maui has to offer, and includes innovative dishes like the coffee-rubbed pork loin and the ulu (breadfruit) gnocchi. The restaurant's location right on the beach provides spectacular views, particularly at sunset, making it a favorite spot for both locals and visitors. The atmosphere is relaxed yet sophisticated, with an emphasis on friendly service and high-quality cuisine.

- **Location:** 505 Front Street, Lahaina, HI 96761
- **Opening Hours:** Daily, 5:00 PM - 9:00 PM
- **Phone Number:** +1 808-667-4341

7. Nalu's South Shore Grill

Nalu's South Shore Grill, located in Kihei, offers a casual yet upscale dining experience with a strong focus on fresh, local ingredients. The restaurant is known for its relaxed atmosphere and farm-to-table approach, with dishes that highlight the flavors of Maui. The menu includes a variety of options, from hearty breakfasts like the Kalua pork benedict to dinner dishes such as the seared ahi or the grass-fed beef burger. Nalu's also offers a selection of fresh smoothies and juices made with locally grown fruits and vegetables. The interior is open and airy, with plenty of natural light, and the outdoor seating area is perfect for enjoying a meal in the warm Maui weather. Nalu's is a great choice for those looking for high-quality, locally sourced food in a laid-back setting.

- **Location:** 1280 S Kihei Road, Kihei, HI 96753
- **Opening Hours:** Daily, 8:00 AM - 9:00 PM
- **Phone Number:** +1 808-891-8650

Seafood Restaurants

Maui's seafood restaurants offer a delightful array of fresh, ocean-inspired dishes, celebrating the island's abundant marine resources. These establishments combine top-notch culinary craftsmanship with the freshest local catches, providing diners with an unforgettable taste of Hawaii's coastal cuisine. Here are some of the best seafood restaurants in Maui:

1. Mama's Fish House

Mama's Fish House is an iconic seafood restaurant on Maui's North Shore, renowned for its commitment to serving only the freshest catch of the day. Located in the charming town of Paia, this oceanfront restaurant offers stunning views of the beach, making it an ideal spot for a memorable dining experience. The menu features a variety of local fish, including mahi-mahi, ahi, and ono, each prepared in unique and flavorful ways. One of the highlights is the stuffed mahi-mahi with lobster and crab, a dish that showcases the richness of Maui's seafood. The restaurant's Polynesian-inspired decor, complete with tropical flowers and island artifacts, creates a warm and inviting atmosphere. The service is impeccable, with staff knowledgeable about the dishes and the stories behind the fishermen who caught the fish.

- **Location:** 799 Poho Place, Paia, HI 96779
- **Opening Hours:** Daily, 11:00 AM - 9:00 PM

- **Phone Number:** +1 808-579-8488

2. Lahaina Grill

Lahaina Grill is an upscale dining establishment located in the heart of historic Lahaina town. While the restaurant offers a wide range of dishes, its seafood options are particularly outstanding. The ambiance is elegant and contemporary, making it a perfect choice for a special night out. The menu features a variety of expertly prepared seafood dishes, such as the seared ahi, served with vanilla bean jasmine rice and a soy-balsamic reduction, and the seafood risotto, packed with fresh island fish, shellfish, and rich flavors. The restaurant's extensive wine list complements the seafood offerings, with selections from around the world. The service at Lahaina Grill is top-notch, ensuring that every guest has a memorable dining experience.

- **Location:** 127 Lahainaluna Road, Lahaina, HI 96761
- **Opening Hours:** Daily, 5:00 PM - 9:00 PM
- **Phone Number:** +1 808-667-5117

3. Paia Fish Market

Paia Fish Market, with locations in Paia, Lahaina, and Kihei, is a must-visit for seafood lovers seeking a more casual dining experience. This beloved local spot is known for serving fresh, generously portioned seafood dishes at reasonable prices. The menu offers a variety of options, from fish tacos and grilled fish plates to hearty seafood pasta and chowder. One of the standout dishes is the fish burger, made with your choice of local fish, including mahi-mahi, ono, or ahi, and topped with house-made tartar sauce. The atmosphere at Paia Fish Market is relaxed and friendly, with picnic-style seating that encourages a communal dining experience. The restaurant's focus on sustainability and fresh, local ingredients makes it a favorite among both locals and visitors.

- **Location:** 100 Baldwin Avenue, Paia, HI 96779
- **Opening Hours:** Daily, 11:00 AM - 9:30 PM
- **Phone Number:** +1 808-579-8030

4. Kimo's Maui

Kimo's Maui is a longstanding favorite in Lahaina, known for its stunning ocean views and commitment to fresh, locally sourced seafood. The restaurant is famous for its laid-back island vibe and warm, welcoming service.

Kimo's menu features a variety of fresh fish, all cooked to perfection, whether you prefer it grilled, baked, or pan-seared. Signature dishes include the macadamia nut-crusted mahi-mahi and the furikake ahi. The restaurant's oceanfront setting provides breathtaking views of the Pacific, especially at sunset, making it an ideal spot for a romantic dinner or a special occasion. In addition to seafood, Kimo's is also known for its Hula Pie, a decadent dessert that is a must-try for anyone visiting Maui.

- **Location:** 845 Front Street, Lahaina, HI 96761
- **Opening Hours:** Daily, 11:00 AM - 9:00 PM
- **Phone Number:** +1 808-661-4811

5. Honokowai Okazuya & Deli

Honokowai Okazuya & Deli, located in the Honokowai neighborhood, is a hidden gem for those seeking delicious, no-frills seafood dishes. This small, take-out-focused spot offers a variety of Hawaiian and Asian-inspired seafood dishes that are big on flavor and freshness. Popular menu items include the sautéed mahi-mahi with lemon caper butter sauce, the garlic shrimp, and the teriyaki ahi. While the setting is simple, the quality of the food more than makes up for it. This is a great option for a quick, satisfying meal that you can enjoy on the go or at the nearby beach. The portions are generous, and the prices are very reasonable, making it a favorite among locals.

- **Location:** 3600 Lower Honoapiilani Road, Lahaina, HI 96761
- **Opening Hours:** Monday to Friday, 10:30 AM - 8:00 PM; Saturday, 10:30 AM - 2:00 PM; Closed on Sundays
- **Phone Number:** +1 808-665-0512

6. Pacific'O Restaurant

Located on the beachfront in Lahaina, Pacific'O Restaurant is a pioneer in Maui's farm-to-table movement, with a strong emphasis on fresh seafood. The restaurant sources much of its produce from its own O'o Farm in upcountry Maui and complements it with the freshest catches from local waters. The menu is seasonal, featuring innovative seafood dishes such as the grilled mahi-mahi with roasted beet puree and the octopus salad with a citrus vinaigrette. The restaurant's location right on the beach provides spectacular views, particularly at sunset, making it a favorite spot for both locals and visitors.

The atmosphere is relaxed yet sophisticated, with an emphasis on friendly service and high-quality cuisine.

- **Location:** 505 Front Street, Lahaina, HI 96761
- **Opening Hours:** Daily, 5:00 PM - 9:00 PM
- **Phone Number:** +1 808-667-4341

7. Fleetwood's on Front St.

Fleetwood's on Front St., owned by the legendary musician Mick Fleetwood, is more than just a seafood restaurant; it's a unique dining experience that combines great food with live music and stunning rooftop views. Located in the heart of Lahaina, this restaurant offers a diverse menu that includes fresh, locally sourced seafood. Signature dishes include the ahi tartare and the lobster mac and cheese. The restaurant's rooftop bar is a highlight, offering panoramic views of the ocean and the West Maui Mountains, making it an ideal spot to watch the sunset while enjoying a cocktail. The ambiance is vibrant and lively, with a mix of locals and tourists enjoying the excellent food and music.

- **Location:** 744 Front Street, Lahaina, HI 96761
- **Opening Hours:** Daily, 11:00 AM - 11:00 PM
- **Phone Number:** +1 808-669-6425

Food Trucks and Local Eateries

Maui's food trucks and local eateries provide a more casual and affordable way to savor the island's diverse culinary offerings. These spots are beloved by locals and visitors alike for their authenticity, creativity, and use of fresh, local ingredients. Below are some of the best food trucks and local eateries in Maui:

1. Geste Shrimp Truck

Geste Shrimp Truck is a legendary food truck located near Kahului Harbor, famous for serving up some of the best garlic shrimp on the island. This no-frills food truck has a loyal following, thanks to its perfectly cooked, succulent shrimp served in various flavors such as spicy pineapple, lemon pepper, and Hawaiian scampi. The shrimp are accompanied by a generous portion of rice and crab salad, making for a satisfying meal that's perfect for enjoying at a nearby beach or park. Despite its humble setting, Geste Shrimp Truck consistently delivers on flavor and freshness, making it a must-visit for seafood lovers on a budget.

- **Location:** Kahului Beach Road, Kahului, HI 96732
- **Opening Hours:** Tuesday to Saturday, 10:30 AM - 5:00 PM; Closed on Sundays and Mondays
- **Phone Number:** +1 808-298-7109

Tip: Arrive early or during off-peak hours to avoid long lines, as this popular food truck can get busy, especially during lunchtime.

2. Tacos of North Shore

Tacos of North Shore, located in the laid-back town of Haiku, is a popular food truck known for its fresh and flavorful tacos. The menu features a variety of tacos, including fish, shrimp, and carnitas, all made with locally sourced ingredients. The fish tacos, made with fresh-caught ahi or mahi-mahi, are a standout, served with a tangy slaw and house-made sauces that perfectly complement the seafood. The food truck's casual, beachy vibe and outdoor seating make it a great spot to relax and enjoy a quick meal while exploring Maui's North Shore. The portions are generous, and the prices are reasonable, making it a favorite among both locals and visitors.

- **Location:** 810 Haiku Road, Haiku, HI 96708
- **Opening Hours:** Monday to Saturday, 11:00 AM - 3:00 PM; Closed on Sundays
- **Phone Number:** +1 808-575-2616

Tip: Pair your tacos with one of their refreshing agua frescas, made with tropical fruits for a taste of Hawaii in a cup.

3. South Maui Fish Company

South Maui Fish Company is a food truck in Kihei that has earned a stellar reputation for its ultra-fresh poke bowls and grilled fish plates. This family-owned and operated business prides itself on using only the freshest local fish, often caught on the same day it's served. The poke is a crowd favorite, featuring cubes of ahi tuna or other fresh fish, marinated in a flavorful sauce and served over rice with a side of seaweed salad. The grilled fish plates are equally popular, offering a healthy and delicious option for seafood lovers. The truck's location near the beach makes it a perfect spot for grabbing a quick and tasty meal after a day in the sun.

- **Location:** 1794 South Kihei Road, Kihei, HI 96753
- **Opening Hours:** Monday to Saturday, 11:00 AM - 3:00 PM; Closed on Sundays
- **Phone Number:** +1 808-875-8888

Tip: Their poke sells out fast, so try to visit earlier in the day to ensure you get a taste of this island favorite.

4. Like Poke?

Like Poke? is a beloved food truck in Kahului that specializes in one thing: poke, and they do it exceptionally well. Their poke bowls are made to order with fresh ahi tuna, seasoned to perfection with soy sauce, sesame oil, and other traditional Hawaiian flavors. Customers can choose from a variety of poke styles, including shoyu, spicy, and ginger. The portions are generous, and the quality of the fish is top-notch, making it a favorite spot for poke enthusiasts. The food truck is located in a parking lot with limited seating, so many customers opt to take their meals to-go and enjoy them at a nearby beach or park.

- **Location:** 591 Haleakala Highway, Kahului, HI 96732
- **Opening Hours:** Monday to Friday, 11:00 AM - 2:00 PM; Closed on weekends
- **Phone Number:** +1 808-344-1040

Tip: Cash is king here, so be sure to bring some with you as this popular food truck does not accept credit cards.

5. Sam Sato's

Sam Sato's is a local institution in Wailuku, known for its saimin (a Hawaiian noodle soup) and manju (a Japanese pastry filled with sweetened bean paste). This family-owned eatery has been serving up hearty, comforting dishes for decades, making it a must-visit for those looking to experience authentic local flavors. The saimin, made with a rich broth, tender noodles, and slices of char siu (barbecued pork), is the star of the menu, perfect for a quick and satisfying meal. The manju, which comes in various flavors, is a sweet treat that should not be missed. The restaurant's simple, no-frills setting is a reflection of its focus on good food and friendly service.

- **Location:** 1750 Wili Pa Loop, Wailuku, HI 96793
- **Opening Hours:** Monday to Friday, 7:00 AM - 2:00 PM; Saturday, 7:00 AM - 12:00 PM; Closed on Sundays

- **Phone Number:** +1 808-244-7124

Tip: Sam Sato's is cash-only and gets busy, so it's a good idea to arrive early to secure a table and enjoy the best of what they offer.

6. Tin Roof Maui

Tin Roof Maui is a casual eatery in Kahului, owned by Top Chef finalist Sheldon Simeon. This popular spot offers a modern take on traditional Hawaiian comfort food, with a menu that features dishes like garlic shrimp, mochiko chicken, and poke bowls. The portions are generous, and the flavors are bold, making it a favorite among both locals and visitors. One of the standout dishes is the pork belly bowl, served with a perfectly soft-boiled egg and house-made pickles. Tin Roof Maui's casual atmosphere and takeout focus make it an ideal spot for grabbing a quick, delicious meal to enjoy at a nearby beach or on the go.

- **Location:** 360 Papa Place, Kahului, HI 96732
- **Opening Hours:** Monday to Friday, 10:00 AM - 2:00 PM; Closed on weekends
- **Phone Number:** +1 808-868-0753

Tip: Tin Roof Maui often has long lines, so ordering online in advance can save you time and ensure you get to try their most popular dishes before they sell out.

7. Local Boys Shave Ice

Local Boys Shave Ice, with locations in Kihei and Lahaina, is the go-to spot for a refreshing Hawaiian treat. While not a full meal, shave ice is an iconic local delicacy that shouldn't be missed when visiting Maui. Local Boys offers a wide variety of flavors, including tropical fruits like mango, passionfruit, and guava, as well as classic options like coconut and vanilla. The shave ice is served with a generous drizzle of sweet syrup and can be topped with extras like condensed milk or ice cream. The friendly service and fun, colorful atmosphere make this a favorite stop for families and anyone looking to cool down on a warm day.

- **Location:** 624 Front Street, Lahaina, HI 96761 (Lahaina location)
- **Opening Hours:** Daily, 10:00 AM - 8:00 PM
- **Phone Number:** +1 808-344-9779

Tip: For an authentic Hawaiian experience, try the shave ice with azuki beans and mochi, a combination that's popular among locals.

Vegetarian and Vegan Options

Maui is a paradise not just for beach lovers but also for those seeking delicious vegetarian and vegan cuisine. The island boasts a range of eateries that emphasize fresh, locally sourced ingredients, offering creative and flavorful plant-based dishes. Here's a look at some of the best vegetarian and vegan options in Maui, each providing a unique dining experience.

1. Moku Roots

Moku Roots is a zero-waste, farm-to-table restaurant located in Lahaina. This eco-conscious eatery focuses on providing creative and flavorful vegetarian and vegan dishes made with locally sourced, organic ingredients. The menu features a wide variety of options, including their famous taro burger, jackfruit carnitas tacos, and zucchini noodle bowls. Moku Roots is also known for its commitment to sustainability, using reusable containers and utensils, and even wrapping its to-go items in ti leaves instead of plastic. The atmosphere is relaxed and welcoming, with a focus on community and environmental responsibility.

- **Location:** 335 Keawe Street #211, Lahaina, HI 96761
- **Opening Hours**: Monday to Saturday, 10:00 AM - 8:00 PM; Closed on Sundays
- **Phone Number:** +1 808-214-5106

Tip: Try their homemade kombucha, a refreshing and healthy drink that pairs perfectly with their plant-based dishes.

2. Choice Health Bar

Choice Health Bar is a beloved vegan café with locations in Lahaina and Paia. Known for its vibrant smoothie bowls, fresh juices, and hearty salads, this café is a favorite among health-conscious locals and visitors. The menu features a variety of raw, vegan, and gluten-free options, all made with fresh, organic ingredients. Popular dishes include the dragon bowl, filled with acai, banana, and house-made granola, and the warrior bowl, packed with greens, quinoa, and avocado. The café's casual, beachy vibe makes it a perfect spot for a post-surf meal or a healthy breakfast to start your day.

- **Location:** 1087 Limahana Place, Lahaina, HI 96761 (Lahaina location)
- **Opening Hours:** Monday to Saturday, 7:30 AM - 3:30 PM; Closed on Sundays
- **Phone Number:** +1 808-661-7711

Tip: Don't miss their raw desserts, like the macadamia nut cheesecake, which are as delicious as they are healthy.

3. Earth Aloha Eats

Earth Aloha Eats is a fully vegan food truck that has quickly become a staple on Maui for plant-based dining. The menu offers a diverse range of vegan comfort foods, from barbecue jackfruit sandwiches to "fish" tacos made with crispy tofu. The food truck is committed to using sustainable practices and compostable packaging, making it a great choice for eco-conscious diners. Earth Aloha Eats regularly moves around the island, with locations in Kihei, Kahului, and Lahaina, so it's a good idea to check their social media for the latest updates on their whereabouts.

- **Location:** Varies (Kihei, Kahului, Lahaina)
- **Opening Hours:** Daily, 11:00 AM - 8:00 PM
- **Phone Number:** +1 808-280-4655

Tip: Follow their Instagram account for daily specials and exact locations—they often feature limited-time dishes that are well worth seeking out.

4. Cafe Des Amis

Located in the charming town of Paia, Café Des Amis is a cozy café offering a delightful fusion of Mediterranean and Indian cuisine, with plenty of vegetarian and vegan options. The menu features flavorful dishes like vegetable curry, hummus platters, and savory crepes stuffed with fresh vegetables and house-made sauces. Café Des Amis has a laid-back, bohemian atmosphere, with indoor and outdoor seating perfect for enjoying a leisurely meal. Their commitment to using fresh, local ingredients ensures that every dish is packed with flavor and nutrition.

- **Location:** 42 Baldwin Avenue, Paia, HI 96779
- **Opening Hours:** Daily, 8:00 AM - 9:00 PM
- **Phone Number:** +1 808-579-6323

Tip: Try their masala dosa, a traditional Indian dish that's both filling and packed with aromatic spices—perfect for a hearty vegetarian meal.

5. Down to Earth Organic & Natural

Description: Down to Earth Organic & Natural is not just a grocery store but also a fantastic spot for vegetarian and vegan dining. Located in Kahului, this store features a large deli offering a wide selection of salads, sandwiches, hot entrees, and fresh juices, all made with organic, plant-based ingredients. The deli's menu changes daily, with options like tofu stir-fry, vegan lasagna, and hearty grain bowls. The store's focus on organic and non-GMO products ensures that everything you eat here is as healthy as it is delicious.

- **Location:** 305 Dairy Road, Kahului, HI 96732
- **Opening Hours:** Daily, 7:00 AM - 8:00 PM
- **Phone Number:** –1 808-877-2661

Tip: Grab a meal to-go and head to a nearby beach park for a scenic picnic—you'll find plenty of ready-made options perfect for a quick, healthy meal.

6. Maui Kombucha

Maui Kombucha in Haiku is a unique spot combining a kombucha brewery with a vegan café. This vibrant eatery offers a variety of vegan dishes, including raw pizzas, sushi rolls, and decadent desserts like chocolate mousse pie. Their kombucha is brewed on-site and comes in a variety of flavors, from classic ginger to more adventurous options like dragonfruit and lavender. The café's cozy, artistic setting makes it a great place to relax and enjoy a healthy meal or snack. Whether you're looking for a full meal or just a refreshing drink, Maui Kombucha has something to satisfy your vegan cravings.

- **Location:** 810 Kokomo Road, Haiku, HI 96708
- **Opening Hours:** Monday to Saturday, 11:00 AM - 6:00 PM; Closed on Sundays
- **Phone Number:** –1 808-575-5233

Tip: Bring your bottle to fill up on their delicious kombucha, a perfect way to stay hydrated and energized while exploring Maui.

Best Breakfast and Brunch Spots

Maui's breakfast and brunch scene is a delightful mix of tropical flavors, local ingredients, and island hospitality. Whether you're looking for a hearty traditional breakfast, a fresh and healthy start to your day, or a laid-back brunch with ocean views, Maui has something to satisfy every craving.

Here's a guide to some of the best breakfast and brunch spots on the island, each offering a unique experience and delicious dishes.

1. Gazebo Restaurant

Nestled along the coastline in Napili, the Gazebo Restaurant is famous for its scenic ocean views and hearty breakfast dishes. This casual, open-air eatery is known for its enormous pancakes, which come in flavors like macadamia nut, pineapple, and white chocolate. The fried rice, loaded with Portuguese sausage, bacon, and green onions, is another crowd favorite. Despite its popularity and long wait times, the friendly service and stunning views make it worth the visit. The atmosphere is relaxed and perfect for a leisurely morning meal.

- **Location:** 5315 Lower Honoapiilani Road, Lahaina, HI 96761
- **Opening Hours:** Daily, 7:30 AM - 2:00 PM
- **Phone Number:** +1 808-669-5621

Tip: Arrive early to avoid long lines, and be sure to try their signature banana macadamia nut pancakes.

2. Kula Lodge & Restaurant

Kula Lodge & Restaurant offers a unique breakfast experience with panoramic views of Maui's Upcountry. Situated at 3,200 feet above sea level, this charming restaurant serves breakfast in a rustic, open-air setting. The menu features a mix of traditional and island-inspired dishes, such as eggs benedict with Maui-grown tomatoes and fresh fruit platters featuring local tropical fruits. The wood-fired oven adds a special touch to their breakfast pizzas, making them a must-try. The serene atmosphere and stunning views of the island make Kula Lodge a perfect spot for a relaxing morning meal.

- **Location:** 15200 Haleakala Highway, Kula, HI 96790
- **Opening Hours:** Daily, 7:00 AM - 11:00 AM (Breakfast)
- **Phone Number:** +1 808-878-1535

Tip: Enjoy a walk through the lodge's garden after your meal, where you can explore the beautiful native plants and flowers.

3. 808 Grindz Cafe

Located in Lahaina, 808 Grindz Café is a local favorite for affordable and delicious breakfast.

This cozy, family-owned restaurant is known for its generous portions and homemade dishes. The menu includes a variety of Hawaiian-style comfort foods, such as loco moco, a traditional dish featuring rice, hamburger patty, egg, and gravy. Their pancakes, especially the macadamia nut variety with homemade coconut syrup, are a hit among both locals and tourists. The casual atmosphere and friendly service make this a great spot for a satisfying and budget-friendly breakfast.

- **Location:** 843 Wainee Street, Lahaina, HI 96761
- **Opening Hours:** Monday to Saturday, 7:00 AM - 1:00 PM; Closed on Sundays
- **Phone Number:** +1 808-868-4147

Tip: Try their specialty, the “Famous 808 Grindz Pancakes,” for a sweet start to your day.

4. Grandma's Coffee House

Tucked away in the small town of Keokea, Grandma’s Coffee House is a charming, family-owned café that has been serving up delicious coffee and breakfast since 1918. The café roasts its coffee beans, grown on nearby farms, ensuring a fresh and flavorful cup of coffee to start your day. The breakfast menu features a variety of homemade pastries, sandwiches, and local favorites like kalua pork omelets and taro pancakes. The rustic, laid-back atmosphere and friendly service make Grandma’s a beloved spot for both locals and visitors.

- **Location:** 9232 Kula Highway, Kula, HI 96790
- **Opening Hours:** Daily, 7:00 AM - 2:00 PM
- **Phone Number:** +1 808-878-2140

Tip: Pair your breakfast with a cup of Grandma’s freshly roasted coffee for an authentic Maui experience.

5. The Plantation House

The Plantation House in Kapalua offers a luxurious brunch experience with breathtaking views of the golf course and the Pacific Ocean. The restaurant is known for its upscale, island-inspired dishes, such as crab cake benedict, smoked salmon, and lilikoi (passion fruit) pancakes. The elegant, open-air setting makes it an ideal spot for a special brunch with friends or family. With a focus on using fresh, local ingredients, the Plantation House offers a menu that reflects the best of Maui’s culinary traditions.

- **Location:** 2000 Plantation Club Drive, Lahaina, HI 96761
- **Opening Hours:** Daily, 8:00 AM - 2:00 PM (Breakfast/Brunch)
- **Phone Number:** +1 808-669-6299

Tip: Make a reservation for brunch to secure a table with the best views of the Kapalua coastline.

6. Cafe Mambo

Café Mambo, located in the vibrant town of Paia, is a colorful, laid-back eatery offering a mix of Mediterranean and island-inspired breakfast and brunch dishes. The menu includes items like huevos rancheros, breakfast burritos, and tropical fruit bowls. The café's funky décor and casual vibe make it a great spot to enjoy a relaxed brunch before hitting the nearby beaches. Café Mambo is also known for its fresh juices and smoothies, perfect for a refreshing and healthy start to your day.

- **Location:** 30 Baldwin Avenue, Paia, HI 96779
- **Opening Hours:** Daily, 8:00 AM - 9:00 PM
- **Phone Number:** +1 808-579-8021

Tip: Try their signature acai bowl, a delicious and energizing option for a light and healthy breakfast.

7. Paia Bay Coffee Bar

Paia Bay Coffee Bar is a hidden gem tucked away in the heart of Paia, offering a tranquil garden setting for breakfast and brunch. The menu features a range of healthy and hearty options, including avocado toast, acai bowls, and breakfast sandwiches. Their coffee is locally sourced and expertly brewed, making it a favorite spot for coffee lovers. The relaxed, bohemian atmosphere, complete with outdoor seating in a lush garden, makes Paia Bay Coffee Bar a perfect spot to unwind and enjoy a leisurely breakfast.

- **Location:** 115 Hana Highway, Paia, HI 96779
- **Opening Hours:** Monday to Saturday, 7:00 AM - 4:00 PM; Sunday, 8:00 AM - 2:00 PM
- **Phone Number:** +1 808-579-3111

Tip: Enjoy your meal in their outdoor garden area for a peaceful and scenic breakfast experience.

Coffee Shops and Cafés

Maui is home to a thriving coffee culture, with numerous coffee shops and cafés offering everything from locally sourced Hawaiian coffee to artisanal pastries and light bites. Each spot provides a unique ambiance, often reflecting the island's laid-back vibe or its stunning natural beauty. Here's a look at some of the best coffee shops and cafés across the island.

1. Grandma's Coffee House

Tucked away in the lush, upcountry town of Kula, Grandma's Coffee House is a charming, family-owned café that has been serving the community since 1918. The coffee is made from beans grown on the slopes of Haleakalā and roasted in-house, giving it a distinctive, rich flavor. The café exudes an old-world charm, with wooden furniture, vintage décor, and a relaxed atmosphere. Visitors can enjoy freshly baked goods like banana bread, scones, and the famous lilikoi (passionfruit) bars, along with hearty breakfast items and sandwiches. The outdoor seating area offers a peaceful spot to savor your coffee while taking in the cool, mountain air.

- **Location:** 9232 Kula Highway, Kula, HI 96790
- **Opening Hours:** Daily, 7:00 AM - 3:00 PM
- **Phone Number:** +1 808-878-2140

Tip: The café's banana bread is legendary, so be sure to grab a loaf to take with you.

2. Paia Bay Coffee Bar

Located in the heart of Paia, a vibrant town known for its surf culture, Paia Bay Coffee Bar is a hidden gem offering a cozy, garden-like setting. This eclectic café serves a variety of coffee drinks made from locally sourced beans, along with an assortment of fresh smoothies, salads, and sandwiches. The outdoor seating area is surrounded by lush greenery, making it a perfect spot to relax and unwind. Inside, the rustic décor and comfortable seating create a welcoming atmosphere. It's an ideal place to start your day with a strong cup of coffee or to hang out with friends over a light lunch.

- **Location:** 115 Hana Highway, Paia, HI 96779
- **Opening Hours:** Daily, 7:00 AM - 4:00 PM
- **Phone Number:** +1 808-579-3111

Tip: Try the acai bowl or avocado toast for a healthy and delicious breakfast option.

3. Island Vintage Coffee

Located in Whalers Village, Island Vintage Coffee is a popular spot for both locals and visitors. Known for its high-quality Hawaiian coffee, the café offers a wide range of beverages, including the signature Island Latte, made with macadamia nut and coconut flavors. The menu also features a selection of gourmet sandwiches, salads, and açai bowls. The café's location near Kaanapali Beach makes it a great place to grab a coffee before heading out for a day of sun and surf. The modern, airy interior, combined with outdoor seating, allows you to enjoy your coffee while taking in the ocean breeze.

- **Location:** 2435 Kaanapali Parkway, Lahaina, HI 96761
- **Opening Hours:** Daily, 7:00 AM - 9:00 PM
- **Phone Number:** +1 808-868-0972

Tip: The Island Latte is a must-try, offering a delicious taste of local flavors.

4. The Coffee Store Napili

The Coffee Store Napili is a beloved neighborhood café located in the Napili Plaza. This casual spot is known for its locally roasted coffee, which is available by the cup or in bulk for those who want to taste Maui home with them. The menu includes a variety of espresso drinks, smoothies, and fresh pastries, including gluten-free options. The friendly staff and laid-back atmosphere make it a favorite among locals. Whether you're stopping by for your morning coffee or looking for a comfortable spot to work, The Coffee Store Napili offers a welcoming space with plenty of aloha spirit.

- **Location:** 5095 Napilihau Street, Lahaina, HI 96761
- **Opening Hours:** Daily, 6:00 AM - 5:30 PM
- **Phone Number:** +1 808-669-4170

Tip: Don't miss the macadamia nut latte, a local favorite that perfectly complements the island vibe.

5. Akamai Coffee Co.

With multiple locations across Maui, Akamai Coffee Co. is known for its commitment to serving high-quality, locally roasted coffee.

The café sources its beans from small, sustainable farms on the island, ensuring that every cup is fresh and flavorful. Each location offers a sleek, modern design with comfortable seating and a relaxed atmosphere. The menu includes a variety of espresso drinks, pour-overs, and cold brews, as well as breakfast items like avocado toast and bagels. Akamai is a great place to enjoy a quick coffee on the go or to sit and enjoy the welcoming ambiance with friends.

- **Location:** 1325 S Kihei Road, Kihei, HI 96753
- **Opening Hours:** Daily, 5:30 AM - 6:00 PM
- **Phone Number:** -1 808-868-3251
- **Tip:** If you're a fan of cold brew, Akamai's nitro cold brew is a standout option.

6. Wailuku Coffee Company

Wailuku Coffee Company, located in the historic town of Wailuku, offers a vibrant, community-focused atmosphere. This local café is known for its strong, flavorful coffee, sourced from small farms on Maui and across Hawaii. The menu features a wide range of coffee drinks, including iced lattes, chai teas, and specialty espresso drinks. Wailuku Coffee Company also offers a selection of breakfast and lunch items, with an emphasis on fresh, locally sourced ingredients. The cozy interior, adorned with local art, and the friendly staff create a welcoming environment where locals and tourists alike can enjoy a great cup of coffee.

- **Location:** 26 N Market Street, Wailuku, HI 96793
- **Opening Hours:** Monday - Saturday, 6:30 AM - 5:00 PM; Sunday, 7:00 AM - 2:00 PM
- **Phone Number:** +1 808-495-0259

Tip: The breakfast burrito is a local favorite and pairs perfectly with a strong cup of coffee.

7. Bad Ass Coffee of Hawaii

Bad Ass Coffee of Hawaii is a well-known chain with a strong presence in Maui, offering a fun and energetic coffee experience. The brand is known for its bold Kona coffee and playful branding. The Maui locations continue this tradition, offering a variety of coffee drinks, from traditional espressos to creative concoctions like the "Bad Ass Mocha," made with Ghirardelli chocolate. The casual, laid-back atmosphere makes it a great spot for a quick pick-me-up or a leisurely coffee break. In addition to coffee, they also serve pastries, breakfast sandwiches, and other light bites.

- **Location:** 671 Front Street, Lahaina, HI 96761
- **Opening Hours:** Daily, 6:00 AM - 6:00 PM
- **Phone Number:** +1 808-667-2004

Tip: Grab a bag of their signature Kona coffee to bring home as a souvenir or gift.

Maui's Farmers Markets

Maui's farmers markets are vibrant hubs where locals and visitors alike can find fresh, locally-grown produce, unique handmade goods, and a taste of the island's agricultural bounty. These markets are more than just places to shop—they offer a genuine experience of Maui's community spirit and a connection to the land. Here's a look at some of the top farmer's markets across the island.

1. Maui Swap Meet

The Maui Swap Meet is one of the island's largest and most diverse farmers markets, held every Saturday morning in Kahului. This bustling market features over 200 vendors selling a wide variety of goods, from fresh fruits and vegetables to homemade crafts, jewelry, clothing, and souvenirs. Local farmers bring their freshly harvested produce, including exotic fruits like rambutan, lychee, and dragon fruit. The market is also a great place to sample local snacks like poke bowls, malasadas, and tropical smoothies. The lively atmosphere, coupled with the sheer variety of products, makes it a must-visit for anyone looking to immerse themselves in Maui's local culture.

- **Location:** 310 W Kaahumanu Avenue, Kahului, HI 96732
- **Opening Hours:** Saturday, 7:00 AM - 1:00 PM
- **Phone Number:** +1 808-244-3100

Tip: Arrive early to get the best selection of produce and avoid the mid-morning crowds.

2. Upcountry Farmers Market

Located in Pukalani, the Upcountry Farmers Market is a favorite among locals, offering a wide range of organic produce, artisanal foods, and handcrafted goods. This market, set in the cooler, scenic area of Upcountry Maui, features farmers who grow their crops in the fertile volcanic soil of the region.

You'll find an abundance of fresh fruits and vegetables, including Maui-grown avocados, sweet Maui onions, and a variety of greens. In addition to produce, vendors are selling freshly baked breads, jams, honey, and other locally made products. The market also has a selection of prepared foods, from vegan dishes to local-style breakfast plates.

- **Location:** 55 Kiopaa Street, Pukalani, HI 96768
- **Opening Hours:** Saturday, 7:00 AM - 11:00 AM
- **Phone Number:** +1 808-269-6723

Tip: Take some time to chat with the vendors; they are often eager to share stories about their farming practices and offer tips on how to prepare and enjoy their products.

3. Kihei Fourth Friday Town Party

While not a traditional farmers market, the Kihei Fourth Friday Town Party is a monthly event that combines a farmers market with a street festival. Held on the fourth Friday of every month in the heart of Kihei, this lively gathering features local farmers selling fresh produce alongside food trucks, craft vendors, and live entertainment. It's a great place to pick up fresh fruits, vegetables, and other locally made products while enjoying live music, performances, and a fun, community-driven atmosphere. The event is family-friendly and offers a true taste of Maui's vibrant South Shore community.

- **Location:** 1279 S Kihei Road, Kihei, HI 96753
- **Opening Hours:** Fourth Friday of each month, 6:00 PM - 9:00 PM
- **Phone Number:** +1 808-270-7710

Tip: Stay for the evening entertainment and enjoy some of the best local food from the various vendors and food trucks.

4. Napili Farmers Market

The Napili Farmers Market is a charming, community-focused market located in West Maui. Held twice a week, this market offers a selection of fresh produce, including organic fruits and vegetables, as well as locally made products like honey, jams, and baked goods. The market has a relaxed, friendly vibe, making it a pleasant place to browse and chat with local farmers and artisans. You'll also find a variety of prepared foods, such as fresh-pressed juices, vegan treats, and local snacks. The market's location, near the beautiful Napili Bay, adds to its appeal.

- **Location:** 4900 Honoapiilani Highway, Lahaina, HI 96761
- **Opening Hours:** Wednesday and Saturday, 8:00 AM - 12:00 PM
- **Phone Number:** +1 808-669-7004

Tip: Combine your visit with a trip to Napili Bay for a relaxing beach day after stocking up on fresh, local goodies.

5. Maui Sunday Market

Held in Kahului, the Maui Sunday Market is a popular evening market that offers a unique combination of a farmers market, food trucks, and live entertainment. Local vendors sell fresh produce, tropical flowers, and handmade crafts, while a variety of food trucks offer a diverse selection of local and international cuisine. The market has a festive atmosphere with live music and cultural performances, making it a great way to end your weekend. This market is a favorite among locals for its variety of food options and relaxed, social atmosphere.

- **Location:** 65 W Kaahumanu Avenue, Kahului, HI 96732
- **Opening Hours:** Sunday, 4:00 PM - 8:00 PM
- **Phone Number:** +1 808-446-9691

Tip: Bring a blanket or lawn chair to relax and enjoy the live entertainment while savoring food from the various vendors.

6. Hana Farmers Market

Located in the remote town of Hana, the Hana Farmers Market offers a more intimate, authentic experience compared to some of the larger markets on the island. This market is held on Fridays and features a selection of fresh produce, much of which is grown in the surrounding lush, tropical environment. You'll find local staples like bananas, taro, and coconuts, along with homemade goods like jams, jellies, and baked treats. The market is small but vibrant, reflecting the tight-knit community of Hana. It's a great place to experience the local culture and support the farmers of this remote area.

- **Location:** 150 Keawa Place, Hana, HI 96713
- **Opening Hours:** Friday, 3:00 PM - 5:30 PM
- **Phone Number:** +1 808-248-8224

Tip: Pair your visit with a trip to nearby Hamoa Beach or Wai'anapanapa State Park for a full day of exploring Hana's natural beauty.

Chapter 14: Shopping in Maui

Local Markets and Souvenirs

Maui Swap Meet

The Maui Swap Meet is a bustling marketplace where local artisans and vendors gather to sell a wide range of products, including handmade crafts, jewelry, clothing, and fresh produce. It's a great place to find unique souvenirs like Hawaiian quilts, local artwork, and traditional Hawaiian apparel. The atmosphere is lively, with vendors often offering samples of local foods and products. The swap meet is held every Saturday morning at the University of Hawaii Maui College campus in Kahului.

- **Location:** University of Hawaii Maui College, Kahului
- **Opening Hours:** Saturdays, 7:00 AM - 1:00 PM

Maui Crafts Guild

Located in the historic town of Paia, the Maui Crafts Guild features a cooperative of local artists showcasing their handmade crafts and artworks. Here, you'll find a variety of unique items such as ceramics, woodwork, glass art, and textiles, all crafted with a distinctly Hawaiian flair. The guild emphasizes high-quality, locally made goods, making it an excellent place to shop for authentic Maui souvenirs that support local artisans.

- **Location:** 120 Hana Highway, Paia
- **Opening Hours:** Daily, 10:00 AM - 6:00 PM

Haleakala Gift Shop

Situated near the entrance of Haleakala National Park, the Haleakala Gift Shop offers a range of souvenirs related to the park and Hawaiian culture. You can find items like t-shirts, hats, books on Hawaiian flora and fauna, and unique gifts inspired by the volcanic landscapes of Maui. The shop is conveniently located for visitors exploring the park and looking to bring home mementos of their Haleakala experience.

- **Location:** Haleakala National Park Visitor Center, Kula
- **Opening Hours:** Daily, 7:00 AM - 3:30 PM

Maui Hands

With multiple locations across Maui (Lahaina, Makawao, and Paia), Maui Hands is a gallery-style shop showcasing a wide array of locally made arts and crafts. Each location features a curated selection of jewelry, paintings, sculptures, and decorative items created by Maui artists. Whether you're looking for a unique piece of jewelry or a vibrant painting inspired by Maui's landscapes, Maui Hands offers a diverse range of authentic souvenirs that reflect the island's artistic community.

- **Locations:** Lahaina, Makawao, Paia
- **Opening Hours:** Varies by location, typically 10:00 AM - 6:00 PM

Maui Ocean Treasures

Located at the Maui Ocean Center in Maalaea, Maui Ocean Treasures specializes in marine-themed souvenirs and gifts. Here, you can find a variety of items such as plush sea creatures, educational books about marine life, apparel featuring ocean conservation messages, and artwork by local artists inspired by Maui's underwater world. The shop is ideal for visitors interested in ocean-related souvenirs and learning more about Maui's marine ecosystems.

- **Location:** Maui Ocean Center, Maalaea
- **Opening Hours:** Daily, 9:00 AM - 5:00 PM

Queen Ka'ahumanu Center

As Maui's largest shopping mall, Queen Ka'ahumanu Center in Kahului offers a mix of retail stores, restaurants, and local boutiques. While it's a modern shopping destination, it also features local vendors and artisans selling Hawaiian gifts and souvenirs. You can explore shops offering Hawaiian clothing, jewelry, artwork, and specialty food items, providing a convenient place to find a variety of Maui-inspired gifts under one roof.

- **Location:** 275 W Ka'ahumanu Ave, Kahului
- **Opening Hours:** Monday-Saturday, 10:00 AM - 9:00 PM; Sunday, 10:00 AM - 5:00 PM

Island Gourmet Markets

Located within The Shops at Wailea, Island Gourmet Markets is a gourmet grocery store offering a selection of locally made products, including Hawaiian snacks, coffee, chocolates, and artisanal gifts. It's a great place to pick up specialty food items unique to Maui, such as Maui-grown coffee beans or locally-produced honey. The market also features a deli and bakery section, making it convenient for grabbing a quick bite while shopping.

- **Location:** The Shops at Wailea, Wailea
- **Opening Hours**: Daily, 8:00 AM - 9:00 PM

Maui Market Co-op

Located in the heart of Lahaina, the Maui Market Co-op is a community-driven marketplace featuring local vendors selling fresh produce, handmade crafts, and artisanal goods. It offers a unique shopping experience where you can interact directly with farmers and artisans, supporting sustainable practices and local entrepreneurship. The co-op often hosts events and workshops, providing insights into Maui's agricultural and artisanal traditions.

- **Location:** Lahaina Gateway, Lahaina
- **Opening Hours:** Monday-Saturday, 9:00 AM - 6:00 PM; Sunday, 9:00 AM - 5:00 PM

Hui No'eau Visual Arts Center

Located in Upcountry Maui, the Hui No'eau Visual Arts Center is both an art gallery and a place where local artists create and showcase their work. The center hosts exhibitions, art classes, and events throughout the year, offering visitors an opportunity to purchase original artworks, ceramics, jewelry, and other handmade items directly from Maui's talented artists. It's a cultural hub where you can immerse yourself in Maui's artistic community and find unique souvenirs.

- **Location:** 2841 Baldwin Ave, Makawao
- **Opening Hours:** Monday-Saturday, 9:00 AM - 4:00 PM; Closed Sundays

Paia Bay Coffee and Gifts

Paia Bay Coffee and Gifts is a charming café and gift shop in the town of Paia, known for its laid-back vibe and proximity to famous surfing spots. It offers a selection of locally roasted coffee beans, Hawaiian-themed gifts, and souvenirs such as t-shirts, hats, and beach accessories.

Whether you're grabbing a coffee to go or browsing for gifts, Paia Bay Coffee and Gifts captures the essence of Maui's surf culture and artistic community.

- **Location:** 115 Hana Hwy, Paia
- **Opening Hours:** Daily, 6:30 AM - 5:00 PM

Handicrafts and Artisanal Products

Maui Gold Pineapple

Maui is renowned for its sweet and succulent pineapples, particularly the Maui Gold variety. Grown in the fertile volcanic soil of Upcountry Maui, these pineapples are celebrated for their exceptional flavor and juiciness. You can purchase fresh Maui Gold pineapples at local farmers' markets, grocery stores, and directly from farms like Hali'imaile Pineapple Company.

- **Location:** Hali'imaile Pineapple Company, 872 Hali'imaile Rd, Makawao, HI 96768
- **Opening Hours:** Monday to Friday, 8:00 AM - 4:00 PM

Koa Wood Products

Koa wood is native to Hawaii and prized for its rich color and unique grain patterns. Artisans on Maui craft a variety of items from Koa wood, including furniture, jewelry, and decorative items. Look for Koa wood products at local galleries, craft fairs, and specialty shops like Maui Hands, which showcases the work of local artists.

- **Location:** Maui Hands, multiple locations including Lahaina, Paia, and Makawao
- **Opening Hours:** Varies by location, typically 10:00 AM - 6:00 PM daily

Ni'ihau Shell Jewelry

Ni'ihau shells are tiny, delicate shells found only on the shores of Ni'ihau, Hawaii's "Forbidden Island." Skilled artisans on Maui create exquisite shell jewelry, including necklaces, earrings, and bracelets. These pieces often feature intricate designs and vibrant colors, making them unique and highly sought after as souvenirs.

- **Location:** Local jewelry stores and galleries in Lahaina, Wailea, and Paia
- **Opening Hours:** Typically, 10:00 AM - 8:00 PM daily

Handwoven Lauhala Products

Lauhala, or pandanus leaves, are used by Hawaiian artisans to create traditional woven products such as hats, baskets, and mats. These items showcase the artistry and cultural heritage of Hawaiian weaving techniques. You can find handwoven Lauhala products at cultural centers, markets, and craft shops across Maui.

- **Location:** Maui Crafts Guild, 69 Hana Hwy, Paia, HI 96779
- **Opening Hours:** Monday to Saturday, 10:00 AM - 6:00 PM; Sunday, 11:00 AM - 5:00 PM

Hawaiian Quilts

Hawaiian quilts are renowned for their intricate designs inspired by native flora and fauna. Traditionally crafted by hand, these quilts feature bold patterns and vibrant colors. Look for Hawaiian quilt shops and galleries where local quilters display and sell their work, often accompanied by stories of Hawaiian culture and history.

- **Location:** Hawaiian Quilt Collection, 1087 Limahana Pl, Lahaina, HI 96761
- **Opening Hours:** Monday to Saturday, 9:00 AM - 5:00 PM; Sunday, 10:00 AM - 4:00 PM

Tapa Cloth

Tapa cloth, known as kapa in Hawaiian, is made from the bark of the mulberry tree and decorated with traditional designs using natural dyes. Artisans on Maui create contemporary versions of tapa cloth, including wall hangings, clothing, and decorative items. Visit art galleries and cultural centers to explore and purchase these unique pieces.

- **Location:** Maui Hands, multiple locations including Lahaina, Paia, and Makawao
- **Opening Hours:** Varies by location, typically 10:00 AM - 6:00 PM daily

Hawaiian Ukuleles

The ukulele is synonymous with Hawaiian music and culture. Handcrafted ukuleles made from local woods like koa are cherished by musicians and collectors alike. Maui is home to several ukulele makers and music shops where you can find a wide selection of instruments, from beginner models to custom-made masterpieces

- **Location:** Mele Ukulele, 1750 Kaahumanu Ave #9, Wailuku, HI 96793
- **Opening Hours**: Monday to Friday, 10:00 AM - 6:00 PM; Saturday, 10:00 AM - 4:00 PM

Maui Goat Milk Soap

Maui is known for its locally produced goat milk soap, crafted from natural ingredients and often scented with tropical fragrances. These soaps are gentle on the skin and popular for their moisturizing properties. Find Maui goat milk soap at farmers' markets, boutique shops, and online stores specializing in Hawaiian skincare products.

- **Location:** Maui Soap Company, available online and at various retailers across Maui
- **Opening Hours:** Online store available 24/7; retail locations vary

Hawaiian Feather Art

Hawaiian feather art, known as kāhili pa'a lima, traditionally adorned Hawaiian ali'i (royalty). Today, contemporary artisans on Maui create stunning feather art pieces using feathers from native birds and dyed feathers from other sources. These artworks are displayed in galleries and cultural exhibitions, showcasing the intricate craftsmanship and cultural significance.

- **Location:** Maui Art Gallery, 25 S Market St, Wailuku, HI 96793
- **Opening Hours:** Monday to Saturday, 9:00 AM - 5:00 PM; Sunday, 10:00 AM - 4:00 PM

Hawaiian Heirloom Jewelry

Hawaiian heirloom jewelry is characterized by intricate designs engraved or etched into precious metals such as gold and silver. These designs often incorporate Hawaiian motifs and can be customized with names or meaningful phrases. Look for jewelry stores and artisans specializing in Hawaiian heirloom pieces, which make cherished gifts and souvenirs.

- **Location:** Maui Divers Jewelry, multiple locations including Lahaina and Wailea

- **Opening Hours:** Varies by location, typically 10:00 AM - 9:00 PM daily

Fashion Boutiques and Beachwear

Mahina:

Mahina offers a blend of Hawaiian-inspired fashion and beachwear, featuring stylish swimwear, breezy cover-ups, and locally made accessories. Their collections emphasize comfort and tropical flair, perfect for both lounging by the beach and exploring Maui's vibrant towns.

- **Location:** Mahina, 24 Baldwin Ave, Paia, HI 96779
- **Opening Hours:** Monday-Saturday 10:00 AM - 6:00 PM, Sunday 11:00 AM - 5:00 PM

Island Gypsy Hawaii:

Located in Lahaina, Island Gypsy Hawaii specializes in bohemian beachwear and unique resort wear. Their collection includes flowy dresses, handcrafted jewelry, and beach accessories sourced from local artisans and international designers.

- **Location: Island** Gypsy Hawaii, 839 Front St, Lahaina, HI 96761
- **Opening Hours:** Daily 9:00 AM - 9:00 PM

San Lorenzo Bikinis:

Known for its trendy swimwear and beach essentials, San Lorenzo Bikinis offers a wide range of bikini styles, from classic cuts to Brazilian-inspired designs. Their boutique in Wailea showcases vibrant prints and high-quality fabrics.

- **Location:** San Lorenzo Bikinis, The Shops at Wailea, 3750 Wailea Alanui Dr, Kihei, HI 96753
- **Opening Hours:** Daily 10:00 AM - 9:00 PM

Nuage Bleu:

Nuage Bleu combines fashion-forward styles with a laid-back island vibe. Located in Paia, this boutique features designer clothing, accessories, and swimwear that reflect Maui's casual elegance and beachside lifestyle.

- **Location:** Nuage Bleu, 76 Hana Hwy, Paia, HI 96779
- **Opening Hours:** Daily 10:00 AM - 6:00 PM

Maui WaterWear:

Maui WaterWear caters to all things beach-related, offering a wide selection of swimwear, board shorts, and beach accessories for men and women. With multiple locations across Maui, it's a convenient choice for beachgoers seeking quality beachwear.

- **Location:** Multiple locations including Lahaina, Kihei, and Kahului
- **Opening Hours:** Varies by location, typically 9:00 AM - 9:00 PM

Sirens & Sailors:

Situated in Lahaina's historic district, Sirens & Sailors showcases a curated collection of coastal-inspired fashion. They feature breezy sundresses, casual beachwear, and accessories perfect for a day at the beach or an evening out.

- **Location:** Sirens & Sailors, 744 Front St, Lahaina, HI 96761
- **Opening Hours:** Daily 9:00 AM - 10:00 PM

Hula Gypsy Boutique:

Hula Gypsy Boutique in Kihei embodies the free-spirited essence of Maui, offering flowy dresses, bohemian jewelry, and beach cover-ups. Their collection reflects a blend of local Hawaiian charm and global boho chic.

- **Location:** Hula Gypsy Boutique, 1913 S Kihei Rd, Kihei, HI 96753
- **Opening Hours:** Monday-Saturday 10:00 AM - 6:00 PM, Sunday 11:00 AM - 4:00 PM

Tamara Catz

Located in Paia, Tamara Catz is renowned for its elegant resort wear and bridal collections. The boutique features sophisticated dresses, resort outfits, and accessories designed with a blend of Hawaiian and international influences.

- **Location:** Tamara Catz, 83 Hana Hwy, Paia, HI 96779
- **Opening Hours:** Daily 10:00 AM - 6:00 PM

Maui Clothing Company:

Offering a wide range of Hawaiian shirts, dresses, and casual wear, Maui Clothing Company is a staple for those seeking authentic Hawaiian apparel. With multiple locations across Maui, they cater to both tourists and locals alike.

- **Location:** Multiple locations including Lahaina, Kihei, and Wailea
- **Opening Hours:** Varies by location, typically 9:00 AM - 9:00 PM

Mana Foods:

While primarily a natural foods store, Mana Foods in Paia also offers a unique selection of locally made clothing, jewelry, and accessories. It's a great spot to find eco-friendly fashion items and support local artisans.

- **Location:** Mana Foods, 49 Baldwin Ave, Paia, HI 96779
- **Opening Hours:** Daily 8:00 AM - 8:30 PM

Shopping Centers and Malls

Whalers Village

Whalers Village in Ka'anapali is a premier shopping destination featuring over 90 shops and restaurants amidst a beautiful oceanfront setting. Here, you'll find a mix of high-end boutiques, local artisans, and popular brands like Louis Vuitton and Tommy Bahama. The open-air layout allows for strolls between stores, with options ranging from fashion and jewelry to beachwear and souvenirs.

- **Location:** 2435 Kaanapali Pkwy, Lahaina, HI 96761
- **Opening Hours:** Monday-Saturday: 9:30 AM - 9:00 PM, Sunday: 10:00 AM - 6:00 PM

The Shops at Wailea

The Shops at Wailea is an upscale shopping center in South Maui, known for its luxurious ambiance and exclusive boutiques. Located near Wailea's resort area, this center features designer brands like Tiffany & Co., Gucci, and Bottega Veneta, alongside fine dining restaurants and art galleries. The beautifully landscaped outdoor mall also hosts cultural events and live music, adding to its appeal as a leisure destination.

- **Location:** 3750 Wailea Alanui Dr, Wailea, HI 96753
- **Opening Hours:** Monday-Sunday: 9:30 AM - 9:00 PM

Queen Ka'ahumanu Center

Queen Ka'ahumanu Center in Kahului is Maui's largest shopping mall, offering a diverse mix of stores, dining options, and entertainment. Anchored by Macy's and Sears, it features over 100 shops ranging from apparel and electronics to local crafts and Hawaiian souvenirs. The mall also hosts events like farmers' markets and cultural performances, providing a community hub for both locals and visitors.

- **Location:** 275 W Kaahumanu Ave, Kahului, HI 96732
- **Opening Hours:** Monday-Saturday: 9:30 AM - 9:00 PM, Sunday: 10:00 AM - 5:00 PM

Maui Mall

Maui Mall offers a laid-back shopping experience with a mix of stores catering to everyday needs and local tastes. Located in Kahului, it features a diverse range of shops including apparel, home goods, and specialty stores like Whole Foods Market and Maui Brewing Co. Visitors can also enjoy dining options ranging from casual eateries to sit-down restaurants.

- **Location:** 70 E Kaahumanu Ave, Kahului, HI 96732
- **Opening Hours:** Monday-Saturday: 9:00 AM - 8:00 PM, Sunday: 9:00 AM - 6:00 PM

Outlets of Maui

Outlets of Maui, located in Lahaina, offers shoppers discounted prices on popular brands like Coach, Michael Kors, and Banana Republic. This outdoor shopping center provides a relaxed atmosphere with views of the ocean, ideal for finding deals on apparel, accessories, and home goods. The center also features dining options and hosts special events throughout the year.

- **Location**: 900 Front St, Lahaina, HI 96761
- **Opening Hours:** Monday-Sunday: 10:00 AM - 9:00 PM

Maui Marketplace

Maui Marketplace in Kahului is a convenient shopping center offering a mix of large retailers, restaurants, and service providers. It's anchored by Walmart and features a variety of stores catering to everyday shopping needs, including apparel, electronics, and home improvement. The mall's central location makes it easily accessible for both locals and tourists.

- **Location:** 270 Dairy Rd, Kahului, HI 96732
- **Opening Hours:** Monday-Sunday: 6:00 AM - 12:00 AM

Lahaina Cannery Mall

Lahaina Cannery Mall offers a blend of shopping, dining, and entertainment in Lahaina's historic district. This indoor mall features Hawaiian-themed stores, local boutiques, and eateries serving both casual and upscale cuisine. Visitors can also enjoy cultural performances and events held regularly at the mall's center stage.

- **Location:** 1221 Honoapiilani Hwy, Lahaina, HI 96761
- **Opening Hours**: Monday-Saturday: 9:30 AM - 9:00 PM, Sunday: 9:30 AM - 5:30 PM

Piilani Village Shopping Center

Piilani Village Shopping Center in Kihei offers a convenient shopping experience with a mix of grocery stores, restaurants, and specialty shops. Located near residential areas, it provides locals and tourists with access to everyday essentials, including clothing, health products, and dining options ranging from fast food to sit-down restaurants.

- **Location:** 247 Piikea Ave, Kihei, HI 96753
- **Opening Hours:** Varies by store; typically, Monday-Sunday: 8:00 AM - 10:00 PM

Azeka Shopping Center

Azeka Shopping Center in Kihei is a bustling community hub offering a variety of shops, eateries, and services. Divided into Azeka Shopping Center Mauka (north) and Azeka Shopping Center Makai (south), it features local boutiques, art galleries, restaurants, and grocery stores. The center also hosts events such as farmers' markets and cultural festivals.

- **Location:** 1279 S Kihei Rd, Kihei, HI 96753
- **Opening Hours:** Varies by store; typically, Monday-Sunday: 8:00 AM - 10:00 PM

Kukui Mall

Kukui Mall in Kihei is a casual shopping center offering a mix of shops, dining options, and entertainment venues. Anchored by Longs Drugs and Safeway, it features a variety of stores including apparel, home goods, and specialty shops.

The mall's central location in Kihei makes it convenient for both residents and tourists exploring the area.

- **Location:** 1819 S Kihei Rd, Kihei, HI 96753
- **Opening Hours:** Varies by store; typically, Monday-Sunday: 9:00 AM - 9:00 PM

Chapter 15: Nightlife and Entertainment

Bars and Beachfront Lounges

Fleetwood's on Front St.

Fleetwood's on Front St., owned by legendary musician Mick Fleetwood, offers a unique blend of live music, excellent food, and stunning ocean views. The rooftop bar is a highlight, providing an unparalleled vantage point to enjoy Lahaina's beautiful sunsets while sipping on craft cocktails or local brews. The venue also features an impressive selection of wines and spirits. Regular live performances and a vibrant atmosphere make Fleetwood's a must-visit spot for an evening out.

- **Location:** 744 Front St, Lahaina, HI 96761
- **Opening Hours:** Daily 11:00 AM – 10:00 PM
- **Phone Number:** (808) 669-6425

Duke's Beach House

Named after the legendary Hawaiian surfer Duke Kahanamoku, Duke's Beach House is a popular beachfront bar and restaurant in Ka'anapali. The open-air setting, with views of the ocean and neighboring islands, creates a relaxed, tropical atmosphere. Enjoy a selection of tropical cocktails, local beers, and island-inspired dishes. Live music and hula performances add to the authentic Hawaiian experience.

- **Location:** 130 Kai Malina Pkwy, Lahaina, HI 96761
- **Opening Hours:** Daily 7:00 AM – 9:00 PM
- **Phone Number:** (808) 662-2900

Monkeypod Kitchen by Merriman

Monkeypod Kitchen by Merriman in Wailea is known for its farm-to-table approach, offering a diverse menu of fresh, local ingredients. The bar boasts an extensive selection of craft beers, cocktails made with local spirits, and a comprehensive wine list. The laid-back atmosphere is complemented by live music performances, making it an ideal spot to unwind after a day on the beach.

- **Location:** 10 Wailea Gateway Pl, Kihei, HI 96753
- **Opening Hours:** Daily 11:00 AM – 11:00 PM
- **Phone Number:** (808) 891-2322

Merriman's Kapalua

Merriman's Kapalua offers breathtaking views of Kapalua Bay, providing an elegant yet relaxed setting for enjoying a drink. The extensive wine list, signature cocktails, and local beers complement the Pacific Rim cuisine perfectly. The open-air bar area is a great place to enjoy a romantic sunset or a casual evening with friends.

- **Location:** 1 Bay Club Pl, Lahaina, HI 96761
- **Opening Hours:** Daily 3:00 PM – 9:00 PM
- **Phone Number:** (808) 669-6400

Leilani's on the Beach

Located at Whalers Village in Ka'anapali, Leilani's on the Beach offers a relaxed, beachfront dining experience. The bar features a wide range of tropical cocktails, local beers, and wines, making it a perfect spot to watch the sunset. The menu includes fresh seafood and traditional Hawaiian dishes, and live music adds to the island ambiance.

- **Location:** 2435 Kaanapali Pkwy, Lahaina, HI 96761
- **Opening Hours:** Daily 11:00 AM – 10:00 PM
- **Phone Number:** (808) 661-4495

The Dirty Monkey

The Dirty Monkey in Lahaina is a lively bar known for its extensive whiskey collection and creative cocktails. The casual, fun atmosphere is perfect for enjoying live sports on multiple screens or participating in trivia nights. The bar also features a range of craft beers and hosts live music and DJ events, making it a popular nightlife destination.

- **Location:** 844 Front St, Lahaina, HI 96761
- **Opening Hours:** Daily 11:00 AM – 2:00 AM
- **Phone Number:** (808) 419-6268

Three's Bar and Grill

Three's Bar and Grill in Kihei combines the culinary talents of three chefs to offer a diverse menu of sushi, seafood, and southwestern cuisine. The bar features a wide range of craft cocktails, local beers, and an impressive wine list.

The outdoor seating area provides a relaxed atmosphere with live music and ocean views, making it a great spot to unwind.

- **Location:** 1945 S Kihei Rd, Kihei, HI 96753
- **Opening Hours:** Daily 8:30 AM – 9:30 PM
- **Phone Number:** (808) 879-3133

The Pint & Cork

The Pint & Cork in Wailea is a gastropub offering a comfortable, upscale atmosphere. The extensive drink menu includes craft beers, signature cocktails, and a curated selection of wines and whiskeys. The pub fare, including burgers, wings, and local specialties, pairs perfectly with the drinks. Multiple screens for sports and a friendly vibe make it a favorite among both locals and visitors.

- **Location:** 3750 Wailea Alanui Dr, Kihei, HI 96753
- **Opening Hours:** Daily 11:00 AM – 11:00 PM
- **Phone Number:** (808) 727-2038

Maui Brewing Company

Maui Brewing Company in Kihei is a must-visit for craft beer enthusiasts. The brewery offers a wide range of locally brewed beers, from IPAs to stouts, all made with island-inspired ingredients. The spacious taproom features a laid-back atmosphere with live music, food trucks, and tours of the brewing facility. It's a great place to sample Maui's best craft beers.

- **Location:** 605 Lipoa Pkwy, Kihei, HI 96753
- **Opening Hours:** Daily 11:00 AM – 10:00 PM
- **Phone Number:** (808) 213-3002

The Mill House

The Mill House, located at Maui Tropical Plantation, offers a unique farm-to-table dining and drinking experience. The open-air bar provides stunning views of the plantation and the West Maui Mountains. Enjoy craft cocktails made with fresh, local ingredients, a curated wine list, and local beers. The tranquil setting and innovative menu make it a memorable destination.

- **Location:** 1670 Honoapiilani Hwy, Waikapu, HI 96793
- **Opening Hours:** Daily 11:00 AM – 9:00 PM

- **Phone Number:** (808) 270-0333

Live Music Venues

Maui's vibrant live music scene offers a range of venues where visitors can enjoy diverse musical performances. Here are some top live music venues in Maui, each providing a unique atmosphere and experience:

Fleetwood's on Front St.

Fleetwood's on Front St. in Lahaina is a premier live music venue owned by Mick Fleetwood of Fleetwood Mac. The venue features a rooftop stage with stunning ocean views where live performances are held regularly. Guests can enjoy a mix of local bands, solo artists, and even surprise performances by Mick Fleetwood himself. The atmosphere is sophisticated yet relaxed, making it an ideal spot for enjoying high-quality music along with great food and drinks.

- **Location:** 744 Front St, Lahaina, HI 96761
- **Opening Hours:** Daily 11:00 AM – 10:00 PM
- **Phone Number:** (808) 669-6425

Charley's Restaurant & Saloon

Charley's Restaurant & Saloon in Paia is a historic venue known for its vibrant live music scene. The saloon has hosted a variety of artists, including Willie Nelson, who is a regular performer. With its laid-back vibe and intimate setting, Charley's is a great place to enjoy live performances ranging from rock and blues to country and Hawaiian music. The eclectic menu and full bar complement the lively entertainment.

- **Location:** 142 Hana Hwy, Paia, HI 96779
- **Opening Hours:** Daily 7:00 AM – 10:00 PM
- **Phone Number:** (808) 579-8085

The Dirty Monkey

The Dirty Monkey in Lahaina is a hotspot for nightlife and live music on Maui's west side. Known for its extensive whiskey collection and creative cocktails, the venue also features live music and DJ performances. The energetic atmosphere, complete with dance floors and multiple screens for sports, makes it a favorite for both locals and tourists. The Dirty Monkey frequently hosts themed nights and special events, adding to its lively appeal.

- **Location:** 844 Front St, Lahaina, HI 96761
- **Opening Hours:** Daily 11:00 AM – 2:00 AM
- **Phone Number:** (808) 419-6268

Kimo's Maui

Kimo's Maui, located on the waterfront in Lahaina, offers live music in a scenic, open-air setting. The venue features a mix of local musicians playing traditional Hawaiian music, contemporary hits, and island-inspired tunes. The relaxed ambiance, coupled with stunning views of the Pacific Ocean, makes Kimo's a perfect spot to enjoy live music while savoring fresh seafood and tropical cocktails.

- **Location:** 845 Front St, Lahaina, HI 96761
- **Opening Hours:** Daily 11:00 AM – 10:00 PM
- **Phone Number:** (808) 661-4811

South Shore Tiki Lounge

South Shore Tiki Lounge in Kihei is a popular spot for live music and dancing. The tiki-themed venue offers a lively atmosphere with regular performances by local bands and solo artists. The outdoor patio provides a casual setting to enjoy reggae, rock, and Hawaiian music. With its fun, tropical vibe and extensive drink menu, South Shore Tiki Lounge is a great place for a night out.

- **Location:** 1913 S Kihei Rd, Kihei, HI 96753
- **Opening Hours:** Daily 11:00 AM – 2:00 AM
- **Phone Number:** (808) 874-6444

Mulligans on the Blue

Mulligans on the Blue in Wailea is a unique venue offering live music with an Irish twist. This Irish pub features performances by local musicians, as well as Irish music and dance. The outdoor stage, overlooking the Wailea Blue Golf Course, creates a picturesque setting for enjoying live entertainment. Mulligans is known for its friendly atmosphere, delicious pub fare, and wide selection of beers and spirits.

- **Location:** 100 Kaukahi St, Kihei, HI 96753
- **Opening Hours:** Daily 11:00 AM – 11:00 PM
- **Phone Number:** (808) 874-1131

Three's Bar and Grill

Three's Bar and Grill in Kihei offers a diverse menu and a vibrant live music scene. The restaurant features performances by local bands and solo artists, playing everything from jazz and blues to rock and reggae. The spacious outdoor seating area provides a comfortable setting to enjoy the music, along with delicious food and drinks. Three's is a popular spot for both dinner and nightlife, attracting a lively crowd.

- **Location:** 1945 S Kihei Rd, Kihei, HI 96753
- **Opening Hours:** Daily 8:30 AM – 9:30 PM
- **Phone Number:** (808) 879-3133

Nalu's South Shore Grill

Nalu's South Shore Grill in Kihei is a casual dining spot known for its live music and laid-back atmosphere. The restaurant features local musicians performing Hawaiian, jazz, and contemporary music. The open-air setting, with views of the garden and ocean, makes Nalu's a great place to enjoy a relaxing meal and live entertainment. The menu includes healthy, locally sourced dishes and a variety of craft cocktails.

- **Location:** 1280 S Kihei Rd, Kihei, HI 96753
- **Opening Hours:** Daily 8:00 AM – 9:00 PM
- **Phone Number:** (808) 891-8650

Hawaiian Moons Natural Foods

Hawaiian Moons Natural Foods in Kihei may primarily be a health food store, but it also features live music on its outdoor patio. Local musicians perform a variety of genres, including Hawaiian, folk, and acoustic. The relaxed, family-friendly environment and healthy food options make it a unique spot for enjoying live music in a more low-key setting. The venue is perfect for those looking for a casual and healthy dining experience with entertainment.

- **Location:** 2411 S Kihei Rd, Kihei, HI 96753
- **Opening Hours:** Daily 7:00 AM – 9:00 PM
- **Phone Number:** (808) 875-4356

The Maui Arts & Cultural Center

The Maui Arts & Cultural Center (MACC) in Kahului is the premier venue for major concerts and live performances on Maui. The center hosts a wide range of events, from local music festivals to performances by internationally renowned artists. The outdoor amphitheater and indoor theaters provide excellent acoustics and a comfortable setting for enjoying live music. MACC is a cultural hub that offers a diverse lineup of entertainment, including traditional Hawaiian music, jazz, rock, and classical performances.

- **Location:** 1 Cameron Way, Kahului, HI 96732
- **Phone Number:** (808) 242-7469

Cultural Performances

Old Lahaina Luau

The Old Lahaina Luau is one of Maui's most authentic and renowned Hawaiian cultural experiences. The evening begins with a traditional Hawaiian feast, featuring kalua pig cooked in an imu (underground oven), poi, and other island specialties. The highlight is the captivating performance of hula and music, tracing the history and legends of Hawaii. The intimate beachfront setting and attention to cultural detail make it a memorable and educational experience for all ages.

- **Location:** 1251 Front St, Lahaina, HI 96761
- **Opening Hours:** Daily 5:15 PM – 8:15 PM
- **Phone Number:** (808) 667-1998

Feast at Lele

Feast at Lele offers a unique and upscale luau experience, combining gourmet dining with a cultural performance. Guests are treated to a multi-course dinner, with each course representing the cuisine of a different Polynesian island. The evening's entertainment features dances and music from Hawaii, Aotearoa (New Zealand), Tahiti, and Samoa, providing a broad overview of Polynesian culture. The oceanfront location in Lahaina adds to the magical ambiance.

- **Location:** 505 Front St, Lahaina, HI 96761
- **Opening Hours:** Daily 6:00 PM – 9:00 PM
- **Phone Number:** (808) 667-5353

Wailele Polynesian Luau at The Westin Maui

The Wailele Polynesian Luau, held at The Westin Maui Resort & Spa, features a thrilling display of Polynesian culture. The show includes traditional Hawaiian hula, as well as dances from other Polynesian islands such as Samoa, Tahiti, and Fiji. The highlight of the evening is the spectacular fire knife dance. Guests also enjoy a sumptuous Hawaiian buffet and tropical drinks, all set against the beautiful backdrop of Ka'anapali Beach.

- **Location:** 2365 Kaanapali Pkwy, Lahaina, HI 96761
- **Opening Hours:** Tuesday, Thursday, and Sunday 5:30 PM – 8:30 PM
- **Phone Number:** (808) 661-2992

The Grand Wailea Luau

The Grand Wailea Luau, also known as 'Aha'aina Wailea, is an elegant luau set in the luxurious Grand Wailea Resort. Guests are greeted with traditional Hawaiian leis and offered a buffet dinner featuring island cuisine. The show tells the story of Maui, the demigod, through hula, chants, and music. The breathtaking oceanfront setting and high-quality production make it a top choice for those seeking a more refined luau experience.

- **Location:** 3850 Wailea Alanui Dr, Wailea, HI 96753
- **Opening Hours:** Monday, Thursday, and Saturday 5:00 PM – 8:00 PM
- **Phone Number:** (808) 875-1234

Maui Arts & Cultural Center

The Maui Arts & Cultural Center (MACC) is the island's premier venue for a wide range of cultural performances, including Hawaiian music, dance, theater, and art exhibitions. The center hosts performances by local and international artists, offering a diverse schedule of events throughout the year. The outdoor amphitheater and indoor theaters provide excellent acoustics and a comfortable viewing experience.

- **Location:** 1 Cameron Way, Kahului, HI 96732
- **Opening Hours:** Event times vary; the box office is open Monday to Saturday 10:00 AM – 6:00 PM
- **Phone Number:** (808) 242-7469

Slack Key Show – Masters of Hawaiian Music

This intimate concert series, held at the Napili Kai Beach Resort, features some of Hawaii's most talented slack key guitarists and musicians. The performances celebrate the traditional Hawaiian art of slack key guitar, characterized by its open tunings and fingerstyle playing. The show also includes storytelling and cultural insights, providing a deeper understanding of Hawaiian music and heritage.

- **Location:** 5900 Lower Honoapiilani Rd, Lahaina, HI 96761
- **Opening Hours:** Wednesday 7:30 PM – 9:00 PM
- **Phone Number:** (808) 669-3858

Ulalena

Ulalena is a theatrical performance that combines traditional Hawaiian music, hula, and acrobatics to tell the story of Hawaii's history and mythology. The production features stunning visuals, original music, and powerful performances that transport the audience through the islands' rich cultural heritage. Held at the Maui Theatre in Lahaina, Ulalena is a must-see for anyone interested in Hawaii's past and present.

- **Location:** 878 Front St, Lahaina, HI 96761
- **Phone Number:** (808) 856-7900

Hula Grill Ka'anapali

Hula Grill Ka'anapali offers nightly hula performances and live Hawaiian music in a casual, beachfront setting. Enjoy delicious island cuisine and tropical cocktails while watching talented dancers perform traditional hula. The restaurant's location on Ka'anapali Beach provides a perfect backdrop for an authentic Hawaiian evening.

- **Location:** 2435 Kaanapali Pkwy, Bldg P, Lahaina, HI 96761
- **Opening Hours:** Daily 11:00 AM – 9:00 PM
- **Phone Number:** (808) 667-6636

Hyatt Regency Maui Drums of the Pacific Luau

The Drums of the Pacific Luau at the Hyatt Regency Maui offers an exciting evening of Polynesian entertainment.

The show includes dances from Hawaii, Tahiti, Samoa, and New Zealand, culminating in a spectacular fire knife dance. Guests enjoy a traditional Hawaiian buffet and tropical drinks, all set in the resort's beautiful oceanfront setting.

- **Location:** 200 Nohea Kai Dr, Lahaina, HI 96761
- **Opening Hours:** Daily 5:30 PM – 8:30 PM
- **Phone Number:** (808) 667-4727

The Shops at Wailea – Concerts at The Shops

The Shops at Wailea hosts free live concerts featuring Hawaiian music, hula, and other cultural performances. These events offer a wonderful opportunity to experience local talent and enjoy a variety of musical styles, from traditional Hawaiian to contemporary island tunes. The open-air setting and relaxed atmosphere make it a perfect way to spend an evening in Wailea.

- **Location:** 3750 Wailea Alanui Dr, Kihei, HI 96753
- **Opening Hours:** Event times vary; typically, in the evening
- **Phone Number:** (808) 891-6770

Night Markets and Events

Maui Swap Meet

The Maui Swap Meet is a popular outdoor market held every Saturday at the University of Hawaii Maui College campus. It features over 200 vendors selling a variety of goods, including fresh produce, local crafts, jewelry, clothing, and unique souvenirs. The market is also a great place to sample local foods and snacks. It's a vibrant gathering spot for both locals and visitors, providing a taste of Maui's diverse culture and community spirit.

- **Location:** University of Hawaii Maui College, 310 W Kaahumanu Ave, Kahului, HI 96732
- **Opening Hours:** Saturdays 7:00 AM – 1:00 PM
- **Phone Number:** (808) 244-3100

Lahaina Second Friday Town Party

Lahaina's Second Friday Town Party is part of the Maui Friday Town Parties series, which takes place in different towns across Maui each Friday. This monthly event transforms Front Street into a lively festival with live music, food vendors, local crafts, and family-friendly activities.

It's an excellent opportunity to experience Lahaina's historic charm, shop for unique items, and enjoy entertainment from local performers.

- **Location:** Front St, Lahaina, HI 96761
- **Opening Hours:** Second Friday of each month, 6:00 PM – 9:00 PM
- **Phone Number:** (808) 667-9175

Makawao Third Friday Town Party

Makawao's Third Friday Town Party is a celebration of this charming Upcountry town's paniolo (Hawaiian cowboy) heritage. The streets come alive with live music, food trucks, local art, and family activities. The event showcases Makawao's unique blend of Hawaiian and cowboy cultures, with vendors offering handmade crafts, jewelry, and delicious local foods. It's a great way to experience the community spirit and artistic flair of Upcountry Maui.

- **Location:** Baldwin Ave, Makawao, HI 96768
- **Opening Hours:** Third Friday of each month, 6:00 PM – 9:00 PM
- **Phone Number:** (808) 270-7710

Kihei Fourth Friday Town Party

Kihei's Fourth Friday Town Party takes place in Azeka Shopping Center and features live music, food booths, arts and crafts vendors, and family-friendly activities. This event highlights the vibrant community of South Maui, offering a diverse selection of local products and entertainment. It's an ideal spot to mingle with locals, enjoy great food, and discover unique gifts and crafts.

- **Location:** Azeka Shopping Center, 1279 S Kihei Rd, Kihei, HI 96753
- **Opening Hours:** Fourth Friday of each month, 6:00 PM – 9:00 PM
- **Phone Number:** (808) 270-7710

Wailuku First Friday Town Party

Wailuku's First Friday Town Party is known for its lively atmosphere, featuring live music, street performers, food vendors, and local crafts. Held in historic Wailuku town, this event showcases the area's rich history and vibrant arts scene. It's a great place to explore unique shops, sample local cuisine, and enjoy entertainment from talented performers.

- **Location:** Market St, Wailuku, HI 96793

- **Opening Hours:** First Friday of each month, 6:00 PM – 9:00 PM
- **Phone Number:** (808) 878-1888

Maui Arts & Cultural Center Events

The Maui Arts & Cultural Center (MACC) hosts a variety of events throughout the year, including concerts, theater performances, film screenings, and cultural festivals. The center's outdoor pavilion, indoor theaters, and art galleries provide a dynamic space for both local and international artists. The MACC's events are a great way to experience Maui's vibrant cultural scene and enjoy world-class performances in a stunning setting.

- **Location:** 1 Cameron Way, Kahului, HI 96732
- **Phone Number:** (808) 242-7469

Hula Shows at Kaanapali Beach Hotel

The Kaanapali Beach Hotel offers complimentary hula shows and Hawaiian entertainment in its open-air courtyard. These performances are a fantastic way to experience traditional Hawaiian dance and music in a relaxed, beachfront setting. The shows often feature talented local dancers and musicians, providing an authentic cultural experience for visitors.

- **Location:** 2525 Kaanapali Pkwy, Lahaina, HI 96761
- **Opening Hours:** Varies, typically evenings
- **Phone Number:** (808) 661-0011

Maui Sunday Market

The Maui Sunday Market, held in Kahului, is a vibrant evening market featuring local food vendors, crafts, and live entertainment. It's a great spot to sample a variety of Hawaiian and international foods, from poke bowls to malasadas. The market also showcases local artisans and their handmade products, making it a perfect place to pick up unique souvenirs.

- **Location:** Kahului Shopping Center, 65 W Kaahumanu Ave, Kahului, HI 96732
- **Opening Hours:** Sundays 4:00 PM – 8:00 PM
- **Phone Number:** (808) 270-7710

Chapter 16: Maui with Family

Family-Friendly Attractions

Maui is a fantastic destination for families, offering a variety of attractions and activities that cater to all ages. Here are some top family-friendly attractions in Maui, with detailed descriptions:

1. Maui Ocean Center

The Maui Ocean Center, also known as the Aquarium of Hawaii, offers a fascinating underwater experience showcasing the diverse marine life found in Hawaiian waters. Highlights include the Living Reef, Turtle Lagoon, and the impressive Open Ocean exhibit, which features a 750,000-gallon tank with a 54-foot-long acrylic tunnel, allowing visitors to walk through and see sharks, rays, and tropical fish up close. Educational programs and interactive exhibits make it a great learning experience for children and adults alike.

- **Location:** 192 Maalaea Rd, Wailuku, HI 96793
- **Opening Hours:** Daily 9:00 AM – 5:00 PM
- **Entry Fee:** Adults $39.95, Children (4-12) $26.95, Under 4 Free

2. Haleakalā National Park

A visit to Haleakalā National Park is a must for families. The park offers a range of activities, from watching the sunrise at the summit to hiking through the stunning landscapes of the volcanic crater. The Hosmer Grove trail is perfect for families, providing a short, easy walk through a unique forest. The park also offers ranger-led programs and educational exhibits at the visitor centers. The drive up to the summit provides breathtaking views and the chance to explore diverse ecosystems.

- **Location:** Haleakalā National Park, Kula, HI 96790
- **Opening Hours:** Open 24 hours
- **Entry Fee:** $30 per vehicle for a 3-day pass

3. Lahaina Banyan Court Park

Home to one of the largest banyan trees in the United States, Lahaina Banyan Court Park is a beautiful spot for families to explore. Planted in 1873, the tree has grown to cover nearly an acre, providing ample shade and a picturesque setting for picnics and relaxation. The park is often the site of local events, art fairs, and cultural activities, offering a glimpse into Maui's vibrant community life.

- **Location:** 671 Front St, Lahaina, HI 96761
- **Opening Hours:** Open 24 hours

4. Maui Tropical Plantation

Maui Tropical Plantation is a great family destination offering a blend of education and entertainment. Take the tram tour to learn about Maui's agricultural history and see crops like pineapples, coconuts, and sugarcane. The plantation also features zip-lining, a farm-to-table restaurant, and lush gardens perfect for a stroll. Children will enjoy feeding the ducks and exploring the grounds.

- **Location:** 1670 Honoapiilani Hwy, Wailuku, HI 96793
- **Opening Hours:** Daily 9:00 AM – 5:00 PM
- **Entry Fee:** Free entry, tram tour $20 for adults, $10 for children (3-12), under 3 free

5. Iao Valley State Park

Iao Valley State Park offers a beautiful natural setting for family outings. The park is known for the iconic Iao Needle, a 1,200-foot rock formation. Families can explore the lush valley, hike the easy trails, and learn about the historical significance of the area. The paved paths make it accessible for strollers, and the small botanical garden near the entrance provides an educational experience about native plants.

- **Location:** 54 S High St, Wailuku, HI 96793
- **Opening Hours:** Daily 7:00 AM – 6:00 PM
- **Entry Fee:** $5 per car for parking

6. Waianapanapa State Park

Waianapanapa State Park is famous for its black sand beach, freshwater caves, and coastal hiking trails. It's a great spot for a family adventure, offering a unique landscape to explore. Kids will love the opportunity to see tide pools, and sea arches, and even spot seabirds. The park has picnic facilities, making it perfect for a day trip along the Road to Hana.

- **Location:** Hana Hwy, Hana, HI 96713
- **Opening Hours:** Daily 7:00 AM – 6:00 PM
- **Entry Fee:** $5 per person for non-residents, $10 per car for parking

7. Maui Arts & Cultural Center

The Maui Arts & Cultural Center hosts a variety of family-friendly events, including concerts, theater productions, and art exhibits. The center's Schaefer International Gallery often features interactive and educational exhibits suitable for children. Outdoor events in the A&B Amphitheater provide a relaxed atmosphere where families can enjoy live performances under the stars.

- **Location:** One Cameron Way, Kahului, HI 96732

8. Maui Dragon Fruit Farm

Maui Dragon Fruit Farm offers a unique experience where families can learn about dragon fruit cultivation. The farm tour includes a walk through the orchards, and tastings of fresh dragon fruit, and other tropical fruits. Kids will enjoy the chance to see the plants up close and learn about sustainable farming practices. The farm also offers activities like zip-lining and aqua ball, adding an element of adventure to the visit.

- **Location:** 833 Punakea Loop, Lahaina, HI 96761
- **Opening Hours:** Daily 8:00 AM – 5:00 PM
- **Entry Fee:** $15 per person for a farm tour, additional cost for activities

9. Kealia Pond National Wildlife Refuge

Kealia Pond National Wildlife Refuge is a great spot for families interested in birdwatching and nature walks. The refuge is home to native Hawaiian bird species, including the Hawaiian stilt and coot. The boardwalk trail provides an easy walk with excellent birdwatching opportunities and educational signage along the way. It's an excellent place to connect with nature and learn about Maui's unique ecosystems.

- **Location:** Milepost 6, Mokulele Hwy, Kihei, HI 96753
- **Opening Hours:** Monday – Friday 7:30 AM – 4:00 PM

10. Pacific Whale Foundation Ocean Discovery Center

The Pacific Whale Foundation Ocean Discovery Center in Ma'alaea Harbor is an educational attraction focused on marine conservation. The center offers interactive exhibits about marine life, conservation efforts, and the foundation's research. Families can also participate in whale-watching tours and eco-adventures organized by the foundation. The center's mission is to inspire and educate visitors about the importance of protecting the ocean.

- **Location:** 300 Maalaea Rd, Wailuku, HI 96793
- **Opening Hours:** Daily 7:30 AM – 5:00 PM

Tips for Traveling with Children

1. Plan Kid-Friendly Activities

Maui offers a plethora of activities suitable for children of all ages. Plan visits to places like the Maui Ocean Center, where kids can learn about marine life through interactive exhibits and aquariums. Beaches with gentle waves, like Baby Beach in Lahaina, are ideal for young swimmers. Also, consider taking a family-friendly hike in Iao Valley State Park, where the trails are short and scenic. Incorporate a mix of educational and fun activities to keep children engaged and entertained.

2. Pack Essentials for Beach Days

A day at the beach can be one of the highlights of a Maui vacation, but it's important to pack everything you'll need to keep the kids comfortable. Bring plenty of sunscreen, hats, and rash guards to protect from the sun. Include beach toys, snorkeling gear, and flotation devices for safe water play. A portable cooler with snacks and drinks, along with a beach umbrella or tent for shade, can make your beach day more enjoyable. Always keep an eye on local weather and ocean conditions to ensure a safe outing.

3. Rent Baby Gear Locally

Traveling with young children often requires a lot of gear, but you can lighten your load by renting items locally. Companies on Maui offer rentals for cribs, strollers, car seats, high chairs, and more. This not only reduces the hassle of traveling with bulky items but also ensures you have access to quality equipment tailored to your needs.

Arrange rentals in advance to have everything delivered to your accommodation, so you can focus on enjoying your vacation from the moment you arrive.

4. Choose Family-Friendly Accommodations

When selecting accommodations, look for family-friendly resorts or vacation rentals. Many resorts offer amenities like children's pools, kids' clubs, and activities that cater to young guests. Vacation rentals can provide more space and convenience, such as kitchens for preparing meals and separate sleeping areas. Locations near beaches or attractions can save travel time and make it easier to manage your schedule. Check reviews and recommendations to ensure the property is well-suited for families.

5. Keep a Flexible Schedule

While it's good to have a plan, maintaining flexibility is key when traveling with children. Kids can get tired or overwhelmed, so be prepared to adjust your itinerary as needed. Allow for downtime between activities, and have a few low-key options on hand, such as a visit to a nearby park or a quiet afternoon at the pool. Flexibility can help prevent meltdowns and ensure that everyone in the family enjoys the trip.

6. Stay Hydrated and Well-Fed

Hawaii's tropical climate means it's important to stay hydrated, especially for young children who may not realize they're thirsty. Carry refillable water bottles and encourage regular sips throughout the day. Pack healthy snacks like fruits, nuts, and granola bars to keep energy levels up between meals. Familiar snacks can also provide comfort in new environments. When dining out, look for restaurants with kids' menus or those known for being family-friendly.

7. Educate Children About Ocean Safety

Maui's beautiful beaches can be tempting, but the ocean demands respect and caution. Teach children about ocean safety, including the importance of swimming in designated areas and never turning their back on the waves. Explain the significance of colored flags and what they indicate about water conditions. Lifeguards are present at many popular beaches, so choose these locations for added safety. Always supervise children closely when they're in or near the water.

8. Prepare for Sun Protection

Maui's sun can be intense, so effective sun protection is essential. Apply broad-spectrum sunscreen with at least SPF 30 to all exposed skin, and reapply every two hours or after swimming. Provide children with sun-protective clothing, such as long-sleeve rash guards and wide-brimmed hats. Sunglasses with UV protection can help protect their eyes. Encourage playing in the shade during peak sun hours (10 AM to 4 PM) to minimize exposure.

9. Engage in Cultural Activities

Incorporate cultural experiences into your trip to help children learn about Hawaiian traditions and history. Attend a family-friendly luau, where kids can enjoy the music, dance, and food while learning about Hawaiian culture. Visit the Lahaina Banyan Court for historical insights, or explore the Bailey House Museum in Wailuku. Participating in a hula lesson or lei-making class can also be a fun and educational activity for the whole family.

10. Have a Travel Kit Ready

A well-stocked travel kit can make all the difference during outings. Include essentials like wipes, hand sanitizer, first-aid supplies, and any necessary medications. Pack a change of clothes for each child, as well as swimwear if you plan to visit the beach. Small toys, books, or electronic devices can help entertain kids during car rides or wait times. Having a travel kit prepared ensures you're ready for any situation and can focus on enjoying your time in Maui.

Kid-Friendly Beaches and Pools

1. Kamaole Beach Park III

Kamaole Beach Park III, also known as "Kam 3," is one of the most family-friendly beaches on Maui. The beach features a large grassy area perfect for picnics and playing games. The gentle waves and sandy shore make it ideal for young children to swim and play safely. Lifeguards are on duty, adding an extra layer of safety for families. There are also playgrounds, barbecue areas, and picnic tables, making it a perfect spot for a full day of fun.

- **Location:** 2800 S Kihei Rd, Kihei, HI 96753
- **Season:** Year-round, best during the summer months
- **Facilities:** Lifeguards, restrooms, showers, picnic tables, barbecue areas, playground

2. Baby Beach, Lahaina

Baby Beach in Lahaina is aptly named for its calm, shallow waters that are perfect for young children. A protective offshore reef breaks the waves, creating a gentle, lagoon-like environment where kids can splash around safely. The beach is sandy and spacious, providing plenty of room for families to set up and relax. It's a favorite among local families and offers stunning views of the neighboring islands.

- **Location:** Kai Pali Pl, Lahaina, HI 96761
- **Season:** Year-round, best during the summer months
- **Facilities:** Limited facilities, restrooms, and parking nearby

3. Napili Bay

Napili Bay is a picturesque beach with calm, clear waters, making it ideal for families with children. The sandy bottom and gentle waves provide a safe environment for swimming and snorkeling. The beach is surrounded by lush greenery and offers plenty of shade, making it comfortable for a day-long visit. The nearby tide pools are also a fun spot for kids to explore marine life.

- **Location:** Napili Pl, Lahaina, HI 96761
- **Season:** Year-round, best during the summer months
- **Facilities:** Restrooms, showers, picnic areas, nearby restaurants

4. Kapalua Bay

Kapalua Bay is renowned for its calm waters and beautiful sandy beaches. The crescent-shaped bay is protected by two outcroppings, which minimize wave action and make it a perfect spot for young children to swim and snorkel. The water is typically clear, providing excellent visibility for snorkeling. The beach is well-maintained and offers stunning views of the surrounding area.

- **Location:** Kapalua, HI 96761
- **Season:** Year-round, best during the summer months
- **Facilities:** Restrooms, showers, parking, beach rentals

5. Wailea Beach

Wailea Beach is part of the luxurious Wailea resort area and offers a beautiful, family-friendly environment. The wide sandy beach and gentle slope into the ocean make it perfect for children. The clear, calm waters are ideal for swimming and snorkeling. The beach is surrounded by upscale resorts and amenities, providing easy access to restrooms, showers, and dining options.

- **Location:** Wailea Alanui Dr, Wailea, HI 96753
- **Season:** Year-round, best during the summer months
- **Facilities:** Restrooms, showers, beach rentals, nearby restaurants and shops

6. Sugar Beach

Sugar Beach, located in North Kihei, is a long stretch of sandy shoreline that is perfect for families. The beach offers shallow waters with gentle waves, making it a safe place for children to swim and play. The beach is less crowded than some of the more popular spots, providing a peaceful environment. It's also a great place for a morning walk or to build sandcastles.

- **Location:** N Kihei Rd, Kihei, HI 96753
- **Season:** Year-round, best during the summer months
- **Facilities:** Limited facilities, restrooms, and parking nearby

7. Charley Young Beach

Charley Young Beach is a family favorite located at the north end of Kamaole I Beach Park. The beach features soft sand and clear, shallow waters perfect for children. The waves are generally gentle, making it safe for swimming and boogie boarding. The beach is spacious and less crowded than some of the more well-known beaches, offering a relaxing environment for families.

- **Location:** 2200 S Kihei Rd, Kihei, HI 96753
- **Season:** Year-round, best during the summer months
- **Facilities:** Restrooms, showers, picnic tables, nearby parking

8. Palauea Beach (White Rock Beach)

Palauea Beach, also known as White Rock Beach, is a hidden gem in the Wailea area. The beach features fine, white sand and calm, clear waters, making it ideal for families with young children. The gentle waves and sandy bottoms provide a safe swimming environment. The beach is relatively secluded, offering a tranquil setting away from the more crowded areas.

- **Location:** Makena Rd, Kihei, HI 96753

- **Season:** Year-round, best during the summer months
- **Facilities:** Limited facilities, street parking, and nearby restrooms

9. Kanaha Beach Park

Kanaha Beach Park, located near Kahului Airport, is a popular spot for families and water sports enthusiasts. The beach features a long stretch of sandy shoreline and shallow waters, making it safe for children to swim. The park offers numerous amenities, including picnic tables, barbecue areas, and playgrounds. It's also a great place to watch windsurfers and kiteboarders.

- **Location:** Amala Pl, Kahului, HI 96732
- **Season:** Year-round, best during the summer months
- **Facilities:** Restrooms, showers, picnic tables, barbecue areas, playground

10. Baldwin Beach Park

Baldwin Beach Park, located in Paia, is a spacious beach with soft sand and clear waters. The beach features a protected lagoon area called Baby Beach, which is perfect for young children. The gentle waves and shallow waters provide a safe environment for swimming and playing. The park also offers ample facilities, including picnic tables, restrooms, and showers.

- **Location:** Hana Hwy, Paia, HI 96779
- **Season:** Year-round, best during the summer months
- **Facilities:** Lifeguards, restrooms, showers, picnic tables, barbecue areas, playground

Parks and Playgrounds

1. Maui Zipline Company

Maui Zipline Company offers an exhilarating zipline adventure set within the lush Maui Tropical Plantation. This family-friendly park features five side-by-side ziplines ranging from 300 to 900 feet, allowing participants to soar over gardens, a lagoon, and tropical landscapes. The knowledgeable guides provide entertaining and educational commentary about the island's flora and fauna. This adventure is suitable for ages five and up, making it a great choice for families looking for a thrilling outdoor activity.

- **Location:** 1670 Honoapiilani Hwy, Wailuku, HI 96793
- **Opening Hours:** Daily 9:00 AM – 5:00 PM

- **Entry Fee:** $150 per person

2. Piiholo Ranch Zipline

Located in Upcountry Maui, Piiholo Ranch Zipline offers an exciting aerial adventure with breathtaking views of the island. The park features multiple ziplines, including one of Hawaii's longest side-by-side ziplines at 2,800 feet. Guests can enjoy panoramic vistas of the Pacific Ocean and the lush landscape below. The zipline tours also include sky bridges and rappels, adding to the adventure. The experienced guides ensure safety and provide interesting insights into the local ecosystem.

- **Location:** 799 Piiholo Rd, Makawao, HI 96768
- **Opening Hours:** Daily 8:00 AM – 3:00 PM
- **Entry Fee:** $185 per person

3. Skyline Hawaii – Haleakala

Skyline Hawaii offers an unforgettable zipline experience on the slopes of Haleakala. This eco-adventure park combines adrenaline-pumping ziplines with stunning natural beauty. Participants can zip through eucalyptus forests, cross swinging bridges, and take in views of the Maui coastline. The park's commitment to sustainability and conservation is evident in its operations. The guides are knowledgeable about the area's geology and history, making the experience both thrilling and educational.

- **Location:** 18303 Haleakala Hwy, Kula, HI 96790
- **Opening Hours:** Daily 8:00 AM – 4:00 PM
- **Entry Fee:** $139 per person

4. Jungle Zipline Maui

Nestled in the lush rainforest of Haiku, Jungle Zipline Maui offers a unique zipline adventure that combines thrills with nature. The park features eight ziplines, multiple aerial bridges, and jungle treetop platforms. The course is designed to blend seamlessly with the natural environment, providing an immersive experience. Participants can learn about native plants and animals while enjoying the rush of zipping through the jungle canopy. The park also offers a walking tour for those who prefer a more relaxed exploration.

- **Location:** 50 E Waipio Rd, Haiku, HI 96708

- **Opening Hours:** Daily 8:00 AM – 3:00 PM
- **Entry Fee:** $139 per person

5. Maui Paintball

For those seeking an action-packed adventure on the ground, Maui Paintball offers an exciting experience in a scenic outdoor setting. The park features multiple themed fields with obstacles and bunkers, providing a variety of strategic gameplay options. It's a great way to enjoy team-based activities and have fun with friends or family. The staff ensures safety and provides all necessary equipment, making it accessible for beginners and experienced players alike.

- **Location:** 814 Honoapiilani Hwy, Lahaina, HI 96761
- **Opening Hours:** Daily 9:00 AM – 5:00 PM
- **Entry Fee:** $50 per person (including equipment rental and paintballs)

6. Flyin Hawaiian Zipline

Flyin Hawaiian Zipline offers a heart-pounding adventure with some of the longest and fastest ziplines in Maui. Located in Waikapu, this zipline tour covers 2.5 miles and includes eight ziplines that offer spectacular views of the central valley, the West Maui Mountains, and the Pacific Ocean. The experience begins with a 4x4 off-road adventure to the starting point, adding to the excitement. The tour also emphasizes environmental education and conservation.

- **Location:** 1670 Honoapiilani Hwy, Wailuku, HI 96793
- **Opening Hours:** Daily 8:00 AM – 4:00 PM
- **Entry Fee:** $199 per person

7. Maui Dragon Fruit Farm

Maui Dragon Fruit Farm is not only a working farm but also an adventure park offering a variety of activities. Visitors can enjoy ziplining, aqua balling (rolling downhill inside a giant inflatable ball), and farm tours. The farm's ziplines provide stunning views of the dragon fruit orchards and the ocean beyond. The aqua ball experience is a unique and fun way to cool off while enjoying the beautiful scenery. The farm tour includes tastings of fresh dragon fruit and other tropical produce.

- **Location:** 833 Punakea Loop, Lahaina, HI 96761

- **Opening Hours:** Daily 9:00 AM – 4:00 PM
- **Entry Fee:** $65 per person for zipline; $55 per person for aqua ball

8. Pacific Whale Foundation Eco-Adventures

Pacific Whale Foundation Eco-Adventures offers a range of eco-friendly outdoor activities, including snorkeling, whale watching, and sailing tours. These adventures provide an opportunity to experience Maui's marine life and stunning coastal views. The foundation's commitment to marine conservation and education ensures that all tours are conducted responsibly. Participants can learn about the local ecosystem and marine wildlife while enjoying a memorable adventure on the water.

- **Location:** 612 Front St, Lahaina, HI 96761
- **Opening Hours:** Daily 8:00 AM – 5:00 PM
- **Entry Fee:** Varies by activity (whale watching from $50, snorkeling from $80)

9. Maui Off-Road Adventures

Maui Off-Road Adventures offers thrilling ATV tours through Maui's rugged terrain. The guided tours take participants on a journey through private lands, offering exclusive access to breathtaking landscapes and hidden gems. Riders can experience the thrill of navigating through dirt trails, mud pits, and scenic overlooks. The tours are suitable for both beginners and experienced riders, with safety equipment and instructions provided.

- **Location:** 3750 Wailea Alanui Dr, Kihei, HI 96753
- **Opening Hours:** Daily 8:00 AM – 4:00 PM
- **Entry Fee:** $175 per person

10. Maui Sunriders Bike Co.

For a unique adventure, Maui Sunriders Bike Co. offers self-paced bike tours down Haleakala, the island's famous volcano. The tour starts with a guided van ride to the summit for sunrise, followed by a thrilling downhill bike ride through scenic landscapes and charming towns. Riders can stop at their leisure to take photos, enjoy a meal, or explore local attractions. The experience combines adventure, stunning views, and cultural exploration.

- **Location:** 71 Baldwin Ave, Paia, HI 96779
- **Opening Hours:** Daily 7:30 AM – 5:00 PM

- **Entry Fee:** $75 per person

Family-friendly Guided Tours and Excursions

Maui offers a range of family-friendly guided tours and excursions that cater to various interests, ensuring memorable experiences for visitors of all ages. Here are some top-rated family-friendly guided tours and excursions in Maui:

Road to Hana Tour

The Road to Hana Tour is a must-do for families visiting Maui. This scenic drive takes you along the lush, coastal Hana Highway, offering breathtaking views of waterfalls, rainforests, and rugged coastline. Guided tours often include stops at key attractions such as the Twin Falls, Waianapanapa State Park (black sand beach), and the Hana Botanical Gardens. Guides provide engaging commentary about the area's natural beauty and cultural significance, making the journey educational and entertaining for both adults and children.

- **Location:** Departs from various locations in Maui
- **Highlights:** Twin Falls, Waianapanapa State Park, Hana Botanical Gardens, scenic coastal views
- **Tour Provider:** Valley Isle Excursions
- **Duration:** 10-12 hours
- **Contact:** +1 808-871-1899 | Valley Isle Excursions

Maui Ocean Center Tour

The Maui Ocean Center Tour provides an interactive and educational experience for families. The tour takes you through the Maui Ocean Center, an aquarium showcasing Hawaii's marine life, including sharks, rays, and colorful fish. Families can explore the Ocean Voyager exhibit, which features a walk-through tunnel offering a 360-degree view of marine life. The center also has touch pools where children can safely interact with starfish and sea urchins. The guided tours include informative presentations about marine conservation and the unique ecosystems of the Hawaiian waters.

- **Location:** 192 Ma'alaea Road, Ma'alaea, Maui
- **Highlights:** Ocean Voyager exhibit, touch pools, marine life education
- **Tour Provider:** Maui Ocean Center
- **Duration:** 2-3 hours
- **Contact:** +1 808-270-7000 | Maui Ocean Center

Whale Watching Cruise

During the winter months, Maui is a prime location for whale watching, and a guided whale-watching cruise offers an exciting and educational experience for families. These tours provide a chance to see humpback whales as they migrate through Hawaiian waters. Experienced naturalists guide the tour, offering insights into whale behavior, biology, and conservation. The tours typically include amenities such as refreshments and on-board commentary to enhance the experience for both adults and children.

- **Location:** Departs from Lahaina Harbor or Ma'alaea Harbor
- **Highlights:** Whale sightings, naturalist commentary, educational insights
- **Tour Provider:** Pacific Whale Foundation
- **Duration:** 2-3 hours
- **Contact:** +1 808-249-8811 | Pacific Whale Foundation

Snorkeling Trip to Molokini Crater

The Snorkeling Trip to Molokini Crater is an adventure that families will enjoy. This tour takes you to Molokini Crater, a crescent-shaped, submerged volcanic caldera known for its clear waters and vibrant marine life. The guided snorkeling trip includes equipment rental, safety briefings, and guided snorkeling sessions in the crystal-clear waters. Families can see colorful fish, sea turtles, and coral reefs. The tour often includes a light breakfast or lunch and provides educational information about the marine environment and conservation efforts.

- **Location:** Departs from Ma'alaea Harbor
- **Highlights:** Molokini Crater, snorkeling with marine life, coral reefs
- **Tour Provider:** Four Winds II
- **Duration:** 4-5 hours
- **Contact:** +1 808-661-5556 | Four Winds II

Upcountry Maui Farm Tour

The Upcountry Maui Farm Tour offers a unique opportunity for families to experience rural Maui. This tour takes you through the scenic Upcountry region, where you'll visit local farms and learn about agriculture in Maui. Highlights include a visit to a working goat farm, where children can interact with goats and see cheese-making demonstrations, and a tour of a lavender farm with beautiful gardens and fragrant fields.

The tour provides a hands-on experience with farming and agriculture, making it both educational and enjoyable for kids and adults alike.

- **Location:** Departs from central Maui
- **Highlights:** Goat farm visit, cheese-making demonstrations, lavender farm tour
- **Tour Provider:** Maui Farm Tours
- **Duration:** 4-5 hours
- **Contact:** +1 808-572-3800 | Maui Farm Tours

Maui Tropical Plantation Tour

The Maui Tropical Plantation Tour offers a fascinating look into Hawaii's agricultural heritage and tropical fruits. This tour takes you through a lush plantation where families can explore various fruit and flower gardens. Highlights include a tram ride around the plantation, providing a comfortable and informative way to see the growing fields of pineapple, sugarcane, and other tropical plants. The tour also features a visit to the plantation's farm stand, where visitors can sample fresh fruits and local products. Guides provide engaging insights into the history and cultivation of these crops.

- **Location:** 1670 Honoapiilani Hwy, Wailuku, Maui
- **Highlights:** Tram ride, fruit and flower gardens, farm stand with fresh produce
- **Tour Provider:** Maui Tropical Plantation
- **Duration:** 1.5-2 hours
- **Contact:** +1 808-244-7643 | Maui Tropical Plantation

Haleakalā Sunrise Tour

The Haleakalā Sunrise Tour offers a breathtaking start to the day with a visit to the summit of Haleakalā National Park. Families can watch the sunrise over the volcanic crater, an experience renowned for its stunning views and dramatic colors. The tour includes transportation to the summit, where guides provide insights into the geology and cultural significance of Haleakalā. After sunrise, the tour often includes a visit to the park's visitor center and a drive through the scenic upcountry region. Warm clothing is recommended as temperatures at the summit can be quite cool.

- **Location:** Departs from various locations in Maui
- **Highlights:** Haleakalā sunrise, volcanic crater views, park visitor center
- **Tour Provider:** Skyline Hawaii
- **Duration:** 6-7 hours
- **Contact:** +1 808-875-2000 | Skyline Hawaii

Maui Sugar Cane Train Tour

The Maui Sugar Cane Train Tour provides a fun and educational journey back in time, showcasing Maui's history of sugar cane production. This tour takes families on a vintage train ride through the scenic landscapes of Lahaina, offering views of sugar cane fields and the island's natural beauty. The train ride includes a narrated history of the sugar industry and its impact on Maui. The tour also features stops at historical landmarks and interactive exhibits that allow children and adults to learn about Maui's agricultural past.

- **Location:** Departs from Lahaina Town
- **Highlights:** Vintage train ride, sugar cane fields, historical narration
- **Tour Provider:** Lahaina Sugar Cane Train
- **Duration:** 1.5-2 hours
- **Contact:** +1 808-661-4300 | Lahaina Sugar Cane Train

Maui Adventure Helicopter Tour

The Maui Adventure Helicopter Tour offers a thrilling and memorable way to see Maui's stunning landscapes from the air. This tour takes families on a helicopter flight over some of the island's most breathtaking scenery, including waterfalls, volcanic craters, and lush rainforests. The helicopter features large windows and comfortable seating, providing panoramic views and a smooth ride. Guides offer informative commentary about the geography and history of the areas viewed, making it an exciting and educational experience for all ages.

- **Location:** Departs from Kahului Airport, Maui
- **Highlights:** Aerial views of waterfalls, volcanic craters, rainforests
- **Tour Provider:** Blue Hawaiian Helicopters
- **Duration:** 50 minutes
- **Contact:** +1 808-877-7005 | Blue Hawaiian Helicopters

Chapter 17: Romantic Experiences in Maui

Best Sunset Spots

Maui offers some of the most breathtaking sunsets in the world, where vibrant colors fill the sky as the sun dips below the horizon. Whether you're looking for a peaceful, secluded spot or a lively beach atmosphere, here are some of the best sunset spots in Maui:

1. Haleakalā Summit

Watching the sunset from the summit of Haleakalā is a mystical experience. At 10,023 feet above sea level, you'll witness a sunset like no other, with the clouds stretching beneath you and the sky transforming into a kaleidoscope of colors. The panoramic views from the summit are surreal, with the vast crater below and the Pacific Ocean in the distance. As the sun sets, the sky turns brilliant shades of orange, pink, and purple, casting a golden glow over the landscape. After the sun dips below the horizon, stay for stargazing, as Haleakalā offers some of the best night sky views on the island.

Location: Haleakalā National Park

Tips: Arrive early to secure a good spot and dress warmly, as temperatures at the summit can drop significantly. Bring a blanket, snacks, and a thermos of hot coffee or cocoa for added comfort.

2. Ka'anapali Beach

One of Maui's most popular beaches, Ka'anapali Beach offers a stunning and lively setting for sunset viewing. The beach stretches for miles along the west coast, providing ample space to find a perfect spot on the sand. As the sun sets over the Pacific Ocean, the golden hues reflect off the water, creating a beautiful and romantic atmosphere. You can watch the sunset from the beach or grab a seat at one of the many beachfront restaurants and bars that line the shore. For added drama, catch the cliff-diving ceremony at Black Rock (Puu Keka'a) just before sunset, where locals dive from the cliffs into the ocean below.

Location: West Maui, near Lahaina

Tips: Parking can be tricky during peak times, so arrive early. For a romantic touch, consider taking a sunset stroll along the beach before settling in to watch the sunset.

3. Makena Cove (Secret Beach)

Tucked away on the southern coast of Maui, Makena Cove—often called "Secret Beach"—is a secluded and picturesque spot for watching the sunset. This small, hidden beach is surrounded by dramatic black lava rock formations and swaying palm trees, creating a truly romantic and intimate setting. The crashing waves against the lava rocks and the pristine white sand add to the beauty of the moment as the sun sets over the horizon, casting a warm golden glow. It's a favorite spot for couples, and many choose to have wedding ceremonies here due to the stunning backdrop.

Location: South Maui, near Makena

Tips: This beach can be difficult to find, so use a map or GPS to navigate. It's small, so come early to secure a good spot and enjoy the peaceful atmosphere.

4. Kapalua Bay

Kapalua Bay is one of the most picturesque beaches on Maui, and it's an ideal spot for sunset viewing. This crescent-shaped bay is framed by palm trees and lush greenery, providing a stunning tropical setting. The gentle waters of the bay reflect the colors of the sky, creating a serene and romantic ambiance as the sun sets behind the island of Molokai in the distance. The beach is less crowded than Ka'anapali, making it a more peaceful and intimate place to watch the sunset. It's also a fantastic spot for snorkeling earlier in the day, so you can make an entire afternoon and evening of your visit.

Location: West Maui, near the Ritz-Carlton Kapalua

Tips: Parking can be limited, so arrive early. Bring a beach blanket and snacks for a relaxed, picnic-style sunset experience.

5. Ho'okipa Beach Park

Located on Maui's north shore, Ho'okipa Beach Park is known for its powerful waves and windsurfing action during the day, but it transforms into a peaceful and scenic sunset spot in the evening. The rocky coastline and dramatic ocean swells make for a stunning backdrop as the sun sets over the water. You can sit on the grassy bluff above the beach for panoramic views or head down to the sand to get closer to the water. On most evenings, Hawaiian green sea turtles come ashore to rest, adding an extra magical touch to the experience.

Location: North Shore, near Paia

Tips: Watch for the turtles on the east side of the beach, but give them plenty of space as they are protected. Bring a jacket, as the north shore can get breezy in the evening.

6. La Perouse Bay

For a more rugged and off-the-beaten-path sunset experience, head to La Perouse Bay, located at the end of the road in South Maui. The bay is part of a natural reserve that features ancient lava fields, crystal-clear waters, and a wild, untouched landscape. As the sun sets, the contrast between the dark lava rocks and the fiery colors of the sky is truly breathtaking. This spot feels remote and isolated, offering a quiet and serene environment away from the crowds. It's a great place for couples looking for a more adventurous and unique sunset experience.

Location: South Maui, past Makena

Tips: The road to La Perouse can be rough, so drive carefully. There are no facilities or amenities, so bring everything you need for the evening, including water and snacks.

7. Wailea Beach

Wailea Beach, located in front of some of Maui's most luxurious resorts, is a beautiful and convenient spot for sunset viewing. The beach is wide and sandy, with calm waters and stunning views of the sun setting over the nearby islands of Lanai and Kahoolawe. You can watch the sunset from the sand or enjoy it from one of the beachfront restaurants or lounges in the area. Wailea Beach offers a romantic and upscale vibe, making it perfect for couples who want to combine a beach sunset with fine dining or a stroll along the scenic Wailea Beach Path.

Location: South Maui, near the Wailea resort area

Tips: For a more private experience, walk down to the quieter sections of the beach. Enjoy a post-sunset dinner at one of the nearby restaurants for a complete romantic evening.

8. Keawakapu Beach

Keawakapu Beach, located between Kihei and Wailea, is a hidden gem for watching the sunset. This long, sandy beach is quieter than some of the more famous beaches, making it a peaceful and romantic spot to watch the sky change colors as the sun sets over the ocean. The beach is known for its soft sand and gentle waves, providing a perfect setting for a sunset walk or relaxing on the sand. The view of the West Maui Mountains in the distance adds to the picturesque scene.

Location: South Maui, between Kihei and Wailea

Tips: Pack a picnic and enjoy a sunset dinner on the beach. The parking lot can fill up quickly, so arrive early.

9. Napili Bay

Napili Bay is a small, crescent-shaped beach on the west side of Maui that offers stunning sunset views. The calm, clear waters, and golden sand create a tranquil and romantic atmosphere as the sun sets behind the island of Molokai. The bay is surrounded by palm trees and lush greenery, making it feel like a hidden paradise. It's also a great spot for swimming and snorkeling during the day, so you can enjoy the water before settling in for the sunset.

Location: West Maui, near Napili Kai Beach Resort

Tips: Napili Bay is a popular spot for visitors, so arrive early to claim a spot on the beach. Bring a towel or beach chair for added comfort.

Couples' Spa and Wellness Retreats

Maui is an idyllic destination for couples seeking relaxation and rejuvenation. The island is home to several world-class spas and wellness retreats that offer luxurious treatments, breathtaking views, and serene environments. Here are some of the best options for couples looking to unwind together:

1. The Spa at Four Seasons Resort Maui at Wailea

The Spa at Four Seasons Resort Maui is a haven of luxury and tranquility, perfect for couples seeking a pampering retreat. The spa offers a range of treatments designed to relax, rejuvenate, and renew. Couples can indulge in a side-by-side massage in a private oceanfront hale (traditional Hawaiian thatched-roof hut), with the sound of the waves providing a soothing backdrop. The spa also features a hydrotherapy circuit, aromatherapy baths, and a steam room. For a truly unforgettable experience, try the "Wailea Cielo" treatment, which includes a massage, body scrub, and facial in a private, open-air setting with stunning views of the Pacific Ocean.

- **Location:** 3900 Wailea Alanui Drive, Wailea, HI 96753
- **Opening Hours:** Daily, 8:00 AM – 7:00 PM
- **Phone Number:** +1 808-874-8000

Tip: Book the couple's treatments well in advance, especially if you want the oceanfront hale experience, as it's incredibly popular and often reserved early.

2. Willow Stream Spa at Fairmont Kea Lani

The Willow Stream Spa at Fairmont Kea Lani in Wailea offers a serene and luxurious environment for couples. The spa's treatments are inspired by the healing traditions of the islands, combining ancient Hawaiian techniques with modern therapies. Couples can enjoy a Lomi Lomi massage together or choose a customized couples' experience that includes massages, facials, and body treatments. The spa features an extensive hydrotherapy circuit, including a hot tub, cold plunge pool, and waterfall massage. The open-air relaxation areas offer breathtaking views of the tropical gardens and ocean, creating a perfect setting for relaxation.

- **Location:** 4100 Wailea Alanui Drive, Wailea, HI 96753
- **Opening Hours:** Daily, 8:00 AM – 6:00 PM
- **Phone Number:** +1 808-875-2229

Tip: Enhance your spa day by enjoying a healthy lunch or smoothie at the spa's wellness café before or after your treatment.

3. Ho'omana Spa Maui

Ho'omana Spa Maui offers an authentic Hawaiian healing experience in a tranquil, upcountry setting. The spa specializes in Lomi Lomi massage, a traditional Hawaiian massage that uses rhythmic, flowing strokes to promote relaxation and healing.

Couples can enjoy a Lomi Lomi massage in a private treatment room surrounded by lush tropical gardens. The spa also offers cultural experiences, such as a Hawaiian herbal medicine workshop, where couples can learn about traditional healing practices.

The intimate and peaceful environment at Ho'omana Spa makes it an ideal retreat for couples looking to connect and unwind.

- **Location:** 1550 Piiholo Road, Makawao, HI 96768
- **Opening Hours:** Monday – Saturday, 9:00 AM – 6:00 PM
- **Phone Number:** +1 808-573-8256

Tip: Consider booking a package that includes a Lomi Lomi massage followed by a traditional Hawaiian bath for the ultimate healing experience.

4. Heavenly Spa by Westin at The Westin Maui Resort & Spa

Located on the famous Ka'anapali Beach, Heavenly Spa by Westin offers a blissful escape for couples. The spa's signature treatments incorporate natural, island-inspired ingredients, such as coconut, aloe vera, and Hawaiian sea salt. Couples can enjoy a side-by-side massage in the open-air cabana, where they can listen to the sounds of the ocean while being pampered. The spa also features a relaxation lounge with ocean views, a whirlpool, and a steam room. For an extra special experience, try the "Heavenly Couples Ritual," which includes a body scrub, massage, and facial designed for two.

- **Location:** 2365 Ka'anapali Parkway, Lahaina, HI 96761
- **Opening Hours:** Daily, 8:00 AM – 7:00 PM
- **Phone Number:** +1 808-667-2525

Tip: After your treatment, take a romantic stroll along Ka'anapali Beach or enjoy a sunset cocktail at one of the nearby beachfront bars.

5. The Ritz-Carlton Spa, Kapalua

The Ritz-Carlton Spa, Kapalua, offers a luxurious wellness retreat inspired by Hawaiian traditions. The spa is set amidst the lush tropical landscape of Kapalua, providing a serene and intimate setting for couples. Signature treatments include the "Lokahi" couples' massage, which uses traditional Hawaiian techniques to restore balance and harmony. The spa also features a eucalyptus steam room, cedar sauna, and relaxation lounges with stunning views of the surrounding gardens. Couples can further enhance their experience by spending time in the spa's private outdoor garden, complete with a whirlpool and cabanas.

- **Location:** 1 Ritz-Carlton Drive, Kapalua, HI 96761
- **Opening Hours:** Daily, 8:00 AM – 6:00 PM
- **Phone Number:** +1 808-665-7079

Tip: Extend your day of relaxation by booking a private cabana at the resort's pool, where you can enjoy poolside service and breathtaking views of the Pacific Ocean.

6. Montage Kapalua Bay – Spa Montage

Spa Montage at Montage Kapalua Bay is a sanctuary of relaxation and rejuvenation. The spa's extensive menu includes a variety of couples' treatments, such as the "Kapalua Escape," which features a full-body massage, facial, and scalp treatment. The spa is renowned for its luxurious facilities, including a eucalyptus steam room, cedar sauna, and outdoor infinity pool with panoramic ocean views. Couples can unwind in the tranquil surroundings of the spa's garden, which features private cabanas and a hot tub. The spa's emphasis on personalized service ensures a truly indulgent experience for couples.

- **Location:** 1 Bay Drive, Lahaina, HI 96761
- **Opening Hours:** Daily, 9:00 AM – 6:00 PM
- **Phone Number:** +1 808-665-8282

Tip: Plan your visit around sunset to enjoy a romantic soak in the infinity pool as the sun sets over the ocean.

7. Travaasa Hana – The Spa at Travaasa Hana

Located in the remote and tranquil town of Hana, The Spa at Travaasa Hana offers a peaceful retreat for couples seeking to disconnect from the outside world. The spa's treatments are inspired by the natural beauty and healing traditions of Hana, incorporating locally sourced ingredients, such as Hawaiian sea salt, coconut oil, and fresh fruit. Couples can choose from a range of massages, facials, and body treatments, including the signature "Hana Ritual," which includes a full-body scrub, wrap, and massage. The spa's serene setting, overlooking the lush gardens and Pacific Ocean, enhances the sense of relaxation and renewal.

- **Location:** 5031 Hana Highway, Hana, HI 96713

- **Opening Hours:** Daily, 9:00 AM – 5:00 PM
- **Phone Number:** +1 808-359-2401

Tip: Extend your visit to Hana by exploring the nearby waterfalls and black sand beaches before or after your spa treatment.

Private Dining and Beach Picnics

Maui offers a variety of private dining experiences and beach picnics that are perfect for couples looking to create unforgettable memories in a romantic setting. From intimate dinners under the stars to gourmet picnics on secluded beaches, here are some of the best options for private dining and beach picnics on the island:

1. Chef's Table Experience at The Restaurant at Hotel Wailea

The Restaurant at Hotel Wailea offers an exclusive Chef's Table experience that is perfect for couples seeking a personalized and intimate dining experience. Set in a private, open-air treehouse overlooking the lush gardens and ocean, this dining experience allows you to enjoy a multi-course meal crafted by the restaurant's executive chef. The menu is customized to your preferences and features locally sourced ingredients, many of which are grown on the hotel's organic farm. The sommelier will pair each course with fine wines, enhancing the flavors and creating a truly unforgettable culinary journey. The romantic ambiance, coupled with the stunning views, makes this one of the most sought-after dining experiences on Maui.

- **Location:** 555 Kaukahi Street, Wailea, HI 96753
- **Opening Hours:** Daily, 5:00 PM – 9:00 PM
- **Phone Number:** +1 808-874-0500

Tip: Book well in advance, as the Chef's Table experience is highly popular and only accommodates a limited number of guests each evening.

2. Private Beachfront Dining at Mama's Fish House

Mama's Fish House, a legendary restaurant in Maui, offers an exclusive private dining experience right on the beach. Located in a secluded area of the restaurant's beachfront property, this dining option is perfect for couples looking to enjoy a romantic dinner with the sound of the waves in the background. The menu features fresh, locally caught seafood, and each dish is prepared with the restaurant's signature Polynesian flair.

The private dining area is adorned with tiki torches and tropical flowers, creating a magical and intimate atmosphere. As you dine, you can watch the sunset over the Pacific Ocean, making for an unforgettable evening.

- **Location:** 799 Poho Place, Paia, HI 96779
- **Opening Hours:** Daily, 11:00 AM – 9:00 PM
- **Phone Number:** +1 808-579-8488

Tip: Request the private beachfront dining experience when making your reservation to ensure you secure this exclusive spot.

3. Romantic Beach Picnic with The Picnic Maui

The Picnic Maui offers customized beach picnic experiences that are perfect for couples looking to enjoy a romantic meal in a beautiful outdoor setting. Whether you choose a sunrise breakfast, a midday lunch, or a sunset dinner, The Picnic Maui will create a luxurious picnic setup complete with blankets, pillows, and a beautifully arranged table. The menu features gourmet dishes made from locally sourced ingredients, including charcuterie boards, fresh salads, sandwiches, and desserts. You can also add on options like a bottle of champagne, fresh flowers, or even a ukulele player to enhance the romantic ambiance. The picnic can be set up on a beach of your choice, allowing you to enjoy the natural beauty of Maui in privacy.

- **Location:** Mobile service throughout Maui
- **Opening Hours:** By appointment only
- **Phone Number:** +1 808-268-1658

Tip: Choose a less crowded beach, such as Makena Beach or Secret Beach, for a more intimate and peaceful experience.

4. Private Oceanfront Dining at The Fairmont Kea Lani

The Fairmont Kea Lani in Wailea offers an exquisite private oceanfront dining experience that is ideal for couples celebrating a special occasion. The dining setup is located on the hotel's private lawn overlooking the ocean, and it is beautifully decorated with candles, flowers, and tiki torches. You'll be treated to a personalized multi-course meal prepared by the hotel's executive chef, featuring fresh, locally sourced ingredients. The meal is paired with fine wines, and the evening is enhanced by the sound of the waves and the warm Hawaiian breeze. The stunning sunset views and the intimate setting make this an unforgettable experience for couples.

- **Location:** 4100 Wailea Alanui Drive, Wailea, HI 96753
- **Opening Hours:** By reservation only
- **Phone Number:** +1 808-875-4100

Tip: Consider booking this experience for a special occasion, such as an anniversary or proposal, to create a truly memorable evening.

5. Private Dining at The Ritz-Carlton, Kapalua

The Ritz-Carlton, Kapalua offers a luxurious private dining experience that can be tailored to your preferences. Whether you prefer to dine on the beach, by the pool, or in a secluded garden, the hotel's culinary team will create a bespoke menu featuring the finest local ingredients. You can enjoy a romantic meal under the stars, with a personal butler attending to your every need. The menu can include a variety of dishes, from fresh seafood to gourmet steaks, all paired with fine wines. The setting is enhanced by candlelight, tropical flowers, and the natural beauty of the surrounding landscape, making it an ideal choice for a romantic evening.

- **Location:** 1 Ritz-Carlton Drive, Kapalua, HI 96761
- **Opening Hours:** By reservation only
- **Phone Number:** +1 808-669-6200

Tip: Enhance your private dining experience by adding a live musician or hula dancer to create an even more enchanting atmosphere.

Secluded Beaches and Hidden Gems

Maui is home to some of the most breathtaking beaches in the world, many of which are hidden away from the crowds, offering a tranquil and intimate experience. These secluded beaches and hidden gems provide a perfect escape for those seeking privacy and natural beauty. Here are some of the best-kept secrets on the island:

1. Makena Cove (Secret Beach)

Tucked away between luxury homes and accessible via a narrow, unmarked path, Makena Cove, often referred to as Secret Beach, is a stunning hidden gem known for its picturesque scenery.

This small, secluded cove is surrounded by lava rock formations, offering a dramatic contrast to the turquoise waters and white sand. The beach is perfect for a quiet day of sunbathing, picnicking, or watching the sunset. The rugged beauty of the cove also makes it a popular spot for wedding photos and romantic escapes. The beach is relatively unknown to most tourists, ensuring that you can enjoy the peaceful surroundings without large crowds.

Location: Off Makena Road, Wailea-Makena, HI 96753

Tip: Visit early in the morning or late in the afternoon to avoid any chance of crowds, and bring your shade as there are no facilities or natural shade available.

2. Honolua Bay

Located on Maui's northwestern coast, Honolua Bay is a secluded paradise for snorkelers and surfers. The bay is part of a Marine Life Conservation District, ensuring that the vibrant coral reefs and abundant marine life are well-protected. The rocky shoreline and lush cliffs create a dramatic backdrop, while the calm, crystal-clear waters are perfect for exploring the underwater world. Honolua Bay is less frequented than other snorkeling spots, making it an ideal location for those looking to enjoy the ocean in solitude. The bay is also a favorite among surfers during the winter months when the waves are at their best.

Location: Mile Marker 32.2, Honoapiilani Highway, Kapalua, HI 96761

Tip: Pack light and be prepared for a short hike from the parking area to the beach. Early morning visits offer the best visibility for snorkeling.

3. Oneuli Beach (Black Sand Beach)

Oneuli Beach, also known as Black Sand Beach, is a hidden gem located within the Makena State Park. This small, often overlooked beach features unique black sand created from the surrounding lava rocks. The beach is ideal for those looking for a quiet spot to relax, sunbathe, or enjoy a peaceful swim. The waters here are clear and calm, making it a great location for snorkeling and diving, especially near the rocky outcrops. The dramatic contrast of the black sand against the blue ocean creates a striking and memorable setting.

Location: Makena Alanui Road, Kihei, HI 96753

Tip: Bring your gear for snorkeling or diving, as there are no rental facilities nearby. The beach is also a great spot for photography, particularly during sunrise or sunset.

4. Red Sand Beach (Kaihalulu Beach)

Red Sand Beach, or Kaihalulu Beach, is one of Maui's most unique and secluded beaches, known for its striking red sand and dramatic cliffs. Located near the town of Hana, this hidden gem is not easily accessible, requiring a short but challenging hike along a rugged, cliffside trail. The secluded nature of the beach and the difficulty in reaching it ensures that it remains relatively uncrowded. The crescent-shaped beach is bordered by jagged volcanic rock, creating a stunning contrast with the deep blue waters of the ocean. The calm waters within the cove are perfect for swimming and snorkeling.

Location: Hana Highway, Hana, HI 96713

Tip: The trail to Red Sand Beach can be treacherous, especially after rain, so wear sturdy shoes and exercise caution. The beach is clothing-optional, and its remote location adds to its off-the-beaten-path appeal.

5. Hamoa Beach

Hamoa Beach, located near Hana, is a secluded crescent-shaped beach surrounded by lush tropical vegetation and towering sea cliffs. The beach's soft, golden sand and gentle waves make it a perfect spot for swimming, bodyboarding, and sunbathing. The beach is often described as one of the most beautiful in Maui, yet it remains relatively uncrowded due to its remote location. The picturesque scenery, with views of the nearby Alau Island, adds to the charm of Hamoa Beach. The beach is easily accessible from the Hana Highway, but its secluded location ensures a peaceful and relaxing experience.

Location: Haneo'o Road, Hana, HI 96713

Tip: There are no facilities at the beach, so bring your food, water, and sunscreen. The waves can be strong, especially in winter, so be mindful when swimming.

6. La Perouse Bay

La Perouse Bay, located at the end of Makena Alanui Road, is a secluded bay surrounded by ancient lava fields from Maui's last volcanic eruption. The rugged, otherworldly landscape contrasts with the clear blue waters of the bay, creating a dramatic and serene environment. The bay is a popular spot for snorkeling, especially in the early morning when the water is calm, and you can often spot dolphins and other marine life. The black lava rock formations, combined with the vibrant ocean, make La Perouse Bay a unique and tranquil spot for those looking to escape the more crowded beaches of Maui.

Location: Makena Alanui Road, Kihei, HI 96753

Tip: The area is remote, with no facilities, so bring everything you need for the day, including plenty of water, snacks, and sunscreen.

7. Waianapanapa State Park

Waianapanapa State Park is home to one of Maui's most famous hidden gems, the black sand beach of Pa'iloa.

This remote and stunning beach is surrounded by lush vegetation, sea arches, and lava caves, offering a sense of seclusion and natural beauty. The black sand contrasts beautifully with the emerald waters, creating a striking visual experience. The park also features hiking trails, freshwater caves, and blowholes, making it a great destination for exploration and adventure. Despite its popularity, the beach's location within the state park ensures that it remains less crowded, especially during the early morning or late afternoon.

Location: Hana Highway, Hana, HI 96713

Tip: The park has basic facilities, including restrooms and picnic areas, but it's best to bring your food and water. Plan to spend a few hours exploring the park's various natural features.

Romantic Hikes and Scenic Drives

Maui is known for its stunning natural landscapes, and it offers some of the most romantic hikes and scenic drives that promise breathtaking views and intimate experiences. Whether you're looking to explore lush rainforests, dramatic coastlines, or volcanic landscapes, these options will ensure a memorable outing with your partner.

Romantic Hikes

1. Sliding Sands Trail

The Sliding Sands Trail, located in Haleakalā National Park, offers a truly unique hiking experience through the volcanic landscape of the island's highest peak. The trail descends into the Haleakalā Crater, where you'll encounter otherworldly scenery of colorful cinder cones and expansive lava fields. The hike provides panoramic views of the crater and the surrounding landscape, making it an ideal choice for a romantic adventure. The trail is approximately 11 miles round trip, but you can choose to hike a shorter section and still enjoy the dramatic vistas. The sunrise and sunset views from the crater are particularly stunning and can create a memorable and intimate experience.

Location: Haleakalā National Park, Kula, HI 96790

Tip: Start early in the morning to avoid crowds and catch the sunrise, or opt for a sunset hike to enjoy the changing colors of the crater. Bring plenty of water and dress in layers as temperatures can vary.

2. Twin Falls Trail

Located on the Road to Hana, the Twin Falls Trail is a relatively easy hike that leads to a beautiful waterfall and swimming hole. The trail is surrounded by lush tropical vegetation, and the waterfalls provide a picturesque and serene backdrop. The hike is about 1.5 miles round trip and is suitable for all skill levels. The tranquil setting of the waterfalls and the opportunity to take a refreshing dip in the pool make this a perfect spot for a romantic outing. The nearby fruit stand offers fresh smoothies and snacks, adding to the charm of the experience.

Location: Mile Marker 2, Hana Highway, Haiku, HI 96708

Tip: Visit early in the day to avoid the crowds, and bring swimwear if you plan to take a dip in the waterfall pool.

3. Iao Valley State Park

The Iao Valley State Park offers several short but scenic hikes through one of Maui's most lush and picturesque landscapes. The park is home to the iconic Iao Needle, a towering spire of rock surrounded by dense rainforest. The easy 0.6-mile Iao Needle Lookout Trail provides stunning views of the Needle and the surrounding valley. For a more immersive experience, explore the Ethnobotanical Loop Trail, which offers insights into the native plants and cultural history of the area. The park's serene environment and verdant beauty create a romantic and peaceful setting.

Location: 54°8'8.06"N, 156°26'50.29"E

Tip: Wear comfortable shoes and bring a light rain jacket, as the weather can be unpredictable. The park can be busy, so visiting early in the day can offer a quieter experience.

4. Pipiwai Trail

The Pipiwai Trail is a stunning hike located in the Haleakalā National Park's Kipahulu District. This 4-mile round-trip trail takes you through a lush bamboo forest and leads to the impressive Waimoku Falls, which cascades over a 400-foot cliff. The trail also passes by the beautiful Pools of 'Ohe'o, where you can take a dip in the natural pools. The combination of diverse landscapes, including bamboo forests, waterfalls, and pools, makes this hike an enchanting and romantic adventure. The journey through the bamboo forest, with the gentle rustling of the stalks, adds to the magical atmosphere.

Location: Kipahulu District, Haleakalā National Park, Hana, HI 96713

Tip: Be prepared for muddy conditions, especially after rain. Bring a swimsuit if you plan to swim in the Pools of 'Ohe'o and be mindful of your footing on the trail.

Scenic Drives

1. Road to Hana

The Road to Hana is one of Maui's most famous scenic drives, offering an unforgettable journey through lush rainforests, cascading waterfalls, and dramatic coastal views. The drive stretches for approximately 64 miles and features over 600 curves and 50 one-lane bridges. Along the way, you'll encounter beautiful beaches, botanical gardens, and charming roadside stands. Key stops include Waianapanapa State Park, where you can see a black sand beach, and the Seven Sacred Pools at Kipahulu. The drive provides numerous opportunities for romantic stops and explorations.

Location: Hana Highway, Maui, HI

Tip: Allow a full day for the drive to fully enjoy the sights and make stops. Start early to avoid the crowds and consider packing a picnic to enjoy at one of the scenic spots.

2. Upcountry Maui Scenic Drive

The Upcountry Maui Scenic Drive takes you through the island's agricultural heartland, offering a different perspective of Maui's diverse landscapes. The drive features rolling hills, lush pastures, and charming towns such as Makawao and Kula. Highlights include the Surfing Goat Dairy, where you can sample artisanal cheeses, and the Ali'i Kula Lavender Farm, where you can stroll through fields of lavender and enjoy the soothing aroma. The scenic views of the central valley and the slopes of Haleakalā add to the romantic ambiance of the drive.

Location: Upcountry Maui, starting in Kula

Tip: Plan your visit to the lavender farm or dairy for specific tour times. The drive is best enjoyed in the morning or late afternoon for the best light and fewer crowds.

3. Hana Highway (Beyond Hana)

For those looking to extend the Road to Hana experience, continue past Hana to explore the less-visited areas of East Maui. This part of the drive features secluded beaches, rugged coastlines, and scenic vistas. Notable stops include the Charles Lindbergh grave at the Palani Lookout and the beautiful Hamoa Beach. The road conditions can be challenging, with unpaved sections and sharp turns, so be prepared for a more adventurous drive. This extended drive offers a more intimate and secluded experience compared to the more traveled sections of the Road to Hana.

Location: Continuing from Hana, Maui, HI

Tip: Ensure your vehicle is suitable for the rougher sections of the road and carries enough fuel and supplies, as services are limited in this area.

Honeymoon Packages and Special Activities

Maui offers a range of honeymoon packages and special activities designed to make your romantic getaway unforgettable. From luxurious resorts with tailored services to unique experiences that capture the essence of the island, these options will ensure a memorable honeymoon. Here's a comprehensive look at some top choices:

Honeymoon Packages

1. Four Seasons Resort Maui at Wailea – Romantic Honeymoon Package

The Four Seasons Resort Maui at Wailea is a top choice for couples seeking luxury and romance. Their Romantic Honeymoon Package includes an ocean-view room or suite, daily breakfast for two, a couples' massage at the resort's renowned spa, and a private sunset dinner on the beach. The package also offers special touches such as a bottle of champagne, chocolate-covered strawberries, and a personalized welcome gift. The resort's idyllic setting, with its pristine beaches and lush gardens, provides a perfect backdrop for a romantic escape.

Location: 3900 Wailea Alanui Drive, Wailea, HI 96753

Tip: Book well in advance to secure availability and inquire about additional romantic enhancements such as helicopter tours or private excursions.

2. Grand Wailea, A Waldorf Astoria Resort – Honeymoon Escape Package

The Grand Wailea offers a luxurious Honeymoon Escape Package that includes accommodations in an oceanfront room, daily breakfast for two, and a $200 resort credit to be used towards dining, spa treatments, or activities. The package also features a romantic turndown service with flower petals and a bottle of champagne. Guests can enjoy the resort's extensive amenities, including its sprawling pools, award-winning spa, and private beach access. The package is designed to provide a blend of relaxation and adventure.

Location: 3850 Wailea Alanui Drive, Wailea, HI 96753

Tip: Use the $200 resort credit strategically for activities like couples' massages or romantic dinners to enhance your experience.

3. Hotel Wailea – Romance Package

Hotel Wailea, an adults-only resort, offers an intimate Romance Package perfect for honeymooners. The package includes a luxurious suite, daily breakfast, a private beach cabana for a day, and a couples' massage. The resort's serene atmosphere, with its lush gardens and panoramic ocean views, provides a secluded and romantic setting. The package also includes a romantic dinner for two at the resort's acclaimed restaurant, which features farm-to-table cuisine and stunning views.

Location: 555 Kaukahi Street, Wailea, HI 96753

Tip: Take advantage of the resort's adult-only policy to enjoy a more tranquil and intimate environment.

4. Andaz Maui at Wailea – Seaside Escape Package

Andaz Maui at Wailea offers a Seaside Escape Package that includes a spacious ocean-view room, a daily breakfast for two, and a $100 resort credit. The package also features a private snorkeling tour and a sunset sail, allowing couples to experience Maui's underwater wonders and picturesque coastlines. The resort's contemporary design and beachfront location provide a chic and romantic atmosphere, perfect for honeymooners.

Location: 3550 Wailea Alanui Drive, Wailea, HI 96753

Tip: Book the private snorkeling tour and sunset sail as early as possible to secure your preferred dates.

Special Activities

1. Private Helicopter Tour

Experience Maui from above with a private helicopter tour that offers breathtaking views of the island's diverse landscapes, including volcanic craters, lush rainforests, and dramatic coastlines. Many tour companies offer customizable itineraries, allowing you to focus on specific areas of interest such as the Hana rainforest or the West Maui Mountains.

The tour provides a unique and romantic perspective of Maui's natural beauty, making it a memorable addition to your honeymoon.

Location: Various operators in Maui, such as Blue Hawaiian Helicopters or Air Maui

Tip: Book your tour in advance and opt for a sunset flight to enjoy the added romance of the setting sun over the island.

2. Sunset Dinner Cruise

A sunset dinner cruise is a classic romantic activity, offering stunning views of the Maui coastline as you sail into the sunset. The cruise typically includes a gourmet dinner, live entertainment, and the chance to spot dolphins or whales. Many operators offer luxury options with fine dining, cocktails, and personalized service. This activity provides a relaxing and intimate way to enjoy Maui's natural beauty and create lasting memories.

Location: Various departure points in Lahaina or Ma'alaea Harbor

Tip: Choose a cruise that offers a private table or cabana for a more intimate experience. Reservations are essential, especially during peak seasons.

3. Couples' Spa Day

Maui's world-class spas offer a range of treatments designed for couples seeking relaxation and rejuvenation. Many resorts feature luxurious spa facilities that offer couples' massages, facials, and wellness treatments. Enjoy a day of pampering with side-by-side massages, followed by a soak in a private hot tub or a relaxing session in a sauna. This experience allows you to unwind together and enjoy a tranquil escape from the stresses of everyday life.

Location: Spa locations vary by resort, including those at the Four Seasons Resort Maui, Grand Wailea, and Andaz Maui

Tip: Book your spa treatments well in advance to ensure availability, and inquire about any special packages or enhancements for couples.

4. Private Beach Picnic

A private beach picnic offers a romantic and intimate dining experience on one of Maui's stunning beaches. Many services provide gourmet picnic setups with fresh local foods, including sandwiches, salads, fruit, and beverages.

The setup often includes a shaded tent, comfortable seating, and a picturesque view of the ocean. Enjoy a leisurely meal together with the sound of the waves and the beauty of the sunset as your backdrop.

Location: Various beach locations, arranged by picnic service providers

Tip: Choose a beach that is less crowded for a more private experience, and coordinate with the picnic service provider to ensure all your preferences are met.

5. Snorkeling Adventure

Discover Maui's vibrant underwater world with a private snorkeling adventure. Explore coral reefs, swim with tropical fish, and if you're lucky, encounter sea turtles and rays. Many tours offer personalized experiences, including guided snorkeling excursions and equipment rental. Snorkeling at spots like Molokini Crater or the Ahihi-Kinau Natural Area Reserve provides a chance to explore some of Maui's best marine environments.

Location: Various operators offer snorkeling tours departing from Lahaina, Kihei, or Ma'alaea

Tip: Check the water conditions and safety recommendations before booking, and ensure that you have adequate sun protection and hydration.

Chapter 18: Health and Wellness

Top Spas and Wellness Centers

Maui offers a range of luxurious spas and wellness centers where you can unwind and rejuvenate amidst the island's serene natural beauty. Whether you're seeking a relaxing massage, a holistic wellness treatment, or a full day of pampering, these top spas provide exceptional experiences tailored to your needs.

1. Spa Montage Kapalua Bay

Spa Montage Kapalua Bay is a premier destination for relaxation and rejuvenation, situated within the luxurious Montage Kapalua Bay resort. The spa offers a comprehensive menu of treatments inspired by the island's natural beauty, including massages, facials, and body treatments. Unique offerings include the Lomi Lomi massage, a traditional Hawaiian technique, and the Makena Beach Body Wrap, which uses local ingredients to nourish the skin. The spa's tranquil setting, featuring ocean views and lush gardens, enhances the experience. Facilities include private treatment rooms, a relaxation lounge, and an outdoor infinity pool.

- **Location:** 1 Bay Drive, Kapalua, HI 96761
- **Opening Hours:** Daily, 9:00 AM - 5:00 PM
- **Phone Number:** +1 808-665-8282

Tip: Book a sunset massage to enjoy stunning ocean views while you relax.

2. Four Seasons Resort Maui at Wailea Spa

The Spa at Four Seasons Resort Maui at Wailea is renowned for its luxurious treatments and stunning oceanfront setting. This full-service spa offers a range of treatments from traditional massages and facials to advanced skincare and wellness therapies. Highlights include the Hawaiian Lomi Lomi massage, the Maui-based Papa'āina body ritual, and personalized skincare treatments using high-end products. The spa features spacious treatment rooms with private lanais, a serene relaxation area, and a variety of wellness classes, including yoga and meditation sessions.

- **Location:** 3900 Wailea Alanui Drive, Wailea, HI 96753
- **Opening Hours:** Daily, 8:00 AM - 7:00 PM
- **Phone Number:** +1 808-874-8000

Tip: Try the signature "Ocean Ritual" for a full-body experience incorporating marine-based products and techniques.

3. Willow Stream Spa at Fairmont Kea Lani

Located within the Fairmont Kea Lani Resort in Wailea, Willow Stream Spa offers a tranquil oasis with a focus on rejuvenating both body and mind. The spa's treatments incorporate natural Hawaiian ingredients and holistic approaches, including the unique "Hawaiian Healing Journey" that combines massage and aromatherapy. Facilities include private treatment rooms, a relaxation lounge, and a hydrotherapy area. Guests can also enjoy the resort's lagoon-style pool and beautiful beachfront.

- **Location:** 4100 Wailea Alanui Drive, Wailea, HI 96753
- **Opening Hours:** Daily, 9:00 AM - 6:00 PM
- **Phone Number:** +1 808-875-2290

Tip: The "Lomilomi Massage" is highly recommended for its deep tissue work and restorative effects.

4. Hale Ho'ola Spa

Hale Ho'ola Spa, located in the heart of Kihei, offers a more intimate and personalized spa experience. The spa focuses on blending traditional Hawaiian healing practices with modern wellness techniques. Services include customized massages, organic facials, and body treatments using locally sourced ingredients.

Hale Ho'ola emphasizes a holistic approach, offering services like energy work and reflexology. The spa's serene ambiance and attentive staff create a peaceful retreat where guests can enjoy a range of treatments.

- **Location:** 1941 S Kihei Road, Kihei, HI 96753
- **Opening Hours:** Monday - Saturday, 9:00 AM - 6:00 PM
- **Phone Number:** +1 808-875-2031

Tip: Opt for a package that combines multiple treatments for a full-day spa experience.

5. The Ritz-Carlton Spa, Kapalua

The Ritz-Carlton Spa, located within the Ritz-Carlton, Kapalua, offers a luxurious escape with a focus on holistic wellness and relaxation. The spa's menu includes a variety of treatments such as massages, facials, and body treatments that utilize local ingredients like Hawaiian honey and volcanic clay. The spa features tranquil treatment rooms, a relaxation lounge, and a beautifully landscaped garden. Guests can also enjoy wellness classes, including yoga and Pilates, and take advantage of the resort's stunning ocean views.

- **Location:** 1 Ritz-Carlton Drive, Kapalua, HI 96761
- **Opening Hours:** Daily, 9:00 AM - 6:00 PM
- **Phone Number:** +1 808-665-7089

Tip: Consider the "Signature Ritual" treatment, which incorporates a range of techniques and local products for a comprehensive experience.

6. Aqua Spa

Aqua Spa, located in Lahaina, offers a serene retreat with a focus on natural and organic treatments The spa features a menu of services including massages, facials, and body scrubs that use locally sourced ingredients and eco-friendly products. Aqua Spa's tranquil environment, complemented by its soothing decor and attentive staff, provides a relaxing experience. The spa also offers wellness workshops and holistic therapies to enhance overall well-being.

- **Location:** 2260 S Kihei Road, Lahaina, HI 96761
- **Opening Hours:** Tuesday - Sunday, 9:00 AM - 5:00 PM
- **Phone Number:** +1 808-667-7321

Tip: The "Tropical Retreat" package combines a variety of treatments for a relaxing day at the spa.

7. Lumeria Maui

Lumeria Maui is a wellness retreat in Makawao that offers a unique combination of spa services and holistic wellness programs. The spa features a range of treatments including massages, facials, and body treatments, often incorporating local, organic ingredients. In addition to individual treatments, Lumeria offers wellness retreats and workshops focusing on yoga, meditation, and personal growth. The serene, natural setting of Lumeria enhances the overall experience, providing a peaceful escape from the hustle and bustle of everyday life.

- **Location:** 1813 Baldwin Avenue, Makawao, HI 96768
- **Opening Hours:** Daily, 8:00 AM - 6:00 PM
- **Phone Number:** +1 808-579-8877

Tip: Join one of the wellness workshops or retreats for a more immersive experience in holistic health.

Yoga and Meditation Retreats

Maui is a paradise for those seeking inner peace and rejuvenation through yoga and meditation. The island offers a variety of retreats that blend the serenity of Maui's natural landscapes with transformative wellness practices. Whether you're a seasoned yogi or a beginner, these retreats provide a sanctuary for healing, relaxation, and spiritual growth.

1. Lumeria Maui

Nestled on the slopes of Upcountry Maui, Lumeria Maui is a luxury wellness retreat offering a range of yoga and meditation programs. The retreat is set on a beautifully restored, six-acre property, surrounded by lush gardens and panoramic ocean views. Lumeria provides daily yoga classes, including Vinyasa, Hatha, and restorative yoga, as well as guided meditation sessions. The retreat also offers wellness workshops, including sound healing, mindfulness practices, and holistic nutrition. The tranquil environment, coupled with the personalized attention of the instructors, makes it an ideal place to deepen your practice and reconnect with yourself.

- **Location:** 1813 Baldwin Avenue, Makawao, HI 96768
- **Opening Hours:** Daily, 8:00 AM - 6:00 PM
- **Phone Number:** +1 808-579-8877

Tip: Book a stay during one of their immersive wellness retreats for a comprehensive experience that includes yoga, meditation, and holistic wellness practices.

2. Maui Healing Retreat

Located in the heart of Maui's lush countryside, Maui Healing Retreat offers personalized wellness programs that focus on yoga, meditation, and holistic healing. The retreat offers custom-tailored yoga sessions designed to meet individual needs, from beginners to advanced practitioners. In addition to yoga, the retreat provides guided meditation sessions, energy healing, detox programs, and life coaching. The serene environment, set amidst the island's natural beauty, enhances the overall experience, providing a peaceful and supportive space for personal growth and healing.

- **Location:** 120 Kainui Loop, Paia, HI 96779
- **Opening Hours:** Daily, 8:00 AM - 6:00 PM
- **Phone Number:** +1 808-870-3711

Tip: Consider enrolling in their "Mindfulness Meditation" program for a deep dive into meditation practices that promote mental clarity and inner peace.

3. Maui Yoga Shala

Maui Yoga Shala is a vibrant community-based yoga studio and retreat center located in the charming town of Paia. The Shala offers a wide variety of yoga classes, including Ashtanga, Vinyasa, Hatha, and aerial yoga. In addition to daily classes, Maui Yoga Shala hosts yoga retreats that combine yoga, meditation, and island adventures such as surfing and hiking. The retreats are designed to help participants reconnect with nature and themselves, providing a holistic approach to wellness. The studio's welcoming atmosphere and experienced instructors make it an excellent choice for both beginners and advanced practitioners.

- **Location:** 381 Baldwin Avenue, Paia, HI 96779
- **Opening Hours:** Daily, 7:00 AM - 7:00 PM
- **Phone Number:** +1 808-283-4123

Tip: Join their "Beach Yoga" sessions for an unforgettable experience of practicing yoga with the sound of the waves and the ocean breeze.

4. Black Swan Temple

Black Swan Temple is a sacred retreat center located in Haiku, offering yoga and meditation retreats in a mystical, serene setting. The temple is surrounded by lush gardens and tropical forests, creating a peaceful atmosphere conducive to deep spiritual practice. Retreats at Black Swan Temple often include daily yoga classes, guided meditation, sound healing, and shamanic practices. The retreats are designed to facilitate personal transformation and healing, with an emphasis on connecting with the divine within. The small, intimate setting ensures personalized attention and a supportive community environment.

- **Location:** 27 Door of Faith Road, Haiku, HI 96708

- **Opening Hours:** Retreats are held throughout the year; inquire for specific dates
- **Phone Number:** +1 808-269-1524

Tip: Participate in their "Goddess Awakening" retreat, which blends yoga, meditation, and sacred rituals designed to empower and uplift.

5. Bikram Yoga Kahului

Bikram Yoga Kahului is the only certified Bikram yoga studio on Maui, offering classes in the traditional 26-posture sequence in a heated environment. While it's not a full retreat center, Bikram Yoga Kahului is an excellent place to dive deep into a disciplined yoga practice. The studio offers daily classes, as well as occasional workshops and events focused on enhancing your practice. The heat and humidity of the studio simulate the conditions of India, making it an authentic experience for those looking to challenge themselves physically and mentally.

- **Location:** 70 E Kaahumanu Avenue, Kahului, HI 96732
- **Opening Hours:** Monday - Friday, 5:30 AM - 8:00 PM; Saturday - Sunday, 8:00 AM - 6:00 PM
- **Phone Number:** +1 808-359-1060

Tip: Stay hydrated and take it slow if you're new to Bikram yoga, as the heat can be intense.

6. Soulasana Yoga Maui

Soulasana Yoga Maui is a modern yoga studio located in Kahului, offering a wide range of classes and workshops focused on yoga, meditation, and holistic wellness. The studio provides a variety of yoga styles, including Vinyasa, Yin, and Power Yoga, as well as meditation sessions designed to reduce stress and promote mental clarity. Soulasana also hosts occasional retreats that combine yoga and meditation with wellness workshops and community activities. The studio's vibrant atmosphere and diverse offerings make it a great choice for both locals and visitors looking to deepen their practice.

- **Location:** 70 E Kaahumanu Avenue, Kahului, HI 96732
- **Opening Hours:** Monday - Friday, 6:00 AM - 8:00 PM; Saturday - Sunday, 8:00 AM - 4:00 PM
- **Phone Number:** +1 808-359-1060

Tip: Take advantage of their first-timer specials, which often include discounted class packages or memberships.

Health and Fitness Classes

Maui offers a wide range of health and fitness classes to keep both residents and visitors active and healthy while enjoying the island's beautiful surroundings. Whether you're interested in high-energy workouts, mindful practices, or outdoor adventures, Maui's fitness scene has something to suit your needs. Below are some of the top options for health and fitness classes on the island.

1. The Gym Maui

Located in Kihei, The Gym Maui is a full-service fitness center offering a variety of group fitness classes, personal training, and state-of-the-art equipment. The gym provides classes such as HIIT (High-Intensity Interval Training), Zumba, Yoga, and Spin, catering to all fitness levels. The facility is known for its welcoming environment and supportive community, making it an ideal place to pursue your fitness goals. Whether you're looking to build strength, improve flexibility, or burn calories, The Gym Maui has a class to fit your needs.

- **Location:** 300 Ohukai Road #101, Kihei, HI 96753
- **Opening Hours:** Monday - Friday, 5:00 AM - 9:00 PM; Saturday, 7:00 AM - 6:00 PM; Sunday, 8:00 AM - 6:00 PM
- **Phone Number:** +1 808-891-8108

Tip: Try the early morning HIIT classes for a challenging workout that kickstarts your day with energy and motivation.

2. Body in Balance

Situated in Lahaina, Body in Balance is a fitness and wellness studio offering a wide range of classes, including Pilates, Barre, Yoga, and TRX Suspension Training. The studio also offers specialty classes such as Aerial Yoga and SurfSET Fitness, which mimics the experience of surfing to improve balance, strength, and agility. Body in Balance prides itself on its personalized approach, with small class sizes ensuring individual attention from instructors. The studio is perfect for those looking to mix up their routine with unique and effective workouts.

- **Location:** 142 Kupuohi Street, Lahaina, HI 96761
- **Opening Hours:** Monday - Friday, 7:00 AM - 7:00 PM; Saturday, 8:00 AM - 2:00 PM; Sunday, Closed

- **Phone Number:** +1 808-661-8700

Tip: Check their schedule for specialty classes like Aerial Yoga, which offer a fun and unique way to enhance flexibility and core strength.

3. Maui Power Yoga

Located in Kahului, Maui Power Yoga offers dynamic yoga classes designed to build strength, flexibility, and endurance. The studio features heated classes including Power Vinyasa and Hot Yoga, which provide a rigorous workout combined with the therapeutic benefits of heat. Maui Power Yoga is known for its vibrant community and skilled instructors who guide participants through challenging sequences in a supportive environment. The studio also hosts workshops and teacher training programs for those looking to deepen their practice.

- **Location:** 101 Lono Avenue, Kahului, HI 96732
- **Opening Hours:** Monday - Friday, 6:00 AM - 7:00 PM; Saturday - Sunday, 8:00 AM - 4:00 PM
- **Phone Number:** +1 808-873-0800

Tip: Join the early morning Hot Yoga sessions to start your day with a revitalizing and sweat-inducing practice.

4. Soulasana Yoga Mau

Soulasana Yoga Maui in Kahului offers a diverse range of classes focused on enhancing physical fitness and mental well-being. The studio provides classes such as Vinyasa Flow, Yin Yoga, and Gentle Yoga, along with meditation sessions and wellness workshops. Soulasana is known for its inclusive and supportive environment, making it accessible to practitioners of all levels. The studio's commitment to community and holistic health is evident in its variety of class offerings and special events.

- **Location:** 70 E Kaahumanu Avenue, Kahului, HI 96732
- **Opening Hours:** Monday - Friday, 6:00 AM - 8:00 PM; Saturday - Sunday, 8:00 AM - 4:00 PM
- **Phone Number:** +1 808-359-1060

Tip: Attend their "Wellness Workshops" to gain additional insights into mindfulness, nutrition, and overall health.

5. Fit Club Maui

Fit Club Maui, located in Wailuku, offers a variety of fitness classes aimed at improving cardiovascular health, strength, and overall fitness. Classes include Boot Camp, Cardio Kickboxing, and CrossFit-style workouts. Fit Club Maui is known for its high-energy atmosphere and motivational instructors who create challenging and fun workout experiences. The club also offers personal training sessions and fitness assessments to help clients reach their individual goals.

- **Location:** 28 E Papa Avenue, Wailuku, HI 96793
- **Opening Hours:** Monday - Friday, 5:30 AM - 8:00 PM; Saturday, 7:00 AM - 2:00 PM; Sunday, Closed
- **Phone Number:** +1 808-244-7800

Tip: Join a Boot Camp class for a high-intensity workout that combines strength training and cardio exercises.

6. Kihei Fitness

Kihei Fitness is a well-equipped gym offering a wide range of group fitness classes including Spin, Zumba, Yoga, and Aqua Fitness. Located in Kihei, the facility provides a welcoming environment with a focus on community and personal fitness. The gym features modern equipment, an indoor pool, and a variety of fitness programs designed to accommodate all levels of experience. Kihei Fitness also offers wellness coaching and nutrition guidance to support overall health.

- **Location:** 2000 Waimahaihai Place, Kihei, HI 96753
- **Opening Hours:** Monday - Friday, 5:00 AM - 9:00 PM; Saturday, 7:00 AM - 6:00 PM; Sunday, 8:00 AM - 4:00 PM
- **Phone Number:** +1 808-891-8181

Tip: Take advantage of their Aqua Fitness classes, which are excellent for low-impact exercise and improving joint mobility.

7. Maui Cycle Studio

Maui Cycle Studio in Lahaina specializes in indoor cycling classes designed to provide a high-energy cardiovascular workout. The studio features state-of-the-art bikes and a dynamic, music-driven environment that makes each session engaging and motivating.

Classes range from high-intensity interval training to endurance rides, with options for all fitness levels. Maui Cycle Studio also offers private and group cycling sessions, as well as specialized events and challenges.

- **Location:** 760 Office Road, Lahaina, HI 96761
- **Opening Hours:** Monday - Friday, 6:00 AM - 7:00 PM; Saturday, 8:00 AM - 2:00 PM; Sunday, Closed
- **Phone Number:** +1 808-661-5550

Tip: Sign up for their "Spin Challenge" sessions to push your limits and track your progress over a series of classes.

8. The Fit Lab

The Fit Lab in Kihei offers a variety of fitness classes and personal training options in a modern, well-equipped space. The Fit Lab provides classes such as TRX, Boot Camp, and Core Strength, as well as individualized training programs tailored to specific goals. The facility is known for its innovative workout methods and supportive atmosphere, making it a great place for both beginners and experienced fitness enthusiasts.

- **Location:** 3150 E Lipoa Street, Kihei, HI 96753
- **Opening Hours:** Monday - Friday, 5:30 AM - 8:00 PM; Saturday, 7:00 AM - 2:00 PM; Sunday, Closed
- **Phone Number:** +1 808-891-8111

Tip: Opt for a personal training session to receive customized workouts and expert guidance tailored to your fitness goals.

Natural Hot Springs and Healing Waters

Maui's natural hot springs and healing waters offer a unique and rejuvenating experience for those seeking relaxation and wellness in a picturesque setting. These natural wonders provide therapeutic benefits and are perfect for unwinding after exploring the island's beauty. Here's a detailed look at some of Maui's notable natural hot springs and healing waters.

1. Alahele Spring

Located in the Upcountry region near Kula, Alahele Spring is a serene natural hot spring known for its mineral-rich waters and tranquil surroundings. The spring emerges from a volcanic rock formation, creating a warm, soothing pool surrounded by lush vegetation and stunning views of the island. The mineral content in the water is believed to have therapeutic properties, promoting relaxation and improving skin health. The setting is quiet and remote, providing a peaceful retreat from the busier parts of the island.

Location: Near Kula, Upcountry Maui (Exact location varies; local maps and guidance recommended)

Tip: Bring your own towels and water shoes, as the area is natural and may not have facilities. The spring is best visited in the morning or late afternoon to avoid peak sun exposure.

2. Waihee Ridge Trail and Springs

While not a traditional hot spring, the Waihee Ridge Trail in the Waihee Valley offers hikers access to natural springs and streams along the trail. The waters from these springs are cool and refreshing, providing a natural way to cool off after a hike. The trail itself offers spectacular views of Maui's lush landscapes, and the stream areas can serve as a relaxing spot to rest and enjoy the beauty of the surrounding nature.

Location: Waihee Valley Road, Waihee, HI 96793

Opening Hours: The trail is open daily from sunrise to sunset

Tip: Wear appropriate hiking gear and bring plenty of water. The streams are not hot springs, but they offer a refreshing natural experience.

3. Hana Lava Tube

The Hana Lava Tube, located in Hana, is a geological marvel formed by lava flow. While not a hot spring, the tube contains cool, underground water pools that offer a unique way to experience Maui's volcanic landscape. The water is cool and clear, providing a refreshing dip after exploring the lava tube's fascinating formations. The surrounding area also includes beautiful rainforests and hiking paths.

Location: 4.4 Miles Hana Highway, Hana, HI 96713

Opening Hours: Daily, 9:00 AM - 5:00 PM

Phone Number: +1 808-248-8260

Tip: Explore the lava tube during a guided tour for a comprehensive understanding of its formation and the surrounding environment.

4. Polipoli Spring State Recreation Area

Located in the Upcountry region of Maui, Polipoli Spring State Recreation Area offers a cooler climate and access to natural springs in a beautiful forested setting. The area features several hiking trails that lead to scenic spots, including natural springs that provide refreshing, cool water. The springs are not hot but offer a pleasant, natural water experience in a lush, forested environment.

Location: Polipoli Spring State Recreation Area, Kula, HI 96790

Opening Hours: Daily, 7:00 AM - 6:00 PM

Phone Number: +1 808-984-8109

Tip: Dress in layers, as temperatures can be cooler in this area. Bring water and snacks for a pleasant hiking experience.

5. Kula Botanical Garden

While not a hot spring, the Kula Botanical Garden features several natural water features and springs that enhance the garden's tranquil environment. Visitors can enjoy walking along the streams and springs that meander through the lush plant life. The water is cool and clear, contributing to the garden's serene atmosphere and providing a soothing experience amidst the beautiful botanical displays.

Location: 638 Kekaulike Avenue, Kula, HI 96790

Opening Hours: Daily, 9:00 AM - 4:00 PM

Phone Number: +1 808-878-1715

Tip: Plan your visit to coincide with a guided tour to learn more about the garden's unique plant life and natural water features.

6. Makena Beach

Makena Beach, also known as Big Beach, is not a hot spring but offers natural, warm waters due to its sheltered location and the presence of shallow areas warmed by the sun.

The beach is known for its stunning views and large, open sandy areas, providing a great spot for swimming and relaxing in warm, gentle waters.

Location: Makena State Park, Makena, HI 96753

Opening Hours: Daily, 7:00 AM - 7:00 PM

Phone Number: +1 808-873-3558

Tip: Visit early in the morning or late in the afternoon to avoid crowds and enjoy the warmest waters. Be mindful of strong currents and tides.

Wellness Resorts and Detox Programs

Maui offers a variety of wellness resorts and detox programs designed to help you rejuvenate, relax, and reconnect with yourself. Whether you're seeking a comprehensive detox retreat or a luxurious wellness resort with a focus on holistic health, Maui has options that cater to a range of wellness needs. Here's a detailed look at some of the top wellness resorts and detox programs on the island:

1. Lanai at Koele, A Four Seasons Resort

The Lanai at Koele offers a luxurious and serene environment for those seeking a comprehensive wellness retreat. Set on the lush island of Lanai, this resort combines luxury with wellness, providing a range of activities such as yoga, meditation, and guided hikes. The resort's spa offers detoxifying treatments including massages, facials, and body scrubs designed to refresh and rejuvenate. The serene environment, coupled with personalized wellness programs, ensures a transformative experience.

- **Location:** 1 Keomoku Highway, Lanai City, HI 96763
- **Opening Hours:** Wellness programs and spa treatments available by appointment
- **Phone Number:** +1 808-565-4000

Tip: Opt for a wellness package that includes a combination of spa treatments and outdoor activities to fully immerse yourself in the resort's holistic approach.

2. The Fairmont Kea Lani

Located in Wailea, The Fairmont Kea Lani offers an exceptional wellness experience with its focus on holistic health and relaxation.

The resort features a full-service spa offering detoxifying treatments, including wraps, scrubs, and massages. The wellness program also includes fitness classes, such as yoga and aqua fitness, designed to enhance physical and mental well-being. The resort's beautiful beachfront location adds to the serene ambiance, making it a perfect spot for relaxation.

- **Location:** 4100 Wailea Alanui Drive, Wailea, HI 96753
- **Opening Hours:** The spa is open daily from 9:00 AM - 6:00 PM; Fitness classes vary
- **Phone Number:** +1 808-875-4100

Tip: Take advantage of the "Wellness Package" that includes daily fitness classes and spa treatments for a comprehensive wellness experience.

3. Maui Wellness Retreat

Maui Wellness Retreat in Upcountry Maui offers specialized detox and wellness programs tailored to individual needs. Their programs include a combination of detoxifying treatments, yoga, meditation, and personalized nutritional guidance. The retreat focuses on holistic healing with an emphasis on detox diets, natural therapies, and mindfulness practices. The tranquil Upcountry setting enhances the retreat experience, providing a peaceful environment for deep relaxation and renewal.

- **Location:** 1438 Baldwin Avenue, Makawao, HI 96768
- **Opening Hours:** Programs available by reservation
- **Phone Number:** +1 808-575-9300

Tip: Book a customized detox program to address specific health goals and enjoy a tailored experience that maximizes the benefits of the retreat.

4. Kapalua Villas Maui

Kapalua Villas Maui offers a wellness-focused retreat experience with its luxurious villas and access to wellness facilities. The resort features a state-of-the-art fitness center, spa services, and wellness programs including yoga and meditation. Guests can also enjoy detoxifying treatments and wellness workshops designed to enhance overall well-being. The resort's beautiful location and private villas provide a serene backdrop for relaxation and rejuvenation.

- **Location:** 300 Kapalua Drive, Lahaina, HI 96761
- **Opening Hours:** Fitness center open daily; Spa services by appointment
- **Phone Number:** +1 808-665-5599

Tip: Consider booking a villa with a private outdoor space to enhance your wellness experience with personal relaxation and meditation.

5. The Ritz-Carlton, Kapalua

The Ritz-Carlton, Kapalua offers an indulgent wellness experience with its luxurious spa and wellness programs. The resort provides a range of detoxifying treatments including organic facials, body wraps, and massages. Wellness programs feature yoga classes, meditation sessions, and fitness workshops designed to promote physical and mental health. The stunning oceanfront setting enhances the wellness experience, allowing guests to enjoy beautiful views while engaging in relaxation and wellness activities.

- **Location:** 1 Ritz-Carlton Drive, Kapalua, HI 96761
- **Opening Hours:** The spa opens daily from 9:00 AM - 6:00 PM; Wellness programs vary
- **Phone Number:** +1 808-669-6200

Tip: Participate in their "Wellness Weekends" which offer a blend of spa treatments, fitness classes, and wellness workshops for a comprehensive retreat experience.

6. Travaasa Hana

Travaasa Hana, located in Hana, offers a tranquil retreat focused on wellness and relaxation. The resort features a full-service spa, fitness classes, and wellness workshops. Detox programs include nutritional counseling, spa treatments, and outdoor activities designed to promote overall health. The remote location and natural surroundings create a serene environment ideal for a restorative escape from daily life.

- **Location:** 5031 Hana Highway, Hana, HI 96713
- **Opening Hours:** Spa and wellness programs available by appointment
- **Phone Number:** +1 808-248-8211

Tip: Make use of the resort's holistic approach to wellness by participating in both spa treatments and outdoor adventure activities.

Chapter 19: Maui Itinerary

5 Days in Maui: The Perfect Maui Itinerary

Maui, known as the "Valley Isle," offers a diverse blend of natural beauty, adventure, and relaxation. A five-day itinerary allows you to experience the best of Maui's beaches, mountains, and cultural sites. Here's a perfect itinerary for exploring Maui in five days:

Day 1: Arrival and West Maui Exploration

Morning: Arrival and Check-In

7:00 AM – 9:00 AM: Arrival at Kahului Airport (OGG)

Your adventure begins as you land at Kahului Airport, the main gateway to Maui. After gathering your luggage, pick up your rental car, which is essential for exploring the island's diverse landscapes. Depending on the time of your arrival, consider a leisurely breakfast near the airport before heading to West Maui.

9:00 AM – 10:00 AM: Breakfast at 808 Grindz Café

Located in nearby Lahaina, **808 Grindz Café** is a local favorite, known for its affordable and hearty breakfast options. Try their famous macadamia nut pancakes or the loco moco, a traditional Hawaiian breakfast dish. The café offers a laid-back atmosphere, perfect for easing into your Maui vacation.

Mid-Morning: Scenic Drive to West Maui

10:00 AM – 11:00 AM: Drive to Lahaina or Ka'anapali

After breakfast, embark on the scenic drive along the **Honoapiilani Highway** (Hwy 30) towards West Maui. This route offers stunning views of the Pacific Ocean on one side and the lush West Maui Mountains on the other. You'll pass by picturesque beaches like **Olowalu** and several viewpoints where you can stop to take photos.

Late Morning: Explore Lahaina Town

11:00 AM – 1:00 PM: Historic Lahaina

Upon arriving in **Lahaina**, check into your accommodation, whether it's a beachfront resort in Ka'anapali or a charming boutique hotel in Lahaina Town.

After settling in, take some time to explore the historic town of Lahaina, which was once the capital of the Hawaiian Kingdom and a bustling whaling village.

Start your exploration at **Lahaina Banyan Court Park**, home to the largest banyan tree in the United States. The sprawling tree covers nearly an acre and provides a cool, shaded spot to relax. Next, visit the Lahaina Heritage Museum to learn about the town's rich history. As you stroll along Front Street, you'll find art galleries, unique boutiques, and historic sites like the Baldwin House Museum.

Afternoon: Beach Time at Ka'anapali

1:00 PM – 2:00 PM: Lunch at Kimo's Maui

For lunch, head to **Kimo's Maui**, a beachfront restaurant with stunning ocean views. Enjoy fresh seafood like the **famous Hula Pie**, or opt for a lighter meal with their **fish tacos** or **poke bowl**. The casual, open-air dining experience is quintessentially Hawaiian, making it a perfect introduction to Maui's culinary scene.

2:00 PM – 5:00 PM: Relax at Ka'anapali Beach

After lunch, make your way to **Ka'anapali Beach**, one of Maui's most famous beaches. With its golden sands and crystal-clear waters, Ka'anapali Beach is ideal for swimming, snorkeling, or simply relaxing under the sun. The Ka'anapali Beachwalk stretches along the shoreline, offering easy access to resorts, shops, and dining options. If you're feeling adventurous, join a catamaran tour or take a snorkeling excursion to Black Rock, a popular spot for seeing colorful marine life.

Evening: Sunset and Nightlife in Lahaina

5:00 PM – 6:30 PM: Sunset at Fleetwood's on Front St.

As the day winds down, head to **Fleetwood's on Front St.**, a rooftop restaurant owned by Mick Fleetwood of Fleetwood Mac. This spot is perfect for watching the sunset while enjoying a cocktail or a glass of wine. The restaurant offers live music most evenings, creating a vibrant atmosphere as you watch the sun dip below the horizon.

6:30 PM – 8:30 PM: Dinner at Lahaina Grill

For dinner, treat yourself to an upscale dining experience at **Lahaina Grill**. Consistently rated as one of the best restaurants in Maui, Lahaina Grill offers a menu of New American cuisine with a Hawaiian twist. Dishes like the **seared ahi tuna** or the **Maui onion** and **sesame-crusted seared ahi** are highly recommended. Pair your meal with a selection from their extensive wine list for a memorable dining experience.

8:30 PM – Late: Nightlife in Lahaina

After dinner, explore Lahaina's nightlife. Visit **Down the Hatch**, a lively bar with a relaxed vibe, great cocktails, and often live music or DJ sets. If you're in the mood for something more laid-back, head to **Pioneer Inn** for a more intimate setting with live local music. End your night with a stroll along Front Street, where the ocean breeze and vibrant atmosphere will leave you feeling refreshed and ready for the days of adventure ahead.

Day 2: Road to Hana Adventure

The Road to Hana is one of Maui's most iconic and scenic drives, offering lush landscapes, cascading waterfalls, and picturesque beaches. This full-day adventure requires an early start to fully enjoy the numerous stops along the way. Remember to pack comfortable clothing, swimwear, towels, snacks, and a camera to capture the breathtaking views.

Early Morning: Start of the Journey

6:00 AM – 6:30 AM: Breakfast at Paia Bowls

Begin your day early by driving to the charming town of Paia, the gateway to the Road to Hana. Stop at **Paia Bowls** for a healthy and energizing breakfast.

Enjoy delicious acai bowls topped with fresh local fruits, granola, and honey, or opt for a smoothie to kickstart your adventure.

6:30 AM – 7:00 AM: Fuel Up and Prepare

Before hitting the road, ensure your vehicle has a full tank of gas, as there are limited fueling options along the route. Stock up on water, snacks, and any essentials you might need for the day. Consider downloading an offline map or guide app specifically for the Road to Hana to help navigate and learn about various points of interest.

Morning: Exploring Natural Wonders

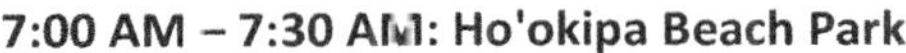

7:00 AM – 7:30 AM: Ho'okipa Beach Park

Just a few miles from Paia, make a quick stop at **Ho'okipa Beach Park**. This renowned surf spot offers early morning views of surfers tackling impressive waves and, if you're lucky, you might spot Hawaiian green sea turtles resting on the shore.

8:00 AM – 8:45 AM: Twin Falls

Your first major stop is **Twin Falls**, located at mile marker 2. This easy hike leads you to beautiful waterfalls and refreshing natural pools where you can take a dip. Enjoy the tranquil surroundings and consider grabbing a fresh coconut or smoothie from the nearby fruit stand operated by local farmers.

9:30 AM – 10:15 AM: Waikamoi Ridge Trail

Stretch your legs at the **Waikamoi Ridge Trail** near mile marker 9. This short loop trail takes you through a lush rainforest showcasing native Hawaiian plants and offers serene viewpoints perfect for nature lovers and photographers alike.

10:30 AM – 11:00 AM: Garden of Eden Arboretum

Explore the beautifully maintained **Garden of Eden**, featuring 26 acres of exotic plants, waterfalls, and stunning vistas including a viewpoint of the famous Puohokamoa Falls. There is an entrance fee, but the scenic beauty and peaceful atmosphere make it worthwhile.

Midday: Cultural and Culinary Experience

11:30 AM – 12:15 PM: Ke'anae Peninsula

Venture down to the **Ke'anae Peninsula** to witness rugged lava rock coastlines and traditional taro fields that offer a glimpse into old Hawaii. Stop by Aunty Sandy's Banana Bread stand to taste what many claim is the best banana bread on the island – a perfect snack to enjoy by the ocean.

12:45 PM – 1:45 PM: Lunch at Nahiku Marketplace

Reach the **Nahiku Marketplace** around lunchtime, a small collection of food stands and local vendors nestled in the rainforest. Enjoy a variety of options such as fish tacos, Thai food, or fresh coconut water. Browse through local crafts and souvenirs while soaking in the vibrant, tropical ambiance.

Afternoon: Beaches and Waterfalls

2:00 PM – 3:00 PM: Wai'anapanapa State Park

Arrive at **Wai'anapanapa State Park**, home to the famous black sand Pa'iloa Beach. Explore sea caves, lava tubes, and blowholes along the coastal trails. The stark contrast between the black sand, blue ocean, and green vegetation provides incredible photo opportunities. Remember to make a reservation in advance as entry is limited.

3:15 PM – 3:30 PM: Hana Town

Drive through the quaint **Hana Town**, a peaceful community that embodies the essence of rural Maui. If time permits, visit the Hana Cultural Center and Museum to learn about the area's rich history and culture.

3:45 PM – 4:00 PM: Wailua Falls

Just past Hana, stop at **Wailua Falls**, one of Maui's most picturesque and easily accessible waterfalls. The 80-foot cascade is visible from the road, but a short path allows you to get closer and even take a refreshing swim at the base, weather permitting.

Late Afternoon: Adventure and Relaxation

4:30 PM – 6:30 PM: 'Ohe'o Gulch (Seven Sacred Pools) and Pipiwai Trail

Proceed to the Kipahulu District of Haleakalā National Park to explore the **'Ohe'o Gulch**, commonly known as the Seven Sacred Pools. These tiered pools offer stunning scenery and, when conditions are safe, opportunities for swimming. For those up for a hike, the Pipiwai Trail is a 4-mile round-trip trek through a majestic bamboo forest leading to the towering Waimoku Falls. Allocate around 2 hours for this hike and ensure you have enough daylight and energy before starting.

Evening: Return Journey

6:30 PM – 7:30 PM: Dinner at Hana Ranch Restaurant

Before heading back, enjoy dinner at **Hana Ranch Restaurant**, offering farm-to-table cuisine with locally sourced ingredients. Relish dishes like grilled fresh catch, burgers, and salads while enjoying views of the Pacific Ocean and surrounding landscapes.

7:30 PM onwards: Return to Accommodation

Begin your return journey carefully as the roads can be challenging to navigate in the dark. Alternatively, consider staying overnight in Hana to explore more the next day and return at a leisurely pace. If you choose to drive back, take your time and drive cautiously, stopping at safe pullouts if needed.

Tips for the Day:

- **Safety:** Drive cautiously as the road is narrow with many curves and one-lane bridges.
- **Timing:** Start early to avoid crowds and have ample time for stops.
- **Reservations:** Book ahead for Wai'anapanapa State Park entry.
- **Supplies:** Bring enough water, snacks, and sunscreen. Restroom facilities are limited along the route.
- **Respect Nature:** Follow posted signs, stay on trails, and respect private properties.

Day 3: Haleakalā Sunrise and Upcountry Maui

Early Morning: Haleakalā Sunrise

2:30 AM – 3:00 AM: Departure from Your Accommodation

Rise early and prepare for the pre-dawn drive to **Haleakalā National Park**. Depending on where you're staying, the drive can take 1.5 to 2.5 hours. Dress warmly, as temperatures at the summit can be freezing before dawn, even in the summer. Bring blankets, hot beverages, and snacks to keep you comfortable.

3:00 AM – 5:00 AM: Drive to Haleakalā Summit

The drive to **Haleakalā's summit** is an adventure in itself, with winding roads and gradually increasing elevation. The higher you go, the more the landscape transforms into an otherworldly terrain. Arrive at the summit's parking lot early to secure a good viewing spot for the sunrise. Reservations are required for sunrise viewing, so make sure to book in advance.

5:00 AM – 6:30 AM: Sunrise at Haleakalā

As dawn breaks, the sky begins to glow with hues of pink, orange, and purple, gradually illuminating the crater below. The experience is often described as spiritual, with the silence of the mountain and the grandeur of the view creating a profound sense of awe. After the sun has risen, take some time to explore the summit area, including the Pu'u'ula'ula (Red Hill) Overlook, the highest point on the volcano at 10,023 feet.

Morning: Descent and Breakfast in Kula

7:00 AM – 8:00 AM: Breakfast at Kula Lodge Restaurant

After descending from the summit, treat yourself to a well-deserved breakfast at **Kula Lodge Restaurant**, located in the heart of Upcountry Maui. The restaurant offers panoramic views of the West Maui Mountains and the Pacific Ocean, making it a perfect spot to relax after your early morning adventure. Enjoy a hearty breakfast with options like **macadamia nut pancakes, eggs Benedict**, or **fresh fruit**.

Mid-Morning: Explore the Ali'i Kula Lavender Farm

8:30 AM – 9:30 AM: Ali'i Kula Lavender Farm

After breakfast, head to the **Ali'i Kula Lavender Farm**, a peaceful and aromatic escape. Stroll through the terraced gardens filled with over 45 varieties of lavender and other beautiful flora. The farm offers guided tours where you can learn about the cultivation and uses of lavender, as well as indulge in lavender-infused products like scones, tea, and essential oils.

Late Morning: Discover MauiWine

10:00 AM – 11:30 AM: MauiWine at Ulupalakua Ranch

Continue your Upcountry exploration with a visit to **MauiWine**, located at the historic Ulupalakua Ranch. The winery is famous for its pineapple wines, but it also produces traditional grape wines. Take a guided tour of the vineyards and the charming **King's Cottage Tasting Room**, where you can sample a variety of wines. The ranch itself is steeped in history, offering a glimpse into Maui's past with its beautifully preserved buildings and serene landscapes.

Midday: Lunch at Ulupalakua Ranch Store

12:00 PM – 1:00 PM: Lunch at Ulupalakua Ranch Store & Grill

For lunch, stay at Ulupalakua Ranch and enjoy a meal at the **Ranch Store & Grill**, where you can savor locally sourced beef, lamb, and elk burgers, or opt for lighter fare like fresh salads and sandwiches. The rustic setting and peaceful surroundings make for a delightful dining experience.

Afternoon: Visit the Enchanting Gardens and Artisans

1:30 PM – 2:30 PM: Explore the Enchanted Floral Gardens of Kula

Head to the **Enchanted Floral Gardens of Kula**, a seven-acre botanical garden that showcases the diverse plant life of Maui. Wander through themed gardens featuring tropical plants, succulents, and colorful flowers, all while enjoying panoramic views of the valley below. This serene environment is perfect for a stroll and photography.

2:45 PM – 4:00 PM: Visit Local Artisans and the Hui No'eau Visual Arts Center

Continue your exploration of Upcountry by visiting the **Hui No'eau Visual Arts Center**, located in a historic estate in Makawao. The center offers art exhibitions, classes, and a gallery shop featuring works by local artists. Explore the beautiful grounds and perhaps pick up a unique piece of art or handmade jewelry as a souvenir.

Late Afternoon: Explore Makawao Town

4:15 PM – 5:30 PM: Stroll Through Makawao

Makawao is a charming, eclectic town known for its paniolo **(Hawaiian cowboy)** heritage and vibrant arts scene. Take a leisurely walk through the town's main street, where you'll find art galleries, boutique shops, and cafes. Don't miss **Komoda Store & Bakery**, a local institution famous for its cream puffs and stick donuts.

Evening: Farm-to-Table Dinner

6:00 PM – 8:00 PM: Dinner at Hali'imaile General Store

End your day with a farm-to-table dinner at the **Hali'imaile General Store**, one of Maui's most celebrated restaurants.

Chef Bev Gannon's menu features locally sourced ingredients prepared with a fusion of Hawaiian, Asian, and American flavors. Signature dishes include the sashimi napoleon, macadamia nut-crusted fish, and Maui pineapple upside-down cake. The restaurant's plantation-style setting adds to the charm of this unique dining experience.

Night: Return to Your Accommodation

8:00 PM onwards: Relax and Unwind

After a full day of exploring Haleakalā and Upcountry Maui, return to your accommodation. Reflect on the day's adventures as you relax and prepare for another exciting day in Maui. The cool, peaceful night air of Upcountry will likely have you drifting off to sleep with ease.

Tips for the Day:

- **Reservations:** Make sunrise reservations for Haleakalā well in advance as they are required.
- **Clothing:** Dress in layers for the sunrise as temperatures can be extremely cold at the summit.
- **Altitude:** Be aware of the altitude changes at Haleakalā, especially if you're sensitive to high elevations.
- **Local Products:** Take the opportunity to buy local lavender products, wines, and handmade crafts as unique souvenirs.

Day 4: Snorkeling and Molokini Crater

Early Morning: Departure and Snorkeling at Molokini Crater

6:00 AM – 6:30 AM: Departure from Your Accommodation

Start your day early and make your way to the harbor for your snorkeling tour. Most tours depart from either **Ma'alaea Harbor** or **Kihei Boat Ramp**, so check your tour details in advance. Be sure to bring sunscreen, a hat, a towel, and your underwater camera to capture the beauty of Molokini.

7:00 AM – 8:00 AM: Boat Ride to Molokini Crater

Embark on a scenic boat ride to **Molokini Crater**. The journey takes about an hour, during which you can enjoy the views of Maui's coastline and the possibility of spotting dolphins or even whales (during the winter months).

Most tour operators offer a light breakfast on board, often including fresh fruit, pastries, and coffee.

8:00 AM – 10:30 AM: Snorkeling at Molokini Crater

Once you arrive at **Molokini Crater**, it's time to dive into the water. The crescent-shaped crater protects the inner reef, providing calm conditions ideal for snorkeling. Visibility can exceed 150 feet on a good day, allowing you to see a wide variety of fish, eels, rays, and sometimes even sea turtles. Take your time to explore the coral gardens and marvel at the diverse marine life.

10:30 AM – 11:30 AM: Snorkeling at Turtle Town

Many Molokini snorkeling tours include a second stop at **Turtle Town**, a coastal area known for its population of Hawaiian green sea turtles (honu). Snorkel alongside these gentle creatures and observe them as they glide gracefully through the water. This is a memorable highlight for many visitors to Maui.

Late Morning: Return to the Harbor and Lunch

11:30 AM – 12:30 PM: Return to Harbor

After your snorkeling adventure, enjoy a leisurely ride back to the **harbor**. Many tours offer refreshments and drinks on the return journey, so you can relax and soak in the sun while reminiscing about your morning underwater.

12:30 PM – 1:30 PM: Lunch at Monkeypod Kitchen in Wailea

Once back on land, head to **Monkeypod Kitchen** in Wailea for a well-deserved lunch. This popular restaurant offers a farm-to-table dining experience with a menu that highlights local ingredients. Enjoy dishes like fresh fish tacos, wood-fired pizzas, or their famous saimin noodles. Pair your meal with a craft beer or one of their signature cocktails, like the Monkeypod Mai Tai.

Afternoon: Beach Time at Makena Beach (Big Beach)

2:00 PM – 4:00 PM: Relax at Makena Beach

After lunch, make your way to **Makena Beach**, also known as Big Beach. This expansive stretch of golden sand is one of the largest and most beautiful beaches on Maui, offering plenty of space to relax and enjoy the afternoon. Whether you want to swim in the clear waters, sunbathe, or take a stroll along the shore, Big Beach is the perfect spot to unwind after your morning adventure.

Optional: Explore Little Beach

If you're feeling adventurous, take the short hike over the hill at the north end of Big Beach to explore **Little Beach**, a smaller, more secluded beach that is popular with those looking for a more free-spirited atmosphere.

Late Afternoon: Explore the Shops at Wailea

4:30 PM – 6:00 PM: Shopping at The Shops at Wailea

Before heading back to your accommodation, take some time to explore The Shops at **Wailea**, an upscale shopping center with a mix of luxury brands, local boutiques, and art galleries. Browse through Hawaiian-made jewelry, and high-end fashion, or pick up some unique souvenirs to take home. If you're interested in art, the galleries here showcase a range of works from local and international artists.

Evening: Seafood Dinner in South Maui

6:30 PM – 8:30 PM: Dinner at Merriman's Kapalua

For dinner, make your way to **Merriman's Kapalua**, located on the western tip of the island. Known for its oceanfront setting and commitment to using locally sourced ingredients, Merriman's offers an unforgettable dining experience. Savor fresh seafood dishes like macadamia nut-crusted mahi-mahi, or indulge in their famous lobster pot pie. The restaurant's open-air design allows for stunning sunset views, making it the perfect place to end your day.

Night: Return to Your Accommodation

8:30 PM onwards: Relax and Reflect

After a full day of snorkeling, beach relaxation, and fine dining, return to your accommodation. Reflect on the incredible marine life you encountered at Molokini Crater and Turtle Town as you unwind and prepare for another day of exploring Maui.

Tips for the Day:

- **Snorkeling Gear:** Most tours provide snorkeling gear, but if you have your own, bring it along for comfort.

- **Sun Protection:** Even though you'll be in the water, sun exposure is intense, so reapply sunscreen frequently.
- **Respect Marine Life:** Observe the marine life from a distance and avoid touching coral or turtles to protect these delicate ecosystems.
- **Hydration:** Keep hydrated throughout the day, especially after spending time in the sun and salt water.

Day 5: Iao Valley and Departure

Your final day on Maui is a blend of serene nature exploration and heartfelt farewells to this island paradise. With your flight likely scheduled for later in the day, you'll have time to visit the lush Iao Valley, soak in the last of Maui's natural beauty, and enjoy a relaxed farewell meal before heading to the airport.

Morning: Visit to Iao Valley State Monument

7:30 AM – 8:30 AM: Breakfast at 808 Grindz Cafe in Lahaina

Start your day with a hearty breakfast at **808 Grindz Cafe**, a local favorite known for its delicious, affordable plates. Enjoy a Hawaiian-style breakfast such as loco moco, pancakes topped with coconut syrup, or their signature corned beef hash. This small, unassuming café is popular, so arrive early to beat the crowds.

9:00 AM – 10:30 AM: Explore Iao Valley State Monument

After breakfast, drive to the Iao Valley **State Monument**, located in Central Maui. This lush, verdant valley is steeped in Hawaiian history and natural beauty. As you approach, you'll notice the iconic Iao Needle, a 1,200-foot-tall rock formation that towers over the valley. Take the short, paved hike up to the viewpoint for a closer look at the Needle and the surrounding landscape. The area is rich with native flora and offers a peaceful atmosphere, perfect for a morning of reflection and connection with nature.

Historical Insight: Iao Valley is not only a place of natural wonder but also a site of historical significance. It was here that the Battle of Kepaniwai took place in 1790, a pivotal conflict in King Kamehameha's campaign to unify the Hawaiian Islands. As you walk through the valley, imagine the history that unfolded in this serene setting.

Tips: The valley can be misty in the morning, so wear appropriate footwear and bring a light jacket. The park's trails are relatively easy but do take your time to fully appreciate the lush surroundings and the sound of the nearby stream.

Late Morning: Return to Kahului and Last-Minute Shopping

11:00 AM – 12:30 PM: Shopping and Lunch at Queen Ka'ahumanu Center

Head back towards Kahului and stop at the **Queen Ka'ahumanu Center**, the largest shopping mall on the island. This is a great place to pick up any last-minute souvenirs or gifts before your departure. The mall offers a mix of local boutiques and national brands, making it easy to find something special to remember your trip.

For a quick lunch, consider grabbing a bite at one of the center's eateries. Koho Grill & Bar offers a variety of options, including fresh salads, sandwiches, and local specialties like poke bowls. Enjoy your meal in the food court or take it to go if you prefer to eat at a nearby park or beach.

Afternoon: Relax and Prepare for Departure

1:00 PM – 2:30 PM: Beach Time at Kanaha Beach Park

With a few hours left before your flight, take one last opportunity to relax by the ocean. **Kanaha Beach Park**, located near the airport, is an excellent spot for this. It's a favorite among locals for windsurfing and kiteboarding, but it also has calm areas perfect for swimming or simply lounging on the sand. The park's facilities include picnic tables, restrooms, and showers, making it a convenient place to freshen up before your journey home.

Late Afternoon: Return the Rental Car and Head to the Airport

2:30 PM – 3:00 PM: Return Rental Car

After your relaxing time at the beach, return your rental car. Most car rental agencies near Kahului Airport are efficient, but it's always good to give yourself a bit of extra time in case of unexpected delays.

3:00 PM – 4:00 PM: Check-in at Kahului Airport (OGG)

Arrive at Kahului Airport with plenty of time to check in, drop off your luggage, and go through security. Kahului is a small airport, but it can get busy, especially during peak travel times. While waiting for your flight, you can browse the airport shops for any last-minute purchases or grab a snack at one of the airport cafés.

Evening: Departure from Maui

4:00 PM – 5:00 PM: Relax Before Your Flight

With everything checked in, take a moment to relax before boarding your flight. Reflect on the amazing experiences you've had over the past five days—from the exhilarating Road to Hana to the peaceful shores of Molokini Crater, to the serene beauty of Iao Valley. As you leave Maui, you'll carry with you not just souvenirs, but memories of an island that truly embodies the spirit of Aloha.

5:00 PM onwards: Departure

Depending on your flight time, prepare for departure. If you have a later flight, take advantage of the airport's amenities or use the time to organize your photos and reminisce about your adventures on Maui.

Tips for Departure Day:

Pack Carefully: Make sure you've packed all your belongings, including any souvenirs or gifts you've purchased during your trip. Double-check your flight details and ensure you have enough time to reach the airport and go through security.

Return Car on Time: Most car rental companies have a grace period, but it's best to return the vehicle on time to avoid any extra charges.

Stay Hydrated: Air travel can be dehydrating, so drink plenty of water before your flight.

Top-Rated Guided Tours

Maui is a haven for guided tours that showcase the island's natural beauty, rich culture, and vibrant history. Here's a detailed look at some of the top-rated guided tours in Maui, each offering a unique experience that captures the essence of this Hawaiian paradise.

1. Road to Hana Tour

The Road to Hana is one of Maui's most iconic drives, and a guided tour is the best way to experience it without the stress of navigating the winding roads yourself. This tour typically includes stops at stunning waterfalls, lush rainforests, and black-sand beaches. Experienced guides share stories about the history and culture of the area, making the journey as informative as it is beautiful.

Many tours also include a visit to the Haleakalā National Park to see the Seven Sacred Pools at Ohe'o.

- **Location:** Starts from your hotel or a designated meeting point
- **Duration:** Full day (10-12 hours)
- **Highlights:** Waterfalls, Hana town, Haleakalā National Park, Seven Sacred Pools
- **Tour Providers:** Valley Isle Excursions, Temptation Tours
- **Contact:** Valley Isle Excursions (+1 808-871-5224), Temptation Tours (+1 808-661-3333)

2. Haleakalā Sunrise Tour

Witnessing the sunrise from the summit of Haleakalā, Maui's highest peak, is an unforgettable experience. This tour takes you to the summit in the early morning hours, where you'll watch the sun rise above the clouds. The guides provide insights into the volcanic landscape and its significance in Hawaiian culture. The tour often includes a visit to the park's visitor center and some short hikes around the crater's rim.

- **Location:** Pickup from various locations around Maui
- **Duration:** 6-7 hours
- **Highlights:** Sunrise at Haleakalā summit, volcanic landscapes, short hikes
- **Tour Providers:** Polynesian Adventure Tours, Skyline Hawaii
- **Contact:** Polynesian Adventure Tours (+1 808-877-4242), Skyline Hawaii (+1 808-518-4189)

3. Molokini Crater and Turtle Town Snorkeling Tour

This snorkeling tour is perfect for marine life enthusiasts. Molokini Crater, a partially submerged volcanic caldera, is one of the top snorkeling spots in Hawaii, known for its crystal-clear waters and diverse marine life. After exploring the vibrant coral reefs of Molokini, the tour typically continues to Turtle Town, where you can snorkel with Hawaiian green sea turtles. Knowledgeable guides provide safety instructions and information about the underwater ecosystem.

- **Location:** Departs from Maalaea Harbor
- **Duration:** 5-6 hours
- **Highlights:** Snorkeling at Molokini Crater, Turtle Town, marine life encounters

- Tour Providers: Pacific Whale Foundation, Maui Snorkel Charters
- **Contact:** Pacific Whale Foundation (+1 808-249-8811), Maui Snorkel Charters (+1 808-244-7333)

4. Maui Pineapple Tour

For something unique, the Maui Pineapple Tour offers a behind-the-scenes look at the island's pineapple industry. This tour takes you to the fields where the famous Maui Gold pineapples are grown. You'll learn about the cultivation process, taste fresh pineapples straight from the fields, and even take home a pineapple as a souvenir. The tour also includes a visit to the packing facility, where you can see how pineapples are prepared for shipping.

- **Location:** Hali imaile, Maui, HI 96768
- **Duration:** 1.5-2 hours
- **Highlights:** Pineapple fields, tasting fresh pineapples, packing facility tour
- **Tour Providers:** Maui Pineapple Tours
- **Contact:** +1 808-665-5491

5. Maui Whale Watching Tour

From December to April, humpback whales migrate to Maui's warm waters, making whale watching a must-do activity. Guided whale-watching tours take you out to sea, where you can observe these majestic creatures up close. Experienced guides provide commentary on whale behavior, biology, and the importance of whale conservation. Many tours guarantee sightings, and some even use hydrophones to listen to whale songs.

- **Location:** Departs from Lahaina or Maalaea Harbor
- **Duration:** 2-3 hours
- **Highlights:** Humpback whale sightings, expert commentary, hydrophone listening
- **Tour Providers:** Pacific Whale Foundation, Ultimate Whale Watch & Snorkel
- **Contact:** Pacific Whale Foundation (+1 808-249-8811), Ultimate Whale Watch & Snorkel (+1 808-667-5678)

6. Iao Valley and Lahaina Tour

This tour takes you on a cultural and historical journey through some of Maui's most significant sites.

Iao Valley is a lush, green area steeped in history, where you'll learn about the Battle of Kepaniwai and the sacredness of the valley to the Hawaiian people. The tour then continues to Lahaina, a historic town that was once the capital of the Hawaiian Kingdom and a bustling whaling port. Here, you can explore landmarks such as the Lahaina Banyan Court, the Old Lahaina Courthouse, and the Baldwin Home Museum.

- **Location:** Pickup from various locations on Maui
- **Duration:** 6-7 hours
- **Highlights:** Iao Valley State Park, Lahaina town, cultural sites, historical landmarks
- **Tour Providers:** Roberts Hawaii, Polynesian Adventure Tours
- **Contact:** Roberts Hawaii (+1 808-539-9400), Polynesian Adventure Tours (+1 808-877-4242)

7. Maui Chocolate Tour

The Maui Chocolate Tour offers a delectable experience for chocolate lovers, guiding you through the process of growing cacao and making chocolate. This tour takes place on a cacao farm, where you'll see how the beans are cultivated, harvested, and transformed into delicious chocolate. The tour includes plenty of tastings, allowing you to sample various types of chocolate made on-site. It's a sweet, educational experience that's fun for all ages.

- **Location:** Lahaina, Maui, HI 96761
- **Duration:** 1.5-2 hours
- **Highlights:** Cacao farm tour, chocolate-making process, tastings
- **Tour Providers:** Maui Ku'ia Estate Chocolate
- **Contact:** +1 808-557-0795

8. Maui Helicopter Tour

For an unforgettable aerial view of Maui, a helicopter tour offers the best perspective. These tours take you above Maui's most stunning landscapes, including the lush rainforests of Hana, the towering cliffs of Molokai, and the dramatic volcanic crater of Haleakalā. Some tours even include a landing in a remote area, allowing you to explore a secluded spot that's only accessible by air. The guides provide informative commentary throughout the flight, making this an educational and awe-inspiring experience.

- **Location:** Departs from Kahului Heliport
- **Duration:** 45 minutes to 2 hours, depending on the tour
- **Highlights:** Aerial views of Haleakalā, Hana, Molokai, waterfalls
- **Tour Providers:** Blue Hawaiian Helicopters, Air Maui Helicopter Tours
- **Contact:** Blue Hawaiian Helicopters (+1 808-871-8844), Air Maui Helicopter Tours (+1 808-877-7005)

9. Maui Ocean Center Tour

The Maui Ocean Center, one of the top-rated aquariums in the world, offers guided tours that provide deep insights into Hawaii's marine life. The tour includes access to exhibits such as the Open Ocean Tunnel, where sharks, rays, and other marine creatures swim overhead. Knowledgeable guides share fascinating information about the marine ecosystems of the Hawaiian Islands, the importance of conservation, and the cultural significance of the ocean to the Hawaiian people.

- **Location:** 192 Ma'alaea Rd, Wailuku, HI 96793
- **Duration:** 1.5-2 hours
- **Highlights:** Open Ocean Tunnel, marine exhibits, cultural stories
- **Tour Providers:** Maui Ocean Center
- **Contact:** +1 808-270-7000

10. Maui Zipline Adventure

For thrill-seekers, the Maui Zipline Adventure is a must-try experience. This tour offers an exhilarating ride over Maui's lush landscapes, with zip lines that stretch across canyons and through treetops. As you soar through the air, you'll be treated to panoramic views of the island's mountains, valleys, and coastline. The guides ensure safety while sharing information about the flora and fauna you'll see along the way. It's an exciting way to combine adventure with the natural beauty of Maui.

- **Location:** 1670 Honoapiilani Hwy, Wailuku, HI 96793
- **Duration:** 2-3 hours
- **Highlights:** Multiple zip lines, panoramic views, safety briefing
- **Tour Providers:** Maui Zipline Company, Skyline Hawaii
- **Contact:** Maui Zipline Company (+1 808-633-2464), Skyline Hawaii (+1 808-518-4189)

Chapter 20: Practical Information

Language and Communication

Maui, like all of Hawaii, has a unique linguistic landscape shaped by its history, culture, and multicultural population. Understanding the language and communication norms in Maui can greatly enhance your experience when visiting the island.

Languages Spoken

English: English is the primary language spoken in Maui and throughout Hawaii. It is used in government, education, business, and everyday interactions. Most residents and visitors are fluent in English.

Hawaiian: Hawaiian is the indigenous language of Hawaii and holds cultural significance. While not as widely spoken as English, efforts to preserve and revitalize the Hawaiian language have increased in recent years. You may encounter Hawaiian words and phrases in place names, cultural contexts, and signage.

Local Dialects and Slang

Pidgin: Pidgin English, often referred to simply as "Pidgin," is a Creole language spoken by some residents in Hawaii, including Maui. It blends English with Hawaiian, Portuguese, Japanese, and Chinese influences. While not everyone speaks Pidgin, you may hear it in informal settings or among certain local communities.

Slang: Like any community, Maui has its own slang and colloquial expressions. These may include terms borrowed from Pidgin or unique to local culture. Learning some common phrases can help you connect with locals and better understand conversations.

Communication Tips

Respect Local Culture: Understanding and respecting Hawaiian culture is essential. The use of Hawaiian words, such as aloha (hello/goodbye/love), mahalo (thank you), and makai (towards the sea), shows cultural sensitivity and appreciation.

Greeting: The Hawaiian tradition of greeting with a warm aloha is common. It's not just a word but a spirit of welcoming and affection. Responding with aloha helps establish positive interactions.

Politeness: Politeness and respect are highly valued in Hawaiian culture. Using please ('olu'olu) and thank you (mahalo) in interactions, whether in English or Hawaiian, reflects cultural norms.

Navigating Language Challenges

Tourist Services: Most tourist services, such as hotels, restaurants, and attractions, are English-speaking and cater to international visitors. English signage and communication are prevalent in tourist areas.

Local Interactions: Engaging with locals can provide insights into Maui's culture. While English is widely spoken, being open to hearing Hawaiian words and phrases enriches cultural exchanges.

Resources for Learning

Language Apps: Apps like Duolingo and Memrise offer Hawaiian language courses. These can help you learn basic phrases and vocabulary before or during your visit.

Local Classes: Some community centers and cultural organizations on Maui offer Hawaiian language classes for beginners. These provide opportunities to learn from native speakers and deepen your understanding of the language.

Cultural Sensitivity

Historical Context: Understanding Hawaii's history, including colonization and cultural suppression, adds context to the importance of language revitalization efforts. Respect for the Hawaiian language and culture demonstrates cultural sensitivity and appreciation.

Safety Tips

Maui is a beautiful destination with diverse landscapes and a welcoming atmosphere, but like any travel destination, it's important to prioritize safety to ensure a smooth and enjoyable trip. Here are comprehensive safety tips to keep in mind while visiting Maui:

1. Ocean Safety

Swimming and Snorkeling: Only swim and snorkel in designated areas with lifeguards present. Follow posted signs and warnings regarding currents, rip tides, and marine life.

Respect Wildlife: Admire marine life from a distance and avoid touching or approaching sea creatures, including sea turtles and monk seals, which are protected by law.

Reef Protection: Avoid standing on coral reefs, as they are fragile ecosystems. Use reef-safe sunscreen to minimize harm to marine life.

2. Beach Safety

Lifeguards and Flags: Swim near lifeguard stations and obey beach warning flags. A red flag indicates dangerous conditions, while a yellow flag advises caution.

Wave Caution: Watch out for powerful shore breaks and sneaker waves, especially on north-facing shores. These can unexpectedly pull swimmers out to sea.

3. Sun Protection

Sunscreen: Wear sunscreen with a high SPF and reapply frequently, especially if swimming or participating in water activities. Protect sensitive areas like ears, nose, and tops of feet.

Sun Exposure: Seek shade during peak sun hours (10 AM to 4 PM) to avoid sunburn and dehydration. Wear a hat, sunglasses, and lightweight, long-sleeved clothing.

4. Driving Safety

Road Conditions: Maui's roads can be narrow and winding, particularly on the Road to Hana and around Haleakala. Drive cautiously, adhere to speed limits, and yield to local drivers.

Rental Vehicles: Familiarize yourself with the rental vehicle's features, such as 4WD or AWD capabilities if exploring off-road areas. Inspect the vehicle for any damage before renting.

5. Hiking and Outdoor Activities

Trail Conditions: Research hiking trails in advance and choose routes suitable for your fitness level. Wear sturdy footwear, bring ample water and snacks, and inform someone of your itinerary.

Weather Awareness: Be prepared for sudden weather changes, especially in higher elevations. Check weather forecasts and avoid hiking during storms or heavy rain.

6. Respect Local Culture

Cultural Sites: Respect sacred and historical sites, such as heiaus (ancient Hawaiian temples) and burial grounds. Observe posted signs and refrain from touching artifacts.

Local Etiquette: Learn about and respect Hawaiian customs and traditions. Ask permission before taking photos of locals or participating in cultural activities.

7. Emergency Preparedness

Emergency Contacts: Save emergency numbers, including 911 for emergencies and local police and medical services. Know the location of the nearest hospital or urgent care center.

Travel Insurance: Consider purchasing travel insurance that covers medical emergencies, trip cancellations, and lost belongings to ensure peace of mind during your trip.

8. Wildlife Encounters

Sharks: While shark attacks are rare, avoid swimming alone or in murky water. Stay informed about any recent shark sightings and follow local guidance.

Jellyfish: Be cautious of Portuguese man-of-war and jellyfish stings, especially during certain seasons. Avoid touching them and seek medical attention if stung.

9. Water Activities

Boating Safety: Follow boating regulations and wear life jackets when boating, kayaking, or participating in water sports. Ensure boats are equipped with safety gear and operated by licensed individuals.

Diving Safety: If diving, choose reputable dive operators certified by organizations like PADI or NAUI. Follow dive guides' instructions and perform equipment checks before diving.

10. General Safety Tips

Secure Valuables: Keep valuables secure in hotel safes or locked compartments in rental vehicles. Avoid leaving belongings unattended on beaches or in public areas.

Local Advice: Seek advice from locals or concierge services regarding safe areas to visit, current conditions, and any specific precautions for remote or less-traveled areas.

Health and Medical Services

When traveling to Maui, it's essential to be aware of the health and medical services available on the island to ensure a safe and enjoyable trip. Here's a comprehensive guide to health and medical services in Maui:

1. Hospitals and Emergency Services

Maui Memorial Medical Center: Located in Wailuku, Maui Memorial Medical Center is the largest hospital on the island. It offers a wide range of medical services, including emergency care, surgery, intensive care, and specialized treatments.

- **Location:** 221 Mahalani St, Wailuku, HI 96793
- **Phone Number:** (808) 244-9056

Kaiser Permanente Maui Lani Medical Office: Provides comprehensive medical services, urgent care, and emergency services for Kaiser Permanente members and non-members.

- **Location:** 55 Maui Lani Pkwy, Wailuku, HI 96793
- **Phone Number:** (808) 243-6000

Emergency Medical Services (EMS): Dial 911 for emergency medical assistance throughout Maui. EMS provides ambulance services and emergency medical care.

2. Urgent Care Centers

Maui Urgent Care: Offers urgent medical care services for non-life-threatening illnesses and injuries. Walk-ins are welcome, and the center provides on-site diagnostic services.

- **Location:** 1325 South Kihei Rd, Suite 103, Kihei, HI 96753
- **Phone Number:** (808) 875-7858

Minit Medical Urgent Care Centers: Multiple locations across Maui offering urgent care services, including treatment for minor injuries, illnesses, and vaccinations.

- **Locations:** Visit Minit Medical Urgent Care for details.

3. Pharmacies

Longs Drugs: A chain pharmacy with multiple locations across Maui. Provides prescription medications, over-the-counter drugs, and pharmaceutical services.

- **Locations:** Visit Longs Drugs Locations for details.

Walgreens: Another chain pharmacy with locations in Maui offering prescription medications, vaccinations, and pharmacy services.

- **Locations:** Visit Walgreens Locations for details.

4. Dental Services

Maui Dental Group: Provides comprehensive dental services, including general dentistry, cosmetic dentistry, and emergency dental care.

- **Location:** 270 Dairy Rd, Suite 204, Kahului, HI 96732
- **Phone Number:** (808) 871-5450

Island Dentistry: Offers a range of dental treatments and emergency dental services for residents and visitors.

- **Location:** 2395 South Kihei Rd, Suite 202, Kihei, HI 96753
- **Phone Number:** (808) 875-7988

5. Travel Health and Vaccinations

Travel Clinics of America - Maui: Provides travel health consultations, vaccinations, and medications tailored to international travel requirements.

- **Location:** 55 Maui Lani Pkwy, Suite 206, Wailuku, HI 96793
- **Phone Number:** (808) 242-3222

Maui County Health Department: Offers information on local health advisories, immunizations, and public health services.

- **Location:** Various locations, check Maui County Health Department for details.

6. Health Insurance

Ensure you have adequate health insurance coverage for your trip to Maui. Verify coverage for medical emergencies, hospitalization, and evacuation if necessary. Many medical facilities in Maui accept major health insurance plans, but it's important to confirm coverage before seeking treatment.

7. Additional Resources

American Red Cross - Maui County: Provides emergency assistance, disaster relief, and community health services.

- **Website:** American Red Cross - Hawaii

Maui Visitors Bureau: Offers visitor information, including health and safety tips for travelers to Maui.

- **Website:** Maui Visitors Bureau

Electricity and Adapters

Understanding the electrical system and adapters in Maui is essential for travelers to ensure their devices can be used safely and efficiently. Here are the key details you need to know:

Electrical System

Maui, like the rest of the United States, operates on a standard electrical system:

Voltage: The voltage in Maui is 120 volts AC, 60Hz.

Plug Type: Electrical outlets in Maui generally use Type A and Type B plugs. Type A plugs are two flat parallel pins, while Type B plugs are similar but with an additional grounding pin (three pins in total).

Frequency: The frequency of the electrical current is 60 Hz.

Most modern electronics and devices, such as laptops, cameras, and mobile phone chargers, are designed to handle a range of voltages (typically 100-240 volts) and frequencies, so they should work without issues when plugged into a compatible adapter.

Power Adapters and Converters

When traveling to Maui, especially from countries with different electrical standards, you may need power adapters and converters:

Power Adapters: If your devices have plugs that are not compatible with Type A or Type B outlets, you will need a power adapter. Adapters allow you to plug your device into Maui's electrical outlets. They do not convert voltage.

- **Type A Adapter:** Converts plugs with two flat pins to fit Type A outlets.
- **Type B Adapter:** Converts plugs with two flat pins and one grounding pin to fit Type B outlets.

Voltage Converters: If your device does not support 120 volts and you're unsure about its compatibility, you may need a voltage converter. Voltage converters can change the electrical voltage from 120 volts to match your device's requirements. However, most modern electronics are dual-voltage and do not require converters.

Universal Adapters: Consider purchasing a universal adapter that includes multiple plug types. This ensures compatibility not only in Maui but also in other countries with different outlet configurations.

Where to Buy Adapters

Adapters and converters can be purchased from various retailers, both online and in physical stores:

Local Electronics Stores: Stores in Maui such as electronics retailers and larger supermarkets often carry adapters and converters.

Airport Shops: Some airports, including Kahului Airport (OGG), may have stores selling travel adapters.

Online Retailers: Websites like Amazon, Best Buy, or travel-specific retailers offer a wide selection of adapters and converters for purchase before your trip.

Tips for Travelers

Check Your Devices: Before traveling, check the voltage specifications on your devices and chargers to ensure they are compatible with 120 volts.

Pack Adapters Early: Don't wait until the last minute to purchase adapters. Pack them with your travel essentials to avoid any inconvenience upon arrival.

Consider a Power Strip: If you have multiple devices to charge, a travel power strip with surge protection and multiple outlets can be useful, especially in hotels with limited outlets.

Tipping Guidelines

Restaurants:

Sit-Down Restaurants:

Standard Tip: 15% to 20% of the pre-tax bill is customary.

Exceptional Service: For exceptional service, especially in higher-end restaurants, tipping 20% or more is appreciated.

Buffet Restaurants:

Buffet Servers: 10% to 15% of the total bill, depending on the level of service provided (e.g., drink refills, clearing plates).

Bars:

Bartenders: $1 to $2 per drink, or 15% to 20% of the total bill if running a tab.

Hotels:

Housekeeping: $2 to $5 per day is standard. Leave the tip in an envelope labeled "Housekeeping" or directly with a thank-you note.

Concierge: Optional, but $5 to $20 for arranging reservations or providing valuable local tips.

Valet: $2 to $5 each time the car is retrieved.

Bell Staff/Porters: $2 to $5 per bag, depending on the size and weight.

Tours and Activities:

Tour Guides: $5 to $10 per person for shorter tours, or 10% to 20% of the tour cost for longer or specialized tours.

Drivers: $2 to $5 per person for shuttle or airport transfers.

Spa and Wellness:

Spa Services: 15% to 20% of the service cost is typical for massages, facials, and other treatments.

General Guidelines:

Service Quality: Tipping is generally based on the quality of service received. Exceptional service may warrant a higher tip.

Cash Preferred: While some places accept tips on credit cards, cash is often preferred for immediacy and convenience.

Group Dining: Some restaurants automatically add a gratuity (usually 18% to 20%) for parties of six or more. Check your bill to avoid double-tipping.

Cultural Sensitivity:

Understanding Aloha: The spirit of "Aloha" includes respect and appreciation for hospitality. Tipping is seen as a gesture of appreciation for good service.

Mahalo: Saying "mahalo" (thank you) when giving a tip is considered polite and reflects gratitude.

Exceptions:

Taxi Drivers: While not mandatory, rounding up the fare is appreciated.

Fast Food and Counter Service: Tipping is not expected unless there is table service or exceptional assistance.

Internet and Wi-Fi Access

Ensuring reliable internet access during your stay in Maui is essential, whether for staying connected, working remotely, or researching local attractions. Here's a comprehensive guide to internet and Wi-Fi access options on the island:

1. Hotels and Resorts

Most hotels and resorts in Maui offer complimentary Wi-Fi for guests. The quality and speed of the internet connection can vary, with higher-end properties typically offering faster speeds and more reliable connectivity. Many resorts also provide internet access in public areas such as lobbies and pool areas.

2. Vacation Rentals

If you're staying in a vacation rental, check with the property owner or management company about the availability and details of Wi-Fi access. Some rentals include Wi-Fi as part of their amenities, while others may charge an additional fee or have limited connectivity options.

3. Coffee Shops and Restaurants

Maui has numerous coffee shops, cafes, and restaurants that offer free Wi-Fi to customers. Popular spots include:

- Akamai Coffee (Kihei)
- Wailuku Coffee Company (Wailuku)
- Sip Me (Makawao)
- Paia Bay Coffee & Bar (Paia)
- Java Jazz & Soup Nutz (Lahaina)

These establishments provide a casual setting to enjoy a meal or coffee while staying connected.

4. Public Libraries

Maui County Public Libraries offer free Wi-Fi access to residents and visitors. While primarily intended for residents, visitors can use the library facilities, including internet access, during operating hours. Some popular libraries include:

- Kahului Public Library (Kahului)
- Makawao Public Library (Makawao)
- Kihei Public Library (Kihei)

5. Co-Working Spaces

For those needing a dedicated workspace with reliable internet access, several co-working spaces are available in Maui. These spaces provide amenities such as high-speed internet, desks, meeting rooms, and sometimes even networking opportunities. Examples include:

- Maui Office Space (Kahului)
- Maui CoWork (Lahaina)
- Makai Coworking (Kihei)

6. Mobile Data and Cellular Service

Maui has good coverage for major cellular carriers like Verizon, AT&T, T-Mobile, and Sprint. If you have a mobile data plan, you can use your smartphone as a mobile hotspot for internet access wherever there is cellular coverage on the island. Be aware of potential data limits and roaming charges if applicable

7. Resort fees

Some hotels and resorts may charge a daily resort fee that includes Wi-Fi access among other amenities. Always check the hotel's policy regarding internet access and any associated fees before booking.

8. Internet Cafes

While less common than in the past, some internet cafes still operate in Maui. These cafes typically offer computer stations for public use and may provide Wi-Fi access for customers with their own devices.

Tips for Using Wi-Fi in Maui:

Security: Always use secure connections (look for HTTPS) when accessing sensitive information such as banking or personal accounts.

Coverage: Wi-Fi coverage can be spotty in remote areas or outdoor locations. Plan accordingly if you need uninterrupted internet access.

Local Resources: Ask locals or hotel staff for recommendations on the best spots for reliable Wi-Fi in the area you're visiting.

Useful Apps and Websites

Planning a trip to Maui involves researching activities, accommodations, dining options, and local tips to make the most of your visit. Here are some comprehensive websites and apps that can enhance your Maui experience:

GoHawaii - Maui

GoHawaii is the official tourism website for the Hawaiian Islands, including Maui. It provides essential information on attractions, activities, events, and accommodations. The website offers travel tips, maps, and guides to help plan your itinerary. Whether you're looking for cultural experiences, outdoor adventures, or relaxation on Maui's beaches, GoHawaii is a valuable resource.

Features:

- Comprehensive travel information
- Detailed guides and maps
- Recommendations for activities and attractions
- Travel tips and local insights

Website: GoHawaii - Maui

Maui Visitors Bureau

The Maui Visitors Bureau website provides up-to-date information on events, festivals, and special promotions on the island. It offers insights into local culture, dining options, shopping, and outdoor activities. The bureau's website is ideal for planning detailed itineraries and discovering hidden gems around Maui.

Features:

- Event calendars and special promotions
- Detailed information on dining and shopping
- Outdoor activities and cultural experiences
- Travel planning resources

Website: Maui Visitors Bureau

Shaka Guide

Shaka Guide offers self-guided audio tours that are perfect for exploring Maui at your own pace. The app provides GPS-based navigation and narrated tours for popular routes such as the Road to Hana, Haleakala National Park, and West Maui. Shaka Guide enhances your experience with local stories, historical insights, and tips for must-see spots.

Features:

- GPS-based audio tours with narration
- Offline maps and navigation
- Insider tips and local stories
- Flexibility to explore at your own pace

Website: Shaka Guide

App: Available on iOS and Android

Maui Now

Maui Now is a comprehensive news and information website that covers local events, weather updates, traffic reports, and community news. It's a valuable resource for staying informed about current events and activities happening in Maui during your visit.

Features:

- Local news updates
- Weather forecasts and alerts
- Traffic reports and road conditions
- Event listings and community updates

Website: Maui Now

Hawaiian Airlines Mobile App

If you're flying to Maui with Hawaiian Airlines, their mobile app offers convenient features for managing your flight bookings, checking in online, and accessing your flight status. The app also provides information on baggage allowances, airport amenities, and Hawaiian Airlines' loyalty program.

Features:

- Flight booking and management
- Online check-in and boarding passes

- Flight status updates and alerts
- Information on airport amenities

App: Available on iOS and Android

Google Maps

Google Maps is essential for navigating Maui's roads and finding attractions, restaurants, and activities. It provides real-time traffic updates, directions, and reviews for businesses. Offline maps are available for areas with limited cellular service, making them a reliable tool for exploring the island.

Features:

- Navigation with real-time traffic updates
- Business reviews and ratings
- Offline maps for areas without internet access
- Street view and satellite imagery

Website: Google Maps

App: Available on iOS and Android

Airbnb Experiences

For unique and authentic experiences on Maui, consider booking through Airbnb Experiences. Local hosts offer activities such as cultural tours, cooking classes, surfing lessons, and nature hikes. These experiences provide opportunities to connect with locals and explore Maui's culture and natural beauty in a personalized setting.

Features:

- Variety of local experiences
- Small group sizes for personalized attention
- Reviews and ratings from previous guests
- Easy booking and secure payment through Airbnb platform

Website: Airbnb Experiences - Maui

Useful Contacts and Numbers

When traveling to Maui, you must have a list of useful contacts and emergency numbers to ensure your safety and convenience. Here is a comprehensive guide to important contacts and emergency numbers you might need while visiting Maui:

Emergency Services

1. Emergency (Police, Fire, Ambulance)

Phone Number: 911

Details: Dial 911 for any emergency that requires immediate assistance from the police, fire department, or ambulance services. This number is toll-free and available 24/7.

2. Maui Police Department

- **Non-Emergency Phone Number:** (808) 244-6400
- **Location:** 55 Mahalani St, Wailuku, HI 96793

Details: For non-emergency police assistance, general inquiries, or to report non-urgent crimes.

3. Maui Fire Department

- **Non-Emergency Phone Number:** (808) 270-7561
- **Location:** Various fire stations across Maui

4. Maui County Civil Defense Agency

- **Phone Number:** (808) 270-7285
- **Location:** 200 South High Street, Wailuku, HI 96793

Details: For information on disaster preparedness, warnings, and emergency management in Maui County.

Medical Services

5. Maui Memorial Medical Center

- **Phone Number:** (808) 244-9056
- **Location:** 221 Mahalani St, Wailuku, HI 96793

Details: The largest hospital in Maui, providing comprehensive emergency, inpatient, and outpatient services.

6. Kaiser Permanente Maui Lani Medical Office

- **Phone Number:** (808) 243-6000
- **Location:** 55 Maui Lani Pkwy, Wailuku, HI 96793

Details: Offers various medical services, including urgent care, primary care, and specialty services.

7. Urgent Care Maui

- **Phone Number:** (808) 667-7676
- **Location:** 2580 Kekaa Dr, Lahaina, HI 96761

Details: Provides urgent care services for non-life-threatening medical issues.

8. Doctors On Call Maui

- **Phone Number:** (808) 667-7676
- **Location:** Whalers Village, 2435 Kaanapali Pkwy, Suite A3, Lahaina, HI 96761

Details: Walk-in clinic offering urgent care, travel medicine, and general medical services.

Tourist Assistance

9. Maui Visitor Information Center

- **Phone Number:** (808) 242-7780
- **Location:** 695 Front St, Lahaina, HI 96761

Details: Provides information on attractions, activities, and accommodations. Staff can assist with travel inquiries and provide local maps and brochures.

10. Hawaii Visitors and Convention Bureau (Maui Office)

- **Phone Number:** (808) 244-3530
- **Location:** 2270 Kalakaua Ave, Suite 801, Honolulu, HI 96815 (Oahu office serving all Hawaiian Islands)

Details: Offers visitor information, travel tips, and support for tourists.

Transportation Services

11. Maui Bus

- **Phone Number**: (808) 871-4838

Details: Provides public transportation services across Maui. Visit their website for routes, schedules, and fare information.

12. SpeediShuttle Maui

- **Phone Number**: (808) 242-7777

Details: Offers airport shuttle services and private transportation around Maui. Bookings can be made online or by phone.

13. Taxi Services

Maui Taxi

- **Phone Number**: (808) 879-4823

Details: Reliable taxi service available 24/7.

Utilities and Essential Services

14. Maui Electric Company (MECO)

- **Customer Service Phone Number:** (808) 871-9777
- **Emergency/Outage Phone Number:** (808) 871-7777

Details: For reporting power outages, electrical emergencies, or customer service inquiries.

15. Hawaiian Telcom

- **Customer Service Phone Number:** (808) 643-3456

Details: For issues related to landline telephone, internet, and cable services.

Other Useful Contacts

16. Maui Humane Society

- **Phone Number:** (808) 877-3680

- **Location:** 1350 Mehameha Loop, Puunene, HI 96784

Details: For reporting lost or found pets, animal control issues, and adopting pets.

17. Lost and Found (Maui Airport)

- **Phone Number:** (808) 872-3421

Details: For inquiries about lost items at Kahului Airport.

18. Maui County Department of Water Supply

- **Customer Service Phone Number:** (808) 270-7730
- **Emergency/After-Hours Phone Number:** (808) 270-7633

Details: For water service issues, billing inquiries, and emergencies.

Visitor Information Centers

Maui Visitor Information Centers provide invaluable resources for tourists looking to make the most of their stay on the island. These centers offer a wealth of information on attractions, activities, accommodations, and local culture, and are staffed by knowledgeable locals who can provide personalized recommendations and assistance. Here are some of the key visitor information centers in Maui:

1. Maui Visitors Bureau

The Maui Visitors Bureau (MVB) is the official tourism agency for Maui. Located in Kahului, the MVB offers comprehensive information on all aspects of travel to the island, including accommodations, activities, dining, and events. Visitors can pick up brochures, maps, and guides, and receive expert advice from the friendly staff. The bureau also promotes sustainable tourism practices to preserve Maui's natural beauty.

- **Location:** 1727 Wili Pa Loop, Wailuku, HI 96793
- **Hours:** Monday to Friday, 8:00 AM - 4:30 PM
- **Phone Number:** (800) 525-6284
- **Website:** Maui Visitors Bureau

2. Haleakalā National Park Visitor Centers

Haleakalā National Park has two main visitor centers: the Park Headquarters Visitor Center and the Haleakalā Visitor Center. These centers provide essential information about the park, including maps, trail guides, safety tips, and educational displays about the park's unique ecosystem. Rangers are available to answer questions and offer guidance on hiking trails, camping, and viewing the sunrise or sunset from the summit.

Park Headquarters Visitor Center: Located at 7,000 feet elevation

- **Hours:** Daily, 8:00 AM - 3:45 PM
- **Phone Number:** (808) 572-4400

Haleakalā Visitor Center: Located at the summit, near the parking lot

- **Hours:** Daily, 6:00 AM - 12:00 PM
- **Phone Number:** (808) 572-4400

Website: Haleakalā National Park

3. Kīhei Visitor Center

The Kīhei Visitor Center is conveniently located in South Maui, providing tourists with information on local attractions, beaches, dining options, and activities. Staffed by knowledgeable locals, the center offers brochures, maps, and personalized recommendations. It is an excellent resource for visitors staying in the Kīhei, Wailea, and Makena areas.

- **Location:** 1794 South Kihei Road, Kihei, HI 96753
- **Hours:** Monday to Friday, 9:00 AM - 4:00 PM
- **Phone Number:** (808) 875-4453

4. Lahaina Visitor Center

Located in the historic town of Lahaina, this visitor center provides a wealth of information on West Maui attractions, including the famous Lahaina Banyan Tree, Lahaina Harbor, and Front Street. The center offers brochures, maps, and information on local tours, activities, and historical sites. It's a great starting point for exploring Lahaina's rich cultural heritage.

- **Location:** 648 Wharf Street, Lahaina, HI 96761

- **Hours:** Monday to Friday, 9:00 AM - 5:00 PM
- **Phone Number:** (808) 667-9193

5. Hana Cultural Center and Museum

While not a traditional visitor center, the Hana Cultural Center and Museum serves as an excellent resource for visitors exploring East Maui and the town of Hana. The center provides information on local history, culture, and attractions. Exhibits include artifacts, photographs, and historical documents that showcase Hana's rich heritage. Staff members are available to answer questions and provide guidance on local points of interest.

- **Location:** 4974 Uakea Road, Hana, HI 96713
- **Hours:** Monday to Friday, 10:00 AM - 4:00 PM
- **Phone Number:** (808) 248-8622
- **Website:** Hana Cultural Center

6. Maui Tropical Plantation

Maui Tropical Plantation, located in Waikapu, is a popular tourist attraction that also serves as an information hub for visitors. The plantation offers tours, activities, and dining options, along with a visitor center that provides information on local attractions, events, and services. It's an excellent place to learn about Maui's agricultural history and plan further excursions on the island.

- **Location:** 1670 Honoapiilani Hwy, Wailuku, HI 96793
- **Hours:** Daily, 9:00 AM - 5:00 PM
- **Phone Number:** (808) 244-7643
- **Website:** Maui Tropical Plantation

7. Whalers Village Information Booth

Located in the heart of Ka'anapali, the Whalers Village Information Booth offers tourists detailed information on shopping, dining, and activities in the area. The booth is a great resource for visitors looking to explore Ka'anapali Beach, nearby hotels, and local attractions. Staff can provide maps, brochures, and recommendations for making the most of your visit.

- **Location:** 2435 Kaanapali Parkway, Lahaina, HI 96761
- **Hours:** Monday to Sunday, 10:00 AM - 9:00 PM
- **Phone Number:** (808) 661-4567

- **Website:** Whalers Village

Packing List: What to Bring for Every Season in Maui

Maui's tropical climate means temperatures are generally warm year-round, but packing appropriately can make your trip more comfortable and enjoyable. Here's a comprehensive packing list of what to bring to Maui for every season:

Clothing

Year-Round Essentials:

Lightweight Clothing: Pack breathable, quick-drying clothes such as shorts, t-shirts, tank tops, and sundresses. Look for materials like cotton, linen, and moisture-wicking fabrics.

Swimwear: Bring multiple swimsuits, as you'll likely spend much time in the water. Consider packing a cover-up for beach days.

Light Jacket or Sweater: Evenings can be cool, especially near the coast or at higher elevations.

Rain Jacket: Maui experiences occasional rain showers, so a lightweight, packable rain jacket is a good idea.

Comfortable Walking Shoes: Essential for exploring towns, trails, and attractions. Opt for sneakers, hiking shoes, or sturdy sandals.

Flip Flops/Sandals: Perfect for the beach and casual outings.

Hat: A wide-brimmed hat or baseball cap to protect you from the sun.

Seasonal Additions:

Winter (December to February):

Warm Layers: If you plan to visit Haleakala or spend time in Upcountry, pack warmer clothing like a fleece jacket, long pants, and a beanie, as temperatures can be much cooler at higher elevations.

Waterproof Shoes: For wet and muddy hikes.

Spring (March to May) and Fall (September to November):

Layering Pieces: Cardigans or light sweaters for cooler mornings and evenings.

Long-Sleeved Shirts: For added sun protection and cooler weather.

Summer (June to August):

Extra Swimwear: More frequent beach days mean you might want a few extra swimsuits.

Lightweight, Breathable Fabrics: Keep cool during the hottest months with moisture-wicking clothing.

Sun Protection Clothing: Long-sleeved rash guards or UV-protective shirts for extended outdoor activities.

Accessories

- Sunglasses: Essential for eye protection against Maui's strong sun.
- Beach Bag: A tote or backpack for carrying your beach essentials.
- Reusable Water Bottle: Stay hydrated while reducing plastic waste.
- Daypack: A small backpack for day trips, hikes, and excursions.
- Waterproof Phone Case: Protect your phone from water and sand.
- Dry Bag: This is for keeping valuables dry during water activities.
- Reusable Shopping Bag: Useful for groceries and shopping.

Toiletries and Personal Items

- Sunscreen: Choose a reef-safe sunscreen to protect Maui's coral reefs.
- Aloe Vera Gel: Helpful for soothing sunburns.
- Bug Repellent: Especially important for evening activities or hikes in lush areas.
- Personal Medications: Bring any prescription medications you need, as well as a basic first aid kit.
- Toiletries: Shampoo, conditioner, body wash, toothpaste, toothbrush, etc. Travel-sized items are convenient.
- Hand Sanitizer: Useful for staying clean on the go.
- Lip Balm with SPF: Protect your lips from sun exposure.

Tech and Gadgets

- Camera: To capture the stunning scenery. Don't forget extra memory cards and batteries.
- Smartphone: For navigation, booking activities, and staying connected.

- Portable Charger: Keep your devices powered on the go.
- Travel Adapter: If you're visiting from outside the United States, you'll need a power adapter.
- Headphones/Earbuds: For entertainment during flights and relaxation.

Beach and Water Gear

- Snorkeling Gear: If you prefer to use your own, bring a mask, snorkel, and fins.
- Beach Towel: Quick-drying towels are practical.
- Beach Blanket: For picnics and lounging on the sand.
- Cooler Bag: Keep your drinks and snacks cool for beach days.

Outdoor and Adventure Gear

- Hiking Gear: Sturdy shoes, moisture-wicking socks, and a hat.
- Water Shoes: Useful for rocky beaches and water activities.
- Binoculars: Great for whale watching (in season) and bird spotting.
- Guidebooks/Maps: Helpful for exploring and learning about Maui's attractions.

Miscellaneous Items

- Travel Documents: Bring your ID, passport (if necessary), travel itinerary, and any booking confirmations.
- Cash and Credit Cards: Some places might be cash-only, so it's good to have both.
- Journal/Notebook: To document your travel experiences.

Conclusion

Maui's diverse landscapes, from the lush Hana Highway to the summit of Haleakalā, offer endless adventures. With pristine beaches, vibrant culture, and world-class dining, Maui is an island that caters to both relaxation and exploration. Whether you're chasing waterfalls, snorkeling in crystal-clear waters, or enjoying local cuisine, Maui provides an unforgettable experience. Embrace the aloha spirit, plan your days with care, and savor every moment on this enchanting island, where natural beauty and island hospitality create lasting memories.

Made in the USA
Monee, IL
24 September 2024